TRADITIONS AND STORIES OF
SCOTTISH CASTLES

Valentine & Sons, Ltd.

FERNIEHIRST CASTLE

Traditions and Stories
of
Scottish Castles

BY

A. H. MILLAR, LL.D.

AUTHOR OF
" GREGARACH " " MARY QUEEN OF SCOTS," ETC.

SANDS & CO.

37 GEORGE STREET, EDINBURGH

AND LONDON

1927

Made in Great Britain.

CONTENTS

CONTENTS

LIST OF ILLUSTRATIONS

Traditions and Stories of Scottish Castles

I

CROOKSTON CASTLE AND CATHCART CASTLE

ONE of the chief peculiarities of the Celtic nations is their fondness for local traditions. Every ruined Keep or dismantled Tower throughout the Highlands has some marvellous tale or romantic incident connected with it, which is lovingly preserved and handed down from generation to generation with undoubting faith and pious care, worthy sometimes of a better cause. The poetical cast of the Celtic mind throws around the most ordinary events a halo of romance which renders attractive many localities that would be otherwise uninteresting ; and even the shrewdly practical Lowland mind, when brought under the influence of the spell, cannot entirely resist the glamour of the times that are gone, or remain indifferent to the tales of love and war, which are sanctified by their removal for several centuries.

9

Yet it needs not that the Lowlander should fly to the fastnesses of the Highland chieftains to feed upon romance, since there is an inexhaustible fund of interest to be found in the Castles within his own territories. Traditions, less mendacious but quite as romantic as the northern stories, are in existence with reference to all the Castles of note in the Lowlands, and require but the collector to rescue them from oblivion in this possibly too practical age. A romantic tale is not less interesting though its date be not that of a far-distant past; and it should be some recommendation if the story be a veritable fact, rather than a notion " all carved from the carver's brain." It is with the purpose of gathering up some of the traditions still preserved in local narratives of some of the historic Castles in all parts of Scotland that this work is written, being sure that these are not without interest to every lover of our country.

There is perhaps no character throughout the whole range of Scottish history that so completely awakens the enthusiasm of Scotsmen as Mary, Queen of Scots. The tale of her gay youth, her happy early years, the heavy clouds of misfortune which encompassed her middle life and deepened into the darkest misery, until finally completed by the thrilling horror of her tragic end—all form a life-drama which cannot fail to move the most stolid hearer to pity. This is not the place to narrate the oft-told tale; but as marking some of the great epochs in her

10

eventful life, attention may be directed to some
of the Castles which are inseparably associated
with her name. The first of these is Crookston
Castle, where she spent her honeymoon with
Henry, Lord Darnley.

CROOKSTON CASTLE.

Three miles south-east from Paisley, on the
Glasgow Road, there stands the ancient Castle
of Crookston, which, though seldom mentioned
in connection with Queen Mary, has still a most
pathetic relation to her history. The green lane,
flanked with hawthorn hedges, which strikes off
the main road at Hillington Bar, leads up a
gentle ascent for about half a mile, bringing the
traveller, somewhat unexpectedly, at once upon
the Castle. Ere reaching this altitude, however,
he must cross the course of the extinct Glasgow
and Ardrossan Canal (now a railway line), and
pass the entrance to Hawkhead, one of the seats
of the Earl of Glasgow. Though thus reached
by an easy slope, and quite free from the appearance of any precipitous elevation, the position
of the Castle is most commanding. Upon three
sides—south, east and west—the fertile fields of
Renfrewshire are stretched at the base of the
hill ; while towards the north the Bowling Braes
stand forth in a bold outline, their base being
laved by the waters of the Clyde. Southwards
no eminence is visible, save the dim figure of
Neilston Pad in the hazy distance ; while the

11

intervening space is filled with "gentle slopes and groves between," giving evidence of a richly fertile soil, and an industrious agricultural population. The gleaming silver line which meanders through the plain marks the course of the White Cart as it "rins rowin' to the sea"; and near the spot where the Castle stands it receives the tributary water of the little rivulet, called the Levern.

Though never of great extent the Castle seems to have been compactly built, and designed in a lawless age to withstand a powerful enemy. Its position as a look-out station has been admirably chosen; and so commanding is the site that a few retainers might have held a considerable force at bay with comparative ease. The first Castle was probably built by Robert de Croc, apparently a scion of a Norman family, who was proprietor of the estate about 1190, and whose name survives in a corrupted form as "Crookstoun." In 1330 the estate was purchased by Sir Alan Stewart, a kinsman of the Stuarts, Seigneurs of D'Aubigny, famous in the history of France and Scotland. Sir Alan, in 1361, granted the Castle and estate to Sir J. Stewart of Darnley; and thus they ultimately came into the possession of Henry, Lord Darnley (1546–67), centuries afterwards, with whom we have to deal.

The remains of the present Castle probably belong to the 13th century (1290–1390), though the exterior arrangements plainly indicate that

CATHICART CASTLE

Valentine & Sons, Ltd.

there was a Keep of some kind here long before
that date, though the ruthless hand of Time has
cleared all the relics away. But in 1488, when
James IV. was fighting for the Crown after his
father, James III., had been killed at Sauchieburn, he attacked his opponent, the Earl of
Lennox, grandfather of Darnley, at Duchal, and
besieged Crookston Castle, bringing " Mons Meg "
from Edinburgh for the purpose. Surely this
shows that even at that time the Castle was of
considerable importance.

The main interest in Crookston of the present
day, this " grey and antique tower," is more
nearly connected with love than war. Here it
was, according to tradition, that the youthful
Henry Darnley, then its lord, led his beauteous
but unfortunate Queen to spend their honeymoon. And those battered and time-worn walls,
through whose " looped and windowed ragged-
ness " the mystic moonlight strays, have resounded to the voice and harp of a Chastelard
or a Rizzio, whilst yet the fortunes of the martyred Queen were unclouded.

Could one gleam of prophetic foresight have
been given to bride and bridegroom to display
the future of either, how incredulous and horror-
stricken would they have been at that festal
hour ! And yet, within a few years, the gay
gallant had descended into the wretched, brutal,
jealous husband, whose insatiable fury was not
restrained from murder, even by the presence of
his Queen. And the loved and lovely bride,

13

whose day-dreams in Crookston Castle were of
love, romance and song, might have shrunk in
terror from the fearful doom which awaited her
newly-wedded lord ; or quailed before the shadow
of the scaffold upon which she must ultimately
meet her own. Yet, as Horace sang of old :—

> " The Deity, prudent and careful,
> Encloses the future in night,"

and so Crookston witnessed nothing save dance
and song ; whilst joy was unconfined during the
few happy days which Mary spent within its
bounds. And when her hard fate was upon her,
not without sad regret must she have thought,
amid the gloom of Fotheringay, upon the pageants
and revelries of Crookston, which had formed for
her a sunny memory of other days. After a visit
to Crookston Castle the Glasgow poet, William
Motherwell, wrote thus :—

> " Beneath yon tree—
> Now bare and blasted—so our annals tell
> The martyr Queen, ere that her fortunes knew
> A darker shade than cast her favourite yew,
> Loved Darnley passing well—
> Loved him with tender woman's generous love,
> And bade farewell awhile to courtly state
> And pageantry for yon o'ershadowing grove—
> For the lone river's banks whose small birds sing,
> Their little hearts with summer joys elate—
> Where tall broom blossoms, flowers profusely spring ;
> There he, the most exalted of the land,
> Pressed with the grace of youth a Sovereign's peerless
>   hand."

14

CATHCART CASTLE.

It is worthy of note that, whilst Crookston Castle witnessed the earlier and happier portion of Mary's variegated life, Cathcart Castle, which is all but visible from it, was the scene of her final downfall. The latter stands about seven miles from Crookston, and nearly two miles south-east of Glasgow, upon the Mearns Road. An inconsiderable pathway which leaves the main road a short space beyond the bridge over the Cart, leads past the Castle gate, which is not surrounded now by any vestige of garden ground. Unlike Crookston, it must have afforded little advantage to its inmates in the matter of defence. It is easily approached on all sides, and is more like a pleasure-palace than a stronghold. There are arrow-slits in the walls, and the appearance of an attempt at fortification; but the surrounding locality affords too easy access for this to have been of much avail. Yet the outlook from one of the windows in the upper chamber, still called Queen Mary's Window, is very lovely. The ground upon which the Castle stands slopes gently down to the river's brink, whose silver sheen glimmers faintly here and there amid the overhanging boughs of birch and ash and nodding beech. Due north from this point of view lies the field of Langside, where was fought the final and decisive conflict which terminated Queen Mary's career in Scotland.

The lands of Cathcart belonged in the 12th century to a family bearing that name, and so continued till 1546, when the Sempill family acquired them through marriage. The original Cathcart family was represented in 1740 by the eighth Baron, who repurchased the ancestral property. The Castle, which had been built in the 15th century, was partly demolished by this Baron Cathcart, and has not since been occupied. In 1814 the tenth Baron was created Earl Cathcart, and the members of the family have long been distinguished in military history. Cathcart House, which took the place of the old Castle, was built by Mr James Hill, Solicitor, Glasgow, who acquired part of the estate in 1788, and from him it passed, in 1801, to Earl Cathcart, when the rest of the estate was purchased by him.

The undulating lea, now called "Battlefield," is completely commanded from "Queen Mary's Window," and it was doubtless from here that the hapless Queen watched with breathless interest the contest upon which her own future depended. After her daring and romantic escape from Lochleven, she made her way to the east coast so as to mislead her pursuers; then doubling back, she sought to reach Dumbarton Castle, which was then held by her partizans. Taking the road by Hamilton, she was soon joined by many of the Lowland gentry, with their retainers, and found herself at the head of a small but well-appointed army. Fearful of risking a conflict with her half-brother, the Regent Moray, who then lay with his troops at Glasgow, she took the south bank of the Clyde, intending to cross to the Dumbarton side when safe from interruption. But the intelligence which Moray had received of her movements enabled him to checkmate her plans. Detaching a strong body of his troops he occupied the field at Langside, which lay directly on her line of march, thus leaving her no option save either to dare the battle or fall helplessly into an ambuscade betwixt the two portions of his army. The confidence of the Queen in her cause decided her to adopt the former course, and in a fatal hour for her the armies engaged in deadly conflict. The position of Cathcart Castle, which overlooked the field of battle, afforded the most favourable spot from which to observe the course of the strife, although, from its proximity to the combatants, perhaps not the safest place for so precious a prize.

That she occupied Crookston Castle for this purpose is not a reasonable supposition, since its distance from Langside and its situation would effectually prevent her from obtaining early intelligence of the course of the battle. And her flight to Dundrennan Abbey after the disastrous issue of the conflict was much more easily accomplished from Cathcart than from Crookston. Yet one must remember that so weighty an authority as Sir Walter Scott mentions the latter place as the position which she held, though perhaps the romantic and poetical contrast between her earlier and later days at Crookston might influence the poet to adopt this theory even though not supported by facts. One thing is certain, that local tradition ascribes this melancholy interest to Cathcart, and even points out the particular spot where the ill-fated Queen beheld the overthrow of all her hopes. And thus, by a curious combination of circumstances, two Castles standing upon the banks of the same river, Cart, and separated by but a few miles from each other, serve as landmarks, tear-fraught and sad, recording the joys and sorrows of Scotland's fairest Queen—her time of love and her time of war.

II

LOCHLEVEN AND BURLEIGH

THE shores of Lochleven, in Kinross-shire, afford
a rich feast to the lover of the picturesque and
romantic. Apart from the interesting associations
which arise from historical events connected with
the locality, there is a peculiar charm to be
found in the combination of mountain, lake, and
stream which make up the scenery presented.
And though the grandeur of the hills and the
gloom of the passes which are to be met with in
the Highlands are alike awanting, there are
more attractive elements of beauty to be seen in
the serenely peaceful villages which are scattered
around the lochside. The quaint old town of
Kinross is itself no uninteresting study. For it
can claim a very respectable antiquity, and has
been frequently the scene of stirring events in
the history of the country. Standing upon the
main highway to the north, and affording a
convenient resting-place between Queensferry
and Perth, it has been often chosen as a rendezvous for troops on the march, or as a place of
ambuscade for purposes of interception. From
very early times the town has been famous for
its cutlery, and its artificers were held in such
high esteem that the name of " Kinrosse " was

borne upon the shield of the Cutlers of Sheffield as being most worthy of renown.

LOCHLEVEN CASTLE.

But the chief point of interest in the neighbourhood is undoubtedly the Castle of Lochleven. No situation could be more romantic than that which it occupies. The loch is dotted here and there with little islands which rise abruptly from the water, bearing scant foliage and displaying no rugged or precipitous rocks. Upon one of these stand the ruins of the Monastery of St Serf or Servanus, whose somewhat unveracious history was recounted by Andrew Wyntoun in his *Orygynale Cronickles of Scotland*, written many centuries ago. One of the largest islands is situated about the centre of the loch, and upon it is erected the Castle of Lochleven, which name has become familiar to every Scottish ear from the historical events of which it has been the witness. Founded in pre-historic times by one of the Scottish chiefs, of whom we have no record save its name, it has stood the brunt of many an angry storm through unnumbered ages ; and though now somewhat battered and decayed, there are still unimpeachable tokens remaining of the strength and durability of masonry erected before the 19th century estimate-work.

The first appearance of Lochleven Castle in credible history is made during the period of the

LOCHLEVEN CASTLE

Valentine & Sons, Ltd.

Balliol dispute in 1333. Throughout Scotland only four Castles supported the claims of Bruce against Balliol and Edward of England, and of these Lochleven was one. To reduce this stronghold to subjection, a body of English, under Sir John de Strivelin, was sent to besiege it; but as the position of the Castle in the centre of the loch prevented any stealthy approach or surprise, the besiegers had to adopt other measures. Finding that the main outlet of the loch was by the little stream of the Leven, the English hit upon the expedient of damming up this outflow with dykes, so that the accumulating waters of the loch might rise above the level of the island, drown the inmates of the Castle, and suffocate Scottish Independence out of existence. But the theory was too correct to be justified by fact, and finally proved the destruction of the attacking forces. The loyal Captain of Lochleven, Alan Vipont by name, sent out at midnight a few of his faithful retainers, who approached the barricade, erected by Strivelin, in a small boat, and, demolishing a portion of the embankment, they caused the pent-up waters of the loch to overwhelm and destroy many of the enemy. Grave doubts have been entertained of the accuracy of this story; but there are not wanting many local antiquaries who can yet indicate the remains of the English dyke, and who cannot tolerate the honest scepticism of any Edie Ochiltree who may "mind the biggin' o't."

It was fitting that so loyal a stronghold should become a Royal Castle. Robert III. occupied it for some time as a Court residence, and the difficulty of access to it in so rude an age may have been found rather an advantage than otherwise. But as civilization advanced the regal taste became more fastidious, and Lochleven soon descended into the position of a state-prison. Whilst in the care of a branch of the Douglas family, it degenerated from its former greatness, and was unhallowed by the presence of Royalty, save under compulsion, and in "durance vile." Every one knows the melancholy story of Mary's incarceration here, and the romantic incident of her escape to still more relentless imprisonment in England. This episode in the history of Lochleven it is needless to relate ; but it may be interesting to note that, with a refinement of cruelty, the dominant party, after her defeat, sent the Earl of Northumberland, who had risen to support her cause in the north of England, to occupy the chambers which the Royal fugitive had tenanted, and to leave them only, like her, that he might die upon the scaffold.

History has not recorded what catastrophe, either in nature or politics, rendered this ancient Keep unfit for habitation. Now there remains little save the square tower and a portion of the outer wall to tell of its former greatness, and to preach to coming generations the mutability of all things. The great hall has now no carpet save the greensward, no roof save the blue vault of heaven ; and the winds sough eerily through the tenantless chambers once resonant with song and revelry. Yet it would be difficult to imagine a spot more calculated to revive the memories of the past ; and here we might look to find some

> " Lady of the Mere
> Lone sitting by the shores of old Romance,"

did we live in other times than the present. But time, the devourer of all things, has laid his destroying hand upon the Castle, and though :—

> " Gothic the pile and high the solid walls,
> With warlike ramparts, and the strong defence
> Of jutting battlements—an age's toil !
> No more its arches echo to the noise
> Of joy and festive mirth. No more the glance
> Of blazing taper through its windows beams
> And quivers on the undulating wave.
> But naked stand the melancholy walls
> Lashed by the wintry tempests, cold and bleak,
> That whistle mournful through the empty halls
> And piecemeal crumble down the tow'rs to dust."

THE NEW HOUSE OF KINROSS.

Directly betwixt the town of Kinross and the shore of Lochleven stands the mansion-house of the locality, commonly called the New House of Kinross. Erected as a residence for the Duke of York (afterwards James II.), it presents all the characteristics of the mansion of the period, though its chambers were long deserted, and the exquisite prospect which it commands of hill and lake was unenjoyed for years by the lawful possessors. A little further around the shores of the loch is situated the old Kirkyard, which contains not a few headstones telling of the virtues of " the rude forefathers of the hamlet." And here, as a memento of semi-barbarous times, there is the house still standing in which the watchers kept ward over the dead to preserve their bodies from the sacrilegious resurrectionists. Close by the kirkyard is pointed out the spot where Mary landed when she made her escape from Lochleven Castle, though the reclamations recently made by drainage of the loch render it difficult to indicate the place with any degree of accuracy.

THE BURGHER BRIG.

Following the pathway by the shore of the loch one soon arrives at the Burgher Brig, a relic of more recent times, but of a period rapidly passing away. Tradition relates that at one time there was no ford over the river North Queich, which runs into Loch Leven, save the precarious passage afforded by stepping stones, which in times of spate were quite impassable. But when the advancing civilization of the district had erected a Burgher Kirk in the neighbourhood, the Lord of the Manor graciously became a Pontifex in his own country, and built a wooden stair-bridge similar to those now seen in Japan, which was ultimately replaced by a stone structure.

BURLEIGH CASTLE.

A little way from this spot stands the ancient Castle of Burleigh. The road which leads from Milnathort around the loch to Scotland-Well, passes this ancient pile, which is placed immediately upon the pathway. The situation is most picturesque. The gable of the Castle towards the road is quite covered with ivy, and the rent and broken portions of the edifice are enlivened and beautified by the subdued tone of the evergreen leaves. By moonlight the scene is romantic in the extreme. The heavy sombre shadows which are thrown across the roadway, and the pale silvery glory which lights up each prominent tower and battlement, give a weird and old-world aspect to the whole place. From time immemorial the Castle of Burleigh has been in the family of the Balfours. Many are the stories related of them, but perhaps none is so sadly romantic as that which is now to be told. In the unsettled times betwixt the abdication of Queen Mary and the settlement of her son, James VI., upon the throne, the young Lord of Burleigh fell under the power of the arch-conqueror Love. The charms of the daughter of the gardener at the Castle had overpowered and captivated him, and reckless of consequences (as

25

lovers ever are) he sought to elevate her to an
equality with himself by honourable marriage.
Her beauty was the theme of every tongue :—

> " Who had not heard
> Of Rose, the gardener's daughter ? Where was he
> So blunt in memory, so old at heart,
> At such a distance from his youth in grief,
> That having seen forgot ? The common mouth
> So gross to express delight, in praise of her
> Grew oratory. Such a lord is love,
> And beauty such a mistress of the world."

But Balfour's affection was not reciprocated
by the maiden, whose heart was already engaged
to another. Deaf alike to his threats and entreaties, she remained steadfast to the lover to
whom she had plighted her troth, and refused to
be swayed from her resolution to live for him
alone. The Lord of Burleigh, finding all his
endeavours to win her hand fruitless, quitted the
paternal roof in the hope that foreign travel
might obliterate her image from his heart, and
hoping that absence, in his case, would prove
the bane of love. But his hopes were doomed
to disappointment, and he returned to his home
with intensified love and increased affection for
the object of his devotion. She, however, had
profited by his absence and was now married to
the man of her choice, who held the position of
schoolmaster at Inverkeithing.

And so, one evening, little dreaming of the
danger which was near them, as the husband and

BURLEIGH CASTLE

Valentine & Sons, Ltd.

wife sat at their own fireside, planning perchance some elaborate scheme for securing the happiness in perpetuity which they then enjoyed, their threshold was darkened by the person of young Balfour of Burleigh. No phantom from the "undiscovered country" could have exercised more power upon the young wife, or paralysed her more completely. Reproach was upon his lips, vengeance was in his eye. The haughty disposition which he had inherited from a remote ancestry was unsoftened even by the influence of love, and now jealousy inflamed him. Drawing a pistol from his bosom, he shot his defenceless rival through the heart, in the presence of his wife, and within his own house. No more dastardly act than this has been recorded in the history of the British nobility. It was only to be expected that so complete a poltroon would seek refuge from the consequence of his guilt in flight and ignominious self-exile. Yet so powerful was the feudal influence of the family that the affair was hushed up and secured from publicity ; and its story now only exists in the traditions of the country, which have been repeated for generations in the field or by the ingle-side.

Pow-MILL.

A short distance from Burleigh Castle stands Pow-mill, whose untiring water-wheel has revolved for over three centuries. The Pow Burn, which forms the motive power of the mill, is one of the *eleven* streams which flow into Loch Leven, from which tradition states (somewhat apocryphally) that the name of *Leven* was derived. The ancient mill, until lately, was in a wonderful state of preservation. The quaint old-fashioned gables and open courtyard remind one forcibly of the mills of Holland and the Low Countries ; and the moss-covered dyke and green-speckled wall still further add to its venerable aspect. As the mill of the district, and therefore a centre of local intelligence, many stories are related of it, one of which is as follows :—

The farm of Pittendreich, in the immediate neighbourhood, was for many generations until lately in possession of a family of the name of White ; and the requirements of their agricultural pursuits naturally made them intimate with the occupants of the mill. During the persecuting times it so happened that Crawford, the miller, took the side of Episcopacy, whilst White, the farmer, was known to be one of the " hill-folk." The characters of the two men gave an index to their religious beliefs ; for White was an upright, God-fearing man, whom even his enemies respected ; but Crawford was rude in speech, loose in morals, and reckless in conduct. In those sad times to be " saintly " in any degree was to provoke the vengeance of one's ill-wishers ; and though long preserved from molestation, White's day of trial at length arrived. A band of troopers, scouring the countryside in search of " conventicle-men," had been directed by some " good-

natured friend " towards Pittendreich; and
White had barely time to escape by a backway and
fly for his life ere they entered his dwelling.

Whilst Crawford the miller stood in his doorway dreamily contemplating the deepening twilight, he beheld a man stealthily creeping along
by the hedge-side, as if fearful of being seen, yet
driven, nevertheless, to compulsory flight. As
the figure came nearer he recognized with some
surprise in the excited and anxious face before
him, his old neighbour White, of Pittendreich.
Hailing him as he sought to pass, the miller
inquired whither he was bound, and despite their
opposition in religion and the risk he thereby
ran, the fugitive declared the cause of his unwilling journey. Nor was his confidence in the
neighbourly feeling misplaced. Touched by the
circumstances of the case, the miller gladly extended his aid to him. " Come in bye," said he,
" for here ye may be safe. They'll never look
for a saint in Hell."

And having seen the farmer safely bestowed,
he resumed his position in the doorway, certain
that his reputation with the troopers would preserve him from molestation. And thus the
" touch of nature " had made even these diverse
characters " Kin," and overcame for the time
their religious animosity. And the record of this
neighbourly action survives to the present day,
though both have long mingled with mother
earth.

The shore of Lochleven from Pow-mill to

Scotland-Well is dotted with picturesque little villages which cannot fail to interest the wayfarer. Little Balgedie, Meikle Balgedie, and Kinnesswood form a continuous link, the last-named being ever memorable as the birthplace of Michael Bruce, the poet, whose Scripture Paraphrases are known throughout the world. The last of the Leven villages is Scotland-Well, the name of which may have been bestowed by the Roman invaders, since Tacitus refers to *Fons-Scotiæ* in his " Annals." The pathway around the eastern end of the loch leads by the base of Bennarty to Paran-Well.

This ancient locality of Paran-Well (erroneously called " Parrot Well " by Sir Walter Scott) was selected for an ambuscade at a very stirring time. The marriage of Mary, Queen of Scots, to Darnley was distasteful to many of her powerful subjects. Amongst these the Earl of Moray, her illegitimate brother, and throughout her life her most implacable enemy, was principally offended by this union. Apart from the fact that Darnley and he were sworn foes, there was the old cry of " the Kirk in danger " to call to his side many wavering vassals. Supported by the Lords of the Congregation, who resented Mary's marriage as endangering the Protestant succession, Moray stationed a body of horse at Paran-Well, under the shadow of Bennarty, to intercept Darnley and his bride whilst on their way from Perth. But accurate intelligence and an early turn out enabled them to defeat the purpose of their enemies, and to escape for a time from their menaces. And thus it appears that every portion of Lochleven is consecrated by some memory of the unfortunate Queen, whose own reminiscences of the locality must have been of the most mournful description.

III

DUMBARTON CASTLE

AMONG the natural phenomena in Scotland the peak of Dumbarton Rock holds no inconsiderable place. Rising abruptly from the banks of the Clyde, and rearing its rugged front erect in solitary state from a comparatively level country, its effect is striking and peculiar. Geologists maintain that they can trace the range of mountains of which Dumbarton is the termination, far away north, through the Kilpatrick and Campsie Hills up to the Grampians.

This uncouth rock is full of memories that carry us far back in the annals of our country, and it forms a connecting link betwixt the chivalrous times that have long vanished and our present utilitarian days. Long before the period of written history Dumbarton existed as a tower of strength for the primitive natives. The misty period of Scottish story, in which Fingal and Ossian with their warlike band appear, is connected with our own times by the hill of Balclutha, the scene of their exploits, the home of their triumph and victory. If corroborative proof were required that this Castle steep was the seat of Fingal, the recent discoveries of canoes and other relics in the district might

DUMBARTON CASTLE

Valentine & Sons, Ltd.

readily afford it. But the songs of Ossian are sufficiently precise to indicate the locality with certainty. And even in those remote times Balclutha was regarded as having existed from far-distant ages, and exhibiting the reverses and vicissitudes common to all earthly things. For thus sings Ossian :—

" I have seen the walls of Balclutha, but they are desolate. The fire had resounded in the halls, and the voice of the people is heard no more. The stream of Clutha was removed from its place by the fall of the walls. The thistle shook there its lonely head ; the moss whistled in the wind. Why dost thou build the wall, son of the winged days ? Thou lookest from thy towers to-day ; yet a few years and the blast of the desert comes. It howls in thy empty courts, and whistles round thy half-worn shield."

A long controversy, began in 1762 and still continued in 1926, arose regarding the authenticity of James Macpherson's translation of the Ossian poems ; but experts in the language maintain that Macpherson founded many of his versions upon Gaelic originals, and in some of them introduced episodes from Irish history. The question will probably never be decided absolutely either way. It is certain, however, that the Ossian poems published by Macpherson were translated into all the European languages, and attained great popularity.

Balclutha formed a stronghold of the aborigines at a very early period, and came under the notice

of the Romans when they invaded Caledonia. A
military nation by profession, such as the Romans
were, could not but perceive its importance as a
fortress. Its commanding site from which the
road and the river could be controlled, would at
once point it out as a most desirable outpost from
which the invaders might menace the inhabitants,
and the difficulty of access which it presented
naturally rendered it almost impregnable. When
Antoninus, therefore, began his great undertaking of the Roman Wall from the Clyde to the
Forth, he selected Dumbarton as the starting-
point, since he there could control all ingress to
Scotland from the Western Sea by the way of the
Clyde. And here was founded the ancient burgh
of Dumbarton, at the base of the rock, which
appears in Roman annals under the name of
"Theodosia," after one of the most eminent
generals commanding the invasion.

And thus, with a continuity which is easily
traced, we find that the Balclutha of Ossian
becomes the Alcluith of the Britons of Strathclyde, the Theodosia of the Romans, the Dun-
brittain of the Scots, and the Dunbartane or
Dumbarton of more recent times. Yet, though
its antiquity is thus established, one hesitates to
accept the statements of Geoffrey of Monmouth,
who gravely records the name of the contemporary of King David of Israel who ruled in his
ancestral halls on the banks of Clyde.

The Roman invasion gave place to the Danish,
and still Dumbarton was esteemed an enviable

point of vantage. In 870 A.D. it endured a siege of four months by the Danes under Olave, and was finally captured by them. From this time onwards the Castle frequently changed its masters, and upon its weather-beaten front was traced the passing history of the country as it alternated betwixt freedom and slavery. It was not, however, until the Earls of Lennox had risen into power that the attention of the Scottish Kings was seriously attracted towards Dumbarton. The title of this ancient house was derived from Levenax or Lennox, the district through which the Leven river flows on its way from Loch Lomond to join the Clyde at the base of the Castle Rock. The Earls of Lennox seemed to have ruled the surrounding country with a high hand, issuing their almost regal mandates from the Castle of " Dunbretane." And so intolerable had the yoke become that in 1238 Alexander II., whilst confirming a charter of land to them, expressly excluded the Castle from it, and retained it as a royal possession. A quarter of a century later it again formed the centre of attack during the Norwegian invasion under Haco. That its importance as a stronghold was thoroughly appreciated in those warlike times we may learn from the fact that Edward I. of England, acting in his self-assumed character of Lord Paramount, directed Nicholas de Segrave, the Castellan, to put Balliol in possession of it.

A peculiar interest attaches to Dumbarton in connection with Sir William Wallace. Sir John

Menteith, his betrayer, or, at least, his captor, was Castellan at the time, and carried the unfortunate patriot to his fortress, under a pledge that he would suffer no harm. But no sooner had he obtained full possession of his person than he handed him over to the English soldiers, and defiled his hands by accepting the bribe of perjury and unfaithfulness. It would be rash to conclude from this transaction that Menteith was other than a brave man in battle, for his later exploits at Bannockburn somewhat atoned for his treachery. But it cannot be denied that the principles of this execrated man were " unstable as water." Indeed, he seems to have been a prototype of the famous American politician, who summed up his creed shortly : " I believe in *one* party, and that is *myself*."

He was untrue to Wallace, faithless to Bruce, treacherous to Edward, and mistrusted alike by countryman and stranger. A curious story is related in connection with King Robert. When that illustrious monarch had made some way in the country south of the Clyde, he crossed to Dumbarton, and, being joined by Malcolm, Earl of Lennox, he laid siege to the Castle, then held by Menteith. Meantime, the Governor, deceived by his past actions, Bruce attempted to bribe ; but the ambitious Castellan would hear of no less a reward than the Earldom of Lennox. The King could not for a moment endure the thought of dispossessing one of his most faithful followers even to gain so important a position, and only the remonstrances of the good Earl Malcolm, who professed himself ready to resign his honours for so desirable an object, at length prevailed. A treaty was made, whereby Menteith undertook to deliver up the Castle to Bruce for the lands and title of Earl of Lennox. But a carpenter named Rolland, who had gained some knowledge of Menteith's designs, warned the King that he would be betrayed unless most watchful.

Nothing daunted, but thoroughly on the alert, the brave Robert Bruce pursued his way to the Castle. He was met at the gate by Menteith, who delivered up the keys with all due pomp and solemnity. But ere sitting down at meat with him the wary King desired to be shown over the Castle. Closely followed by his own attendants, he inspected every corner of the fortress, and noticed with rising doubt that Menteith carefully avoided opening the door of one cellar in particular. His suspicions were aroused, and, calling his guard to arms, he forced the door and found within the chamber a body of English troops, who were doubtless secreted there so as to take the citadel by surprise. The unhappy Governor, who had thus over-reached himself, was at once secured. But those were times in which strict justice might not be done, and Bruce could ill afford to execute one valiant knight, however grave his misdemeanour. Menteith was promised a full pardon for his treason if he would join the Scottish Army on the eve of Bannockburn. And so mightily did he wield his sword on that memorable occasion that he was not only restored to liberty, but also loaded with honour.

A romantic story connected with Dumbarton is still preserved in the traditions of the Castle. When David II. returned from England, there followed in his train a Welshwoman named Catherine Mortimer, upon whom he had bestowed tokens of favour. Jealous of her influence with the King, the ambitious Earl of Angus hired two ruffians to accomplish her assassination. Apprised by their employer of her movements, they waylaid her upon a lonely moor near Melrose, and murdered her in cold blood. A deed so abhorrent, even in that lawless age, called loudly for vengeance, and as the complicity of Angus was an open secret, the enraged King ordered him to be confined in Dumbarton Castle, whilst the remains of his victim were interred with great solemnity at Dunfermline. But the year 1361, which succeeded his incarceration, was a fatal one for the Lennox country, as the plague broke out there with great virulence, destroying nearly one-half of the inhabitants, and numbering amongst its victims the unhappy Earl of Angus.

It would be tedious to relate all the sieges which this venerable Castle has endured ; but the story of the connection of James IV. with it must not be omitted. At the Court of this unfortunate monarch no nobleman was more beloved and respected than Lord Darnley, afterwards Earl of Lennox. His youth, his talents, and the promise of success which they afforded, pointed him out

as one of the men whom the King delighteth to
honour. And thus, among other munificent gifts,
we find that in 1479 " the Castell of Dunbretane,"
with all the revenues pertaining to it, was bestowed upon him by his too generous sovereign.
For nine years did Darnley bask in the sunshine
of the royal countenance ; but

> " Vaulting ambition that o'erleaps itself
> And falls on t'other side "

at length overcame him. In 1488 his plots
against the King were discovered, and he was
degraded from his rank. Fortune played shuttle-
cock with him in the following year. In February
all the Acts of Parliament against him were
rescinded, and he was restored to favour ; but
in July of the same year orders were given to
besiege the Castle of Crookston, Dumbarton and
Duchall, which belonged to himself and his sons,
and to execute the extreme penalties for treason
against them. So great was the feeling adverse
to Darnley that King James himself took horse
to lead the attack. Assembling his troops at
Glasgow, he marched first against Duchall, which
he reduced in seven days. Directing his army
against Crookston, he soon forced a capitulation,
and, with the laurels from these victories fresh
upon him, he joined with the Earl of Argyll
against Dumbarton. But here, though ultimately successful, he found victory not so easy
as he had anticipated. Despite the assistance

which the King had of all the Scottish artillery, including Mons Meg from Edinburgh Castle, it took a considerable time to reduce the garrison. In despair the King was at last compelled to raise the siege and confess himself foiled by his powerful subject. Returning, however, in the month of September, he again opened his battery against Dumbarton, and succeeded in obtaining possession of it, though only upon the conditions of a full pardon for Darnley, now Earl of Lennox.

Whether the difficulty of conquering it had endeared the Castle to him or not it is not possible to tell, but certainly Dumbarton became one of the most cherished residences of King James IV. after this time. It is interesting to notice how frequently Dumbarton appears in the Records of the Chancellor of the Exchequer, whose debit and credit accounts afford much information to the historian. For instance, there is this curious entry :—

"1494–5, Mars. 19. Item, To the Pyper of Dumbartane, be the King's command, xiiij sh'."

Whether this piper was the famous Rory Murphy, whose name still exists in local song and story, is not recorded.

After the lamentable death of King James at Flodden the country was rent by the several factions of the Queen-Mother and the Earl of Arran, who both strove for the Regency. The latter nobleman, assisted by the Earls of Lennox and Glencairn, attacked Dumbarton successfully. In the quaint words of the chronicler of that time :—In ane mirk, wyndy nicht, the xij of Januar (1514), they under-myndit the nedder-pole of the yett of Dunbartane, and enterit thairat, and tuik the Castell, and put furth the Lord Erskine, then Capitane thereof." But their triumph was of short duration, as the arrival of Albany caused the overthrow of the Earl of Arran, and Lennox was imprisoned in Edinburgh until he delivered up Dumbarton.

For thirty years after, the possession of this Castle indicated the supremacy of the one or the other party. The political principles of the nobility of those days were very slip-shod indeed, and Earl Lennox was a type of his peers. In 1526 he again took and fortified the Castle, holding it for the young Queen of Scots. But shortly after he listened to the charming voice of Henry of England, who sought to conquer Scotland by marrying Queen Mary to his son Edward. Meanwhile the Chevalier de Brosse had been despatched from France to Dumbarton with stores and treasures to assist the cause of the Queen; and, unaware of the change in the political opinions of Lennox, he was induced by that wily nobleman to place his precious load in the Castle for safety. No sooner had this been done than the Earl quietly took possession of the treasure in the name of Henry VIII., and turned the duped and bewildered Chevalier out of Dumbarton.

In 1547 the unfortunate young Queen was conveyed to Dumbarton, as affording the most secure shelter for her from English force and fraud, and it was here that she suffered from an attack of smallpox, which was then the scourge of Scotland. And in a melancholy hour did she embark for France from Dumbarton, taking leave of the Queen-Mother on the greensward at the base of the Rock, and bidding a gay farewell to Scotland as her barque floated swiftly down the Clyde. To this regal residence she returned no more, for her next attempt to reach it was foiled at Langside, and she never again beheld the rugged rock, and her hospitable refuge, from which she had first set out in all the bloom of youth and hope.

For two years after her flight to England Lord Fleming held the Castle in her name, and defeated the besiegers under the Regent Moray, who strove for its possession. But it was wrested from him by one of the boldest assaults recorded in history. In 1571, whilst Lennox lay ill at Glasgow, having been injured by a fall from his horse, this forlorn hope was planned, and entrusted for its execution to Captain Crawford of Jordanhill. It was proposed to attempt the Castle by escalade. One of the soldiers of the Castle, whose wife had been whipped by the Governor for some trifling offence, deserted, and joined the proposed assaulting party, acting as their guide. Late in the evening, while the mist hung over the hill-top, the band set forth upon their perilous expedition, marching in single file, the foremost of the party carrying the ladders, and all keeping together in the darkness by holding a rope which passed from man to man. Stealthily approaching the base of the rock, they

42

began to tie their ladders together, and to place them in position at the most precipitous portion of the mountain. The reason for thus multiplying the difficulty of the adventure was a sound one, as the event proved, and Crawford's own words show that the scheme had been deeply pondered : " Because thai suspectit nocht the heighest pairt o' the craig, thair was not ane watche in that pairt of the wall above, within sex scoir of futes to the pairt that we entered."

The ascent began under evil auspices, for the first ladder broke with the weight of the men ere one had reached a landing-place. When tied and eked as well as possible it was still two fathoms short of the point they wished to reach. The leader and one of his men, therefore, boldly clambered up the face of the rock to an overhanging tree which grew in a cleft above, and, swinging the ladder by ropes tied thereto, thus enabled the band to attain another eminence. But here an unlooked for difficulty arose. One of the men was subject to epilepsy, and the excitement of the attack had brought on a fit whilst he was in the act of ascending the ladder. Humanity and prudence alike forbade that he should be thrown to the ground, and yet their own safety must be secured by their ascending over him. Fertile in expedients, the Captain directed that he should be tied to the ladder with ropes, and then, by turning it the whole of the men were enabled to pass over his body without injuring him. When they reached the summit two of the band leaped over the wall and slew the nearest sentinel, so that the entire troop entered the Castle ere an alarm had been given, and possessed themselves of it with comparative ease. No one who has examined the appearance of the rock at the point of assault will doubt the bravery of Captain Crawford and his gallant followers.

With one other story of bloodless capture this record of Dumbarton Castle may be concluded. In the troublous times when the dominant party sought to force Episcopacy upon the Scottish nation, the burgh of Dumbarton was governed by Provost Sempill, a tried and trusty Covenanter, whilst the Castellane was Sir William Stewart, as faithful an Episcopalian. Shortly after the Assembly of Glasgow had abolished the new form of religion and denounced the Bishops, the Provost and Council of Dumbarton concluded that it was their duty to take their venerable fortress out of the keeping of a recusant who differed from them in religious matters. They therefore met one Sunday in the house of the Provost, and sent an invitation to Sir William Stewart to dine there after service in the Chapel. Suspecting no treachery, he came unattended amongst them, and was at once met with a demand for the keys of the Castle. In vain he protested that he had them not, and he was ultimately compelled to send a messenger to procure them. Then, under threat of instant death in case of betraying them, he was forced to give the password for the night, and to exchange clothes with one of his captors.

In the twilight the sham Governor easily gained an entrance to the Castle, and soon placed his party in possession of it, without the shedding of blood.

The romance of Dumbarton Castle has to a large extent departed since the transference of the Scottish Court to London. No longer a kingly residence, it has only been visited once by royalty since Queen Mary abode there, when in 1847 the late Queen Victoria inspected the ancient fortress. But its importance as a bulwark against invasion is greater now than in the time of Hako the Dane, since a foreign foe, if unopposed there, may enter by the Clyde to the richest portion of Scotland, and over-run and devastate the very heart of the kingdom. And any system of shore fortification which does not include Dumbarton invites invasion by negligence. The wisdom of our fathers in this respect was greater·than ours, and they would not have left so important a post to be defended by cannons with oxidized touch-holes, loaded with balls which may have stood exposed to the storm since the 19th century was young. If these are to form our defensive artillery, let us discard our latest machine-guns, and return to more primitive weapons, and then

" At the sight of Dumbarton once again,
   We'll cock up our bannets and march amain ;
   Wi' braid claymores hangin' doun to our heel,
   To whang at the bannocks o' barley-meal."

IV

NEIDPATH CASTLE

THE watershed of the southern part of Scotland presents some curious phenomena to the observer of Nature. The country south of the Forth, though elevated somewhat above the sea-level, is so uniform in its altitude that no towering peaks or colossal mountain ranges may be found sufficiently pronounced to account for the courses which the mightier rivers of the locality take. It is easy for the geographer to explain why the Amazon river flows right across the continent of South America, for the flat pampas to the east of the great western range could offer no impediment to the foaming torrent which owed its birth to the cloud-daring Andes. Nor is there much difficulty in framing theories as to the more notable rivers of Europe in this way, which have at least probability to recommend them. But the Border Country is a greater enigma to the physical-geographer than its inhabitants will readily believe ; and the discovery of the minute causes at work to determine the direction of some of the greater streams demands the labours of the geologist as well as the topographer. Examine on the map the wayward careers of the three great southern rivers—Clyde, Tweed and Annan

46

—and the difficulty will be at once apparent. The Lowther Hills, situated about midway between the North Sea and the Atlantic Ocean, and forming almost a central point between the Firths of the Forth and the Solway, contain the springs from which these rivers originate, although the one takes its course due south, whilst the other two debouch upon the east and west coasts respectively. And the traditional rhyme is not without foundation when it declares that

> " Annan, Tweed and Clyde
> A' rise oot o' ae hillside."

An impeding rock, a protuberance in the mountain, a gentle slope in the valley, has determined the final destination of each of these majestic rivers ; and the impetuous waters, dashing with resistless force through the fertile plains which they have encountered, have now, by their own augmented energy, scooped out the three great districts of Tweeddale, Clydesdale and Annandale, each presenting characteristics of scenery diverse from the others. The Annan, flowing rapidly

> " Without stop or stay down the rocky way "

which leads to the Solway, has a briefer career than either of the other streams, whilst the Clyde wanders undecidedly first northward, then westerly, and finally due south, to lose itself in the raging Atlantic Ocean. But the Tweed enjoys a more equable existence than its compeers, and, gathering to itself the waters of many tributary streams, it meanders placidly, with many a winding link and crook, through the rich pastoral country which intervenes betwixt its well-spring and the sea.

> " Bosom'd in woods where mighty rivers run,
> Kelso's fair vale expands before the sun ;
> Its rising downs in vernal beauty swell,
> And, fringed with hazel, winds its flowery dell ;
> Green spangled plains to dimpled lawns succeed,
> And Tempé rises on the banks of Tweed.
> Blue o'er the river Kelso's shadow lies,
> And copse-clad isles amid the waters rise."

Nor is the country upon the banks of Tweed memorable only for its picturesque scenery. The whole of the valley through which it flows is haunted by literary memories, and the Yarrow, the Ettrick, and the Tweed recall irresistibly the hallowed names of Leyden, of Hogg, and of Scott, whose powers of description in prose and poetry have alike been expended upon this locality. As the chosen home of Border minstrelsy, and the abode of the heroes who figure in these ballads, Tweedside occupies a prominent position in this department of literature ; for the many towers and keeps which overlook its waters, and are reflected in its crystal stream, have each their tale of other days to him who cares to listen.

The human heart, like the Æolian lyre, may be roused to martial ardour by the fierce blast of the

48

NEIDPATH CASTLE

Valentine & Sons, Ltd.

stormy nor'-east wind, and resound in boldest tones the triumph of war; but it can also be thrilled responsively by the magic touch of the zephyr, which gently plays upon its sensitive strings some Lydian measure, until they murmur forth the praise of love. The noise of the fatal fray may be hushed for a time to allow of a tale of love, of faith, and of sorrow—the story of the hapless " Maid of Neidpath."

The Tweed for a large part of its course is studded with Castle-Towers or *Peels*, which were used in former times as beacon-lights to warn the Border clans of invasion, or to call them to rendezvous for a raid or foray. Every here and there in the line of the Peels might be found a commodious Castle, the property of the feudal superior and the rallying point for his vassals, to which they would repair, clad in their huge jack-boots, buff jerkins, and morions, ready to die at their lord's bidding.

There are several noticeable Castles of this description on Tweedside, and Neidpath was one of these. A few miles west of the town of Peebles the Tweed takes a south-eastward bend, and here, upon a gentle eminence whose grassy slope runs down to the river's brink, stands Neidpath Castle. Its massive walls and turrets, some of which are over ten feet in thickness, show that it has been a keep of great strength, the oldest part apparently dating from the 14th century, and probably erected by Edmund de Mortimer, who was third Earl of March, and died in 1381, as this would be the western boundary of the March country over which he ruled. After the death, in 1425, of the fifth Mortimer, Earl of March, Neidpath came into the possession of the Hays of Yester, and remained with that family for centuries.

The Hays of Yester were originally Norman Barons, who came to England in 1066 with William the Conqueror. Some of them seem to have been intimate with David I. of Scotland when he was at the English Court, and returned with him when he came back to his own kingdom, and received many grants of land. The Hay family is now represented by the present eleventh Marquess of Tweeddale, descended from the Hays of Yester and the first Marquess of Tweeddale. The Hays, while Earls of March, had their principal seat at Dunbar Castle, and sometimes retired to the seclusion of Neidpath.

The most sequestered spot on earth is not secure from the insidious advances of sorrow and suffering, and the Castle of Neidpath, however powerful to resist an armed foe, could not withstand the silent canker of despair, as the story which is linked inseparably with these ruined walls sufficiently testifies. The Earl of March, who was once Lord of the Castle, was, like "Jephthah, Judge of Israel," in this at least, that

> " He had one only daughter, and no mo,
> The whitch he loved passing well."

Born amid wealth and reared in luxury as that time afforded, the lovely heiress of Dunbar and Neidpath attained to budding womanhood without having experienced one cloud upon her fortunes, or cherished a desire that was not speedily gratified. As the only successor of an ancient lineage, it may be supposed that the Earl looked to her to uphold the dignity which her birthright thrust upon her, and hoped that his honoured name would still descend through her offspring to distant time. Doubtless many ambitious schemes of matrimonial alliance passed through his mind in her early days.

The scheming father who dotes upon his child, and conjures up airy castles to delight his imagination, is ever the chosen sport of Cupid.

> " O love will venture in
>   Whaur it daurna weel be seen ;
>   O love will venture in
>   Whaur wisdom aince had been ; "

and the fair Maid of Neidpath fell a victim to his wiles. The young Laird of Tushielaw, in Ettrick Forest, had met her when upon one of her visits to her Tweedside retreat, and ere long they had confessed to each other their mutual flame.

Though the Scotts of Tushielaw were of an ancient and honourable strain, and had made their name known in Border warfare, the youthful lover was no match, so far as rank was concerned, for the heiress of Dunbar and Neidpath. And perhaps the knowledge of this fact made them endeavour to conceal their passion from the parent whose cooler judgment was likely to dispel their day-dream of happiness. Their clandestine meetings, their whispered farewells by the banks of Tweed, or in the shade of Ettrick Forest, served to knit their hearts closer together in the bonds of true affection. Heedless of the danger they dared, and under the glamour of resistless love, they suffered themselves to drift ecstatically with the stream until the current carried them far beyond the hope of rescue, and they found themselves ensnared votaries of Cupid.

The great gift of true and lasting affection was theirs, since they had discovered of what it consists, so admirably described by the poet in these lines :—

> " It is not Phantasy's hot fire,
>   Whose wishes, soon as granted, fly ;
> It liveth not with fierce Desire,
>   With dead Desire it doth not die.
>
> It is the secret sympathy,
>   The silver link, the silken tie,
> Which heart to heart and mind to mind
>   In body and in soul can bind."

But their dreams, however rapturous, could not last, and they were destined to endure a rude awakening. Their secret vows and stolen interviews, though long hidden from profane eyes, at length were revealed, and the Earl learned with rage and indignation that the son of a Border Chief had won the heart of his daughter, from whom he had anticipated accumulated honours for his house. To forbid their meeting was his first step, and to enforce their separation by threats of dire and summary vengeance was the method he adopted. The timid and retiring maiden, unused to violence directed against herself, shrank in terror from her infuriated parent, and at once informed her lover, not without tears, that their time of love was over. The fear for his personal danger prompted her to counsel his withdrawal from his native country for a time, till changing scenes or altered circumstances should obliterate her from his memory, or prepare the way for a glad reunion. And the young Borderer, powerless against fate, bade farewell to the scenes of his infancy which love had hallowed, and took his mournful departure, like the hero of the old ballad :—

> " For I will into some far countrye,
>   Where noe man shall me knowe."

Perhaps the hardest lot is hers who must bide at home, with every well-known spot before her to recall forgotten pleasures, and unable to escape by the most frantic effort from inevitable despair. Yet, unwilling to show the depth of her misery, she assumed a placid demeanour which belied the tumult within :—

" I'll bid my heart be still,
        And check each rising sigh ;
    And none e'er shall know
    My heart's long-cherished woe
        When the first tears of sorrow are dry."

The inward grief which finds no outlet is the
most wearing and dangerous of all, and so it
proved with the daughter of the Earl of March.
" The course of true love " thus rudely interrupted had wrought a change in her which could
not long be concealed. The pale, ivory-like brow,
the hectic cheek, the attenuated frame all told
that the reversal of the current of her being was
wearing out the frail body which her lofty spirit
had once animated. At last her father, no longer
blind to the change which had taken place in her,
and terrified lest his precipitancy might have
destroyed his hopes of her, consented that the
exiled lover should be recalled and accepted as
her affianced husband. What was the pride of
birth compared with the life of his daughter ?
The heiress of so ancient a name as hers might
ennoble the man of her choice by marriage.

The message was soon conveyed to young Scott,
and he returned on the speedy wings of love to
his native land and his loving bride. Hastening
from the east coast, on which he had landed, he
rode " with loose rein and bloody spur " on the
way to Neidpath Castle. Meanwhile the maid had
thought to plan a glad surprise for him, and removed to the Earl's house in Peebles, which lay

upon the road which he must take. Worn and emaciated as she had been, the vigour seemed to have returned to her frame and the fire to her eyes once more as she sat by the balcony waiting, waiting to hear the beat of the horse's hoofs which should prelude their meeting, with a thousand conflicting emotions surging through her bosom.

> " And hopes, and fears that kindle hope,
>   An undistinguishable throng.
> And cherished wishes, long subdued,
>   Subdued and cherished long."

With feelings strung to a pitch of intense excitement, she sat listening eagerly for every sound which might tell of his proximity. At length she heard the hasty hoof of a horse impelled by some urgent rider, which drew nearer and nearer to the spot where she waited. Straining her eyes to catch the first glance of her lover, she recognised him a long way off, and felt her heart's blood pulse more quickly through her veins. Now had come the long-expected period of his return, and love and joy should thenceforth be their portion. But the sound of that rapid hoof ceased not even at her threshold, and the eyes of the rider, intent upon the way to Neidpath, never once glanced upon her. Could it be that the dream of her life had been visionary indeed ? Was there no faith in mankind ? Were the vows, plighted in Ettrick and sworn by Tweed, after all but a hollow mockery ? The revulsion of her feelings was too much for her overstrung system, reduced by disease as it had been, and ere the hollow beat of the foaming steed's frantic gallop had been wholly lost upon the air, while bearing her love onward, as he thought, to meet her, the desire of his heart, the hope of his life, was no more !

" Oh, lover's eyes are sharp to see,
 And lover's ears in hearing ;
And love in life's extremity
 Can lend an hour in cheering.
Disease had been in Mary's bower,
 And slow decay from mourning,
Though now she sits on Neidpath's tower
 To watch her love's returning.

. . . . .

He came—he passed—a heedless gaze,
 As o'er some stranger glancing ;
Her welcome, spoke in faltering phrase,
 Lost in his courser's prancing—
The Castle arch, whose hollow tone
 Returns each whisper spoken,
Could scarcely catch the feeble moan
 Which told her heart was broken."

V

DUNNOTTAR CASTLE

In ancient times, when lance and spear, claymore and dirk were the favourite weapons of war, few Castles could lay claim to greater strength than Dunnottar, in Kincardineshire, not far from Stonehaven. The peninsula on which it stands rises to a considerable height above the sea-level, and the stormy waves of the North Sea break into foam upon three sides of its base. The deep chasm which intervenes betwixt the Castle and the mainland, like some Californian *canon*, plainly exhibits its volcanic origin. And a very tyro in military affairs may perceive that the only approach to the Castle which is possible from the land might be defended at close quarters, as Thermopylæ was of old, by a mere handful of resolute patriots. But against the heavy ordinance of modern times the most elaborate fortifications which are on a lower level than the surrounding country are practically powerless. The long-range guns and rifles of these latter days have done more to demolish chivalrous bravery and hardihood than may be at first supposed. And the magnificent game of war, which once gave scope to the most daring and courageous of heroes, is now reduced to a mere mathematical problem, founded upon distances, paraboles, expansive forces, and impenetrability. All these achievements in mechanical warfare put to flight the great deeds of our ancestors, and thus earthly glory passeth away. As students of humanity, then, it is to older times that we must turn if we wish to see the truest examples of personal prowess and endurance, and Dunnottar Castle has preserved for us not a few of these.

The Keiths, Earls Marischal of Scotland, the feudal proprietors of this fortress, have afforded some renowned names to grace the annals of Scottish history. From a very early date they were entrusted with the hereditary office of Marischal at the Court, and were thus the custodians of the regal honours of the kingdom— the Crown, the Sceptre, and the Sword of State, which once bore sway in Scotland. The first name among the Keiths which is brought prominently into notice is immediately connected with Dunnottar. Despite its inaccessible position, it appears that the site of the Castle was at one time occupied by the Parish Church of the district. But about 1292 Sir William Keith, then Earl Marischal, knowing the disturbed state of the country, and appreciating the importance of the ground on which the church stood for the purposes of defence, built an edifice more easy of access near Stonehaven, and persuaded many of the parishioners to perform their devotions there.

Taking possession of the cliff, he transformed

58

the church into a private chapel, and surrounded it by those buildings necessary to render it at once habitable and defensible. Judging from the ruins which now exist, the erections must have been considerable, for the appearance of the Castle and outworks, even in their present demolished condition, is rather that of a ruined hamlet than a single fortress. The necessity for extensive buildings, even for stores, may be understood when we remember that the only communication by land could be easily cut off, and the Castle placed in a state of close siege by a very small opposing force.

An unlooked for adversary arose to this scheme in the person of the Bishop of the diocese. This ecclesiastic, jealous of any encroachment by the temporal on the spiritual power, took action against Sir William, and solemnly excommunicated him by bell, book and candle for trespassing upon consecrated ground. The Earl, usually brave enough in secular matters, was timorous with those who wielded the power over the soul. Fearful of the doom fulminated against him, he sought the protection and absolution of Pope Benedict XIII., explaining that ere he touched the ancient church he had provided for the spiritual wants of the parish, and insisting that the times demanded that there should be some such fortress as he had erected in that quarter for the preservation of the lives of the parishioners. Benedict XIII., in the spirit of a wily Italian Pope, made capital out of both the blunders of

Bishop and warrior Earl, for he decreed that the sentence of excommunication should be taken off the latter, and that upon the payment of a fine to the Church the Earl should be allowed to enjoy the Castle unmolested. And thus Sir William's yearly ransom enabled him to preserve his body from his foes in this world, and his soul from the Enemy in the next.

This chapel was the scene of a very tragic occurrence a few years later. In 1297 the English had gained possession of Dunnottar, and placed a strong garrison there. But the dauntless Wallace had made his way even into this strong fortress, and spread dismay among the southern soldiers. The greater portion of them sought refuge near the altar, trusting that the superstition of the time would prevent the Scottish hero from violating the sanctity of that holy place. This intrepid leader, however, had advanced too far thus to retire, and he braved the terrors of the spiritual powers by enclosing these fugitives within the church, and setting fire to it. From their dreadful fate no escape was possible. The sacred structure overhung the raging waves of the North Sea, and the only exit by land was guarded by the relentless Wallace and his followers, and thus, by fire, by water, and by the sword, perished four thousand of the English invaders. Ere blaming Wallace too severely for this deed, we should remember the critical period in which he lived, and the great stake of home and fatherland for which he played.

Nor should we forget the long arrears of crime and oppression which the English had incurred, and which only the most stringent measures could repress. Harshness was not habitual with him, and there are times when leniency is the worst form of mercy. And we may believe that he had to steel his heart against compassion and discard all thoughts of tenderness when he remembered his murdered wife, his slain father and brethren, and his desolate and bleeding country.

> " Not few nor slight his burdens are
>   Who gives himself to stand
> Steadfast and sleepless as a star
>   Watching his fatherland.
> Strong must his will be, and serene,
>   His spirit pure and bright ;
> His conscience vigilant and keen,
>   His arm an arm of might."

The Castle, though frequently employed as an asylum for the neighbouring inhabitants during the raids of lawless Highland chieftains, does not appear conspicuously in history until the time of the Civil Wars. The rapid changes in political faith which then took place amongst the nobility rendered their Castles the frequent scenes of retribution for crimes committed within their walls. And thus the dungeons of Dunnottar Castle were tenanted alternately by Covenanters and Episcopalians as either of these parties gained the ascendancy. The traditional policy of the Keith family was distinctly Tory in its tendency, and

even when the existing holder of the title in 1645
had declared for the Covenant, it was but a half-
hearted support which he gave to the Lords of
the Congregation. When, therefore, the Marquess
of Montrose, who had been won over to the King,
was on his way from the North and called upon
Dunnottar to surrender in the name of King
Charles, it was with much difficulty that the
possessor of that fortress was prevented from
declaring himself the vassal of His Majesty. The
persuasive eloquence of the Presbyterian clergymen, his companions in the Castle, at length
overcame his scruples, and he fortified the place
against the great Marquess, and put him to defiance. Finding that he had no time to spend
upon a formal siege of Dunnottar, and doubting
its importance in the guerilla warfare which he
then pursued, Montrose avenged himself by devas-
tating the surrounding country, and supplied the
necessities of his army from the produce of the
inhabitants.

But "the whirligig of Time brings in his re-
venges," and so it happened shortly after that
the Castle changed hands and found a new master,
who was as vigorous a persecutor as its former
one had been a saint. Even yet among the ruins
is shown the "Whig's Vault," in which, according
to tradition, a number of the hill-folk were confined, and subjected to extreme trials of fortitude
and endurance. Torture was freely resorted to,
and boots, thumbkins, and racks were called into
requisition to provoke an abjuration of Presby-

terianism. The rings are yet shown to which prisoners were chained, and the " Martyrs' Monument," in the ancient churchyard, serves to localise the tradition.

The historical incident, however, which is most distinctly associated with the name of Dunnottar is the preservation of the regalia during the invasion of Cromwell. When the Lord Protector had " crossed the Rubicon " and openly broken with the Presbyterian party in the north, he found that it was necessary for the establishment of his prestige to strike a vigorous and decisive blow at the strength of the Scottish Independents. The English leader was essentially a man of war, so he buckled on his armour, and ere the Lords of the Congregation had finished their stormy deliberations he had entered the country with fire and sword. Here he found himself opposed by both the Tory and Whig parties; yet, as these two would not coalesce against the common foe, the strength of the country was divided, and he marched triumphantly through Scotland, as he did through Ireland, making his name a terror to the people. To General Monck he entrusted the reduction of the Castles of Scotland which still held out against the Parliament, and this victorious leader subdued them, one after the other, meeting with little resistance from the people. Dunnottar was the last of the Castles to be attacked, in 1652, and to its siege a particular interest was attached.

Since the Union of the Crowns in the person of

James VI., half a century before this time, the Scottish nation had watched over the regalia of the kingdom with peculiar jealousy. They had not succeeded in retaining the ancient " Stone of Destiny " at Scone Palace, upon which the Kings of Scots from time immemorial had been crowned, and the superstition of the age led them to imagine that the luck of the kingdom would depart if the Crown Jewels and Insignia were removed. After the disastrous battle of Dunbar the Scottish leaders cast about for a suitable place of safety for these precious relics, and the Castle of Dunnottar was selected as the strongest fortress in their possession. The emblems were conveyed thither in secrecy and dispatch, and handed over to Lord Keith.

The place of their seclusion, however, was soon discovered, and, as the cupidity of the English had been excited by extravagant accounts of the value of the jewels, these became a special object of interest to them. They laid close siege to the Castle, and prepared for a long campaign. Sir George Ogilvy of Barras, then Governor, at once put Dunnottar in a state of defence, and endeavoured to establish communications with the land by the seaward side of the Castle. In this attempt he was foiled, and the English Army, trusting to conquer by protracting their blockade, resolutely encamped before the fortress. Even so extensive a storehouse as Dunnottar must ultimately fail if sufficient time be spent upon it, and when the stores at length gave token of

DUNNOTTAR CASTLE

reaching a speedy termination, it became necessary to provide for the safe keeping of the national honours. A very bold and daring scheme was conceived and executed by the Governor, with the assistance of the Rev. Mr. Grainger, minister of Kinneff, and his wife, then confined to the Castle. For the purpose of putting the besiegers off their guard, a report was circulated that the regalia had been sent to the Continent in the charge of Sir John Keith, a brother of the Earl's. So industriously was this report spread that the vigour of the siege was relaxed, and a fuller communication with the land permitted.

In these circumstances the courageous Mrs. Grainger applied to General Monck for permission to remove some bundles of lint from the Castle, to which she made claim, and, as he was more noted for gallantry than any other of the Parliamentary generals, her request was readily granted. With the sword and the sceptre enclosed in the bundles which her servant carried, and with the crown secreted about her own person, she boldly made her way through the English camp, receiving, it is said, special attention from the general himself, and, taking the road to Kinneff Church, where her husband awaited her, she finally deposited her charge there. Mr. Grainger removed some of the flagstones in the floor of the church, and, wrapping the precious articles in fine linen, he deposited them there, where they lay unmolested until after the Restoration of Charles II.

Meanwhile the Castle of Dunnottar, after a

brave defence, was compelled to surrender, and great was the disappointment of the English when they found themselves checkmated. The unfortunate Governor was subjected to close examination, and even, it is alleged, to the torture, but he held his secret unflinchingly. The minister and his wife were likewise ill-treated, but they steadfastly refused to betray the hiding-place wherein they had disposed the valuable honours. And thus the siege of Dunnottar, from which the Parliamentarian Army had expected to reap such glorious spoils, became nothing but a barren victory, and the sagacious leaders had to confess themselves outwitted by a woman.

The end of the history of Dunnottar Castle came in the year 1715, a date ever memorable in Scottish annals. The tenth Earl Marischal, who then held sway there, was sufficiently ill-advised to join the rash noblemen who took the field at that time in support of the Chevalier de St George (James VIII.). Ever noted for their devotion to the House of Stuart, the Keiths were easily led into the Jacobite Rising, and George, Earl Marischal, remained faithful to his troth until the end. After the collapse of that unfortunate expedition the Earl was attainted of treason, tried, and condemned, and as he was then upon the Continent, and could not conveniently suffer beheading, it was decided that Dunnottar Castle should be dismantled. And thus this ancient fortress, which had for more than four hundred years maintained a bold front against

invasion and rebellion, was taken when defenceless by the soldiers of the new dynasty, the
fortifications razed to the dust, and its halls left
roofless and uninhabitable. The ruthless spirit of
oppression, stimulated by fear, which character-
ized the government of that time, could not
suffer so venerable a stronghold of the Stuart
family to remain unmolested. And it was the
consideration of such revengeful demolitions of
ancient landmarks which prompted the old
Jacobite ballad which runs thus :—

> " Our ancient Crown's fa'en in the dust ;
>   De'il blin' them in the stour o't,
> An' write their names in his black book.
>   Wha ga'e the Whigs the pow'r o't.
>
> Our sad decay in Kirk and State
>   Surpasses my descrivin' ;
> The Whigs cam' ower us for a curse,
>   An' we ha'e dune wi' thrivin'."

VI

CASTLE CAMPBELL

THE Ochil Hills bear much the same relation to
the East Coast of Scotland as the Kilpatrick Hills
do to the West. Though not in themselves privi-
leged to give rise to an extensive stream, they are
both inseparably associated with the noble rivers,
the Forth and the Clyde, which sweep majestic-
ally past their several bases on their way to the
eastern and western seas. But in point of
grandeur the Ochils transcend the western range,
even as they are themselves dwarfed into insig-
nificance by the loftier hills of the north.

Opposed by the Pentland Hills, which limit the
southern basin of the Forth, the Ochils form a
lofty barrier between the valleys of the Forth and
the Tay, and send tributary streams to swell the
volume of both of these rivers. Three minor ranges
of the Sidlaws, the Ochils, and the Pentland Hills
thus enclose between them the two noblest rivers
on the East Coast of Scotland, and direct their
course to the North Sea. The Ochils, unlike the
more northern mountains, are clad with verdure
almost to their summits, and though bold in
outline and varied in colour, they have not the
sterile majesty of the peaks of Aberdeenshire. At
their base lie many little hamlets and towns,

whose subsistence is drawn rather from their manufactures than from agriculture. Tillicoultry and Alva are alike famous for their productions in the woollen trade, and the extensive factories which here exist show that the introduction of steam as a motive power has rather increased than diminished the number of weavers.

Pre-eminent among the Ochil towns stands Dollar, picturesquely situated upon one of the innumerable " crooks of Devon," which claims remembrance from many causes. The educationalist will think of it as the site of the famous Academy, to which many Scottish men of letters owe their mental birth ; the poet will remember it as the residence of Tennant, the inimitable author of " Anster Fair," and the immortalizer of " Maggie Lauder " ; and the Waltonian will never forget that in its neighbourhood he has bagged the finest trout which the streams of Scotland afford. For down by the very doors of the inhabitants of Dollar flows the lovely river Devon, whose name is not unknown among the lyrics of Scotland, since of it does our National Bard sing in his well-known lay :—

" How pleasant the banks of the clear winding Devon,
  With green spreading bushes and flowers blooming fair."

It is not easy to find a more purely Scottish stream than this same Devon river, which calls forth the enthusiasm of the tourist. Taking its rise in the eastern end of the Ochil range, it wanders by the natural dip of the land towards

Lochleven ; but a peculiar geological formation interposes a barrier and diverts the stream westward, so that, instead of having a short-lived existence ere it lost itself in the loch, it " meandering flows " through many miles of varied scenery, until at length it becomes tributary to the Forth. Nowhere does it attain considerable size, but everywhere it presents the essential phenomena of the Scottish stream. From the Crook of Devon, which is literally the turning-point of its existence, it wanders placidly between the banks with verdure crowned, until it nears Rumbling Bridge.

Here the rapid descent of the valley of Dollar causes it to assume a more turbulent character, and, dashing through the " Devil's Mill," where its stream is not seen, but heard as some weird subterranean " voice of many waters," it hurries on towards the Cauldron Linn. The force of the water, continuously rushing for centuries, has hollowed a vast basin in the sandstone rock, and the stream now pours through a contracted aperture, with the force of a water-spout, sheer over the precipice. From this point it descends more gently through the valley of Dollar, presenting all the characteristics of a Scottish salmon-stream, and realizing Tennyson's description of " The Brook " :—

> " I wind about, and in and out,
>   With here a blossom sailing,
> And here and there a lusty trout,
>   And here and there a grayling."

70

Passing near the town of Dollar, it takes a south-westerly direction toward the Forth, merely catching a glimpse of the picturesque Castle Campbell, which stands amid the green woodland of the hill.

Viewed from a distance, this ancient Keep might readily be mistaken for some retiring mansion-house, embowered in a miniature forest of larch and beech, or, by a stretch of the imagination, to the poet's mind it might seem

> " A palace, lifting in eternal summer
> Its marble head from out a glossy bower
> Of leaves."

Yet a nearer acquaintance with its topography will speedily dispel this illusion. The approach to the Castle soon alters from the mild river-side way with which it begins, to the rugged and stern mountain path which terminates at the ruin. The " bower of leaves " becomes a gloomy forest, and the " marble palace " vanishes into a grim and solitary ruin, which frowns defiantly from the summit of a precipice, apparently inaccessible. The road is now narrowed to its minutest limit, and crosses the fearful chasm which partly surrounds the Castle by one of those shaky wooden bridges which terrify the soul of the timorous tourist. But the view to be obtained from this spot is well worth the trouble thus occasioned. In the valley of the Devon its glistening stream appears, disappears, and re-appears far below the spectator ; and the spires of Dollar and the factories of Tillicoultry, the scenes of the triumph of head and hand, are at once visible. Over the rising ground which lies between the Devon and Alloa, the estuary of the Forth may be seen, now expanded into a noble firth ; while westward the levelling country indicates the proximity of the fertile Carse of Stirling.

Nearer the point of vision the two streams which flow around the Castle and fall into the Devon a short way from it have been named by some romantic native in pre-historic times, the Water of Care and the Burn of Greif (Gryfe) ; while the ancient title of the ruin itself was " the Castle of Gloom," and the site of the melancholy trio was " the Valley of Dolour." This poetical combination, however, like so many fanciful tales, has collapsed before the searching examination of this practical age, and a new interpretation must now be given. The name of Castle Gloom is probably a corruption of the Gaelic *Chleum* or *Coch Leum*—the Mad Leap, though the origin of that title is lost in obscurity. The Water of Care was most likely applied to the stream after the building of the edifice, as it seems an easy transition from *Caer*, the Celtic prefix for a castle and its surroundings. Dollar is now supposed to have been originally *Balor*, the high field—a title which its position justifies ; and thus the tender element of romance evaporates beneath analysis.

The date of the erection of the Castle is now

CASTLE CAMPBELL

undiscoverable, nor has the most elaborate investigation thrown much light upon its origin. There is a tradition still current which declares that it was a portion of the dowry which King Robert the Bruce bestowed upon his sister, Lady Mary Bruce, on the occasion of her marriage with Sir Neil Campbell of Lochow. But if this was the case it must have gone out of the possession of the family afterwards, for it was certainly held by Archbishop Schevet, of St Andrews, and was gifted by him to the head of the Campbells in his time as a bribe to secure his support on a special occasion. The Archbishop died in 1498 at an advanced age. In 1493 an Act of Parliament was passed to enable the proprietor (apparently the second Earl of Argyll) to change its name from " Castle of Gleume " to " Castle Campbell," by which designation it is still known. And though it must have been peculiarly convenient for a powerful western clan to have a stronghold of such security in the eastern district, whereby disaffection might be overawed, the isolation of the Castle from the main body of the Clan Campbell frequently exposed it to danger, and finally brought about its destruction.

The rivalry between the clans of the east and the west of Scotland raged with violence for centuries, and the untutored clansmen pursued their feuds with the same deep spirit of revenge as a Corsican follows the vendetta of his family. When, therefore, the Covenanters in the time of Charles I. included two such eminent men as

Montrose and Argyll, the leaders of the Grahams and the Campbells, who had been sworn foes for a lengthened period, it was soon evident that they could not long remain devoted to the same cause. Their traditional enmity effectually prevented them from coalescing, and the crafty spirit of Argyll led him to attempt

> " Ways that are dark,
> And tricks that are vain,"

The haughty soul of Montrose recoiled from his leadership and renounced the Covenanting cause which he had espoused. His overtures to the King were well received at Court, for his reputation as a warrior had gone before him, and he was looked upon as a Chevalier Bayard, *sans peur et sans reproche.*

The exploits of the great Marquess of Montrose in Scotland read more like a romance of olden times than veritable history; and his heartfelt devotion to the King in good or ill-fortune elevate him to the position of a hero. But the sun of the Stewart family was then under eclipse; and it was not given to Montrose to be the instrument of their restoration to power, however strenuous his endeavours for that purpose; though, perhaps his cruel and ignominious death did as much to forward the Royal Cause as his most brilliant victory on the field of battle. The history of Montrose, however, is not to concern us at present, save in its relation to Castle Campbell.

The period of Scottish history which treats of the Civil War during the time of Charles I. and the Commonwealth, shows distinctly that the gratification of private revenge and the settlement of family feuds largely influenced the combatants. The wavering fortunes which inclined now to the Covenanters and anon to the Royalists soon reduced the land to the state in which Judæa was placed when " there was no King in Israel." Argyll had his own traditional enemies, but so also had every prominent man in his retinue ; and thus vengeance was widely spread, and never lacked opportunity. The history of the time was a constant record of murder and rapine, of insult and reprisal, until the condition of the country became absolutely deplorable. The opposing forces soon reached that stage at which no sense of honour restrains from excess, and when the claims of family ties and blood relationships are boldly set at naught or publicly outraged. And it was during this fearful time, and as a result of this melancholy and fratricidal position that Castle Campbell fell a victim to the general fury.

The Campbells, as already mentioned, were at feud with the Grahams, but they were also sworn foes to the Ogilvies, another powerful eastern clan, which commanded a large portion of Forfarshire. The Earl of Airlie, leader of this clan and a devoted adherent of Charles I., had removed to England early in the struggle of 1640, fearing that the Covenanters would insist upon his signature. His Castles of Airlie and Forter were left in charge of his son, Lord Ogilvy, and as they were well-garrisoned, he thought they might escape the rage of the enemy. But the Committee of Estates, undaunted by the check which the young Lord had given them, issued a Commission of Fire and Sword to Argyll, authorizing him to capture both these strongholds. The task was a congenial one to the ruthless Argyll; and with fiendish glee he set about its accomplishment. Directing an overwhelming force against the Castle of Airlie, he compelled Lord Ogilvy to withdraw, and then, in pursuance of his instructions from the Committee, he proceeded to raze the walls and battlements.

A contemporary writer records that " Argyll was seen taking a hammer in his hand, knocking down the hewed work of the doors and windows till he did sweat for heat at his task." And the ancient ballad from which the following verses are quoted, details, with perhaps some superfluous exaggerations, the poetical aspect of the grim scene :—

" It fell on a day, and a bonnie simmer day,
    When green grew aits an' barley,
That there fell oot a great dispute
    'Tween gleyed Argyll an' Airlie.

Argyll has raised ane hunder men,
    Ane hunder harnessed rarely ;
An' he's awa' by the back o' Dunkeld
    To plunder the Castle o' Airlie.

Lady Ogilvy looks ower her bower window,
  An' O, but she looks wearily ;
An' there she spied the great Argyll,
  Come to plunder the bonnie house o' Airlie.

' Come down, come down, my Lady Ogilvy,
  Come down an' kiss me fairly.'
' O, I wadna kiss the fause Argyll
  Tho' he shouldna leave a standin' stane in Airlie.'

. . . . . .

' O, I ha'e seven braw sons,' she said—
  ' The youngest ne'er saw his daddie ;
But tho' I had ane hunder mae
  I'd gi'e them a' to King Charlie.

' But gin my gude Lord had been at hame,
  As this nicht he is wi' Charlie,
There durstna a Campbell in a' Argyll
  Ha'e plundered the bonnie house o' Airlie.

' Gif my gude Lord was noo at hame,
  As he is wi' King Charlie,
The dearest blude o' a' thy kin
  Wad slocken the burnin' o' Airlie ! ' "

Thus runs the old song, and though there seems
too strong a flavour of the Trojan dame in this
Scottish matron, the strain proved prophetic,
for her Lord had the privilege on the bloody
field of Kilsyth of executing summary vengeance
upon the Campbell clan in open battle.

Meanwhile, a partial revenge had been taken
upon the unfortunate Castle Campbell by the
followers of Montrose. After the " glorious

victory " at Aulderne, that intrepid leader descended by the east coast to the Forth, and then, striking across the country by way of Kinross and Devon Valley, he thought to surprise and capture Stirling with little effort. In his progress westward he had to pass this stronghold of Argyll ; and as the ruthless conduct of the cross-eyed Earl at Airlie had been detailed to Montrose, he relaxed discipline to allow the Ogilvies, who were with him, to indulge their revengeful spirit. These were joined by the followers of the Earl of Stirling, whose house of Menstrie, at the base of the Ochils, had been relentlessly destroyed by the same hand. And as these avengers of blood marched boldly up the narrow path towards the ancient Castle of Gloom, well might the Campbells within its walls tremble

" To see the gallant Grahams come hame.

I'll crown them east, I'll crown them wast,
    The bravest lads that e'er I saw ;
They bore the gree in free fechtin',
    An' ne'er were slack their swords to draw.

They won the day wi' Wallace wight.
    They were the lords o' the south countrie ;
Cheer up your hearts, brave cavaliers,
    The gallant Grahams ha'e come ower the sea ! "

The resistance offered to the assault must have been slight, since the position of the Castle might have rendered defence easy. But the name of

Montrose acted as a magic spell upon his enemies ; and this token of western power fell into the hands of the warriors of the east, and was laid waste by fire and sword. Nor have its lofty battlements since borne the Banner of Argyll, with the Galley of Lorne, and the proud motto of the Campbells, *Ne obliviscaris.*

VII

ROTHESAY CASTLE

As the County of Kinross, one of the smallest
in area of the divisions of Scotland, contains
within its limited space variety of scenery and
wealth of historic association unequalled by
larger counties, so Bute, one of the least considerable of the islands of the west, appears to
the intelligent observer as a miracle of loveliness,
teeming with facts and fancies of olden times.
The River Clyde, which here debouches into the
Atlantic Ocean, surrounds the islands of Bute,
Arran, and the Cumbraes, each presenting a
different type of beauty from the others, and
claiming diverse meads of praise. The scenery
of Arran, whose bold outline of rugged alpine
peaks in barren grandeur is thrown against the
sky, contrasts with the commonplace elevation
of the Cumbraes, whose gentle, undulating
eminences are too fruitful and well-cultivated
to become the home of romance. To Bute is
reserved that combination of wild, unsophisticated
nature and extreme civilization which holds the
greatest charm for the tourist of modern times.
From the inconsiderable heights which this
island affords, you may overlook the broad
expanse of water which lies betwixt Bute and

ROTHESAY CASTLE

the Ayrshire coast, whose continuous outline
becomes reduced shorewards, until it terminates
in the distant point of Port Crawford; or,
looking northward, the grim desolation of the
Cowal shore presents a different scene. There
the o'ertopping Argyll mountains fade away into
obscurity, filling in the distant background with
some far-remote Ben, which none save an expert
will venture to name. There are not many
places in Scotland where, at one moment, we
may find ourselves—

> " Far 'lone amang the Hieland hills
>   'Mid Nature's wildest grandeur ; "

and at the next may turn to view—

> " The cloud-capped towers, the gorgeous palaces,
>   The solemn temples "

of a very advanced civilization. Yet these are
points in the island of Bute from which the
beholder may elect either to feast his eyes upon—

> " The hills embrowned with brackens' rusty gold,
>   And the bell-heather,"

telling of the scanty pasturage and waste lands
which produce the men of war ; or to turn his
gaze upon the—

> " Deep waving fields and pastures green,
>   With gentle slopes and groves between,"

of a highly-civilized land, which exhibits the
blessings of peace.

From a slight elevation the eye may at one glance see the ancient town of Rothesay, stretching around the shore of its crescent-shaped bay, and uplifting its multi-form spires and towers above the din and tumult of constant traffic; and at the same time it may rest upon the placid waters of Loch Ascog or Loch Fad, embosomed amid the uplands of the island, and reposing as tranquilly as though they were situated in the least-frequented hills of the Northern Highlands.

The summit of the heath-clad steep of Barone Hill permits a very wide expanse of country to be seen; and topographers of an arithmetical turn may reckon up twelve counties as being thus brought within the range of vision. The receding coast of Ayrshire allows a broad sheet of water to extend southwards to the horizon; and the Argyll shore, suddenly trending westward, and terminating in the elongated peninsula of Cantyre, leaves Bute standing alone amid the surrounding element—

"A priceless gem, set in a silver sea."

The very minuteness of the separate portions of the scene gives a kind of fairy charm to it. For it seems as if one were looking upon some exquisite model of Scottish landscape, wherein might be seen, upon a reduced scale, the loch, the hillside, and the river, with every distinctive characteristic which belongs to "the land of the mountain and the flood." And so this lovely islet is but a microcosm, a toy-model of Scottish scenery. One is not astonished, therefore, to find that Bute has some pre-historic ruins of a religious establishment, whose unwritten story must be of a remote date.

The remains of the ancient Chapel of St Blane may still be seen nestling in a sequestered dell in the southern part of the island ; and here, if tradition may be believed, the holy Blane has peacefully reposed for these last thirteen centuries. The architecture of the Chapel certainly belongs to an era of comparative antiquity, though the dates of some of the earlier chroniclers of the Saints are no more reliable than the chronology of the Chinese historians. The story of Saint Blane as now preserved in the traditions of the island must be taken with " a pinch of salt," as the Romans used to say. A certain bishop from Ireland (these Irish people early found the way to Caledonia), called St Chattan, had selected this part of Bute as his residence, and here he settled with his sister Erca, resolved to effect the conversion of the pagans of Scotland to the true and universal faith. Whatever effect the ministrations of the holy man may have had upon the natives is now unknown ; but it is recorded that whilst he was powerless to win over the King of Scots to his religion, the beauty of his sister enticed that sovereign from the path of rectitude. The unhappy Erca, when her crime could no longer be hid, was visited with the punishment then deemed the best corrective for errors of judgment. She was placed in a coracle, or boat of skins, and set adrift upon the bosom of the Clyde, a living Elaine in search of her faithless Lancelot. The wind and the tide bore her far away southwards, and cast her, with her helpless babe, upon the hospitable shore of Ireland.

Here she was rescued by two generous Hibernian monks, who baptized the little stranger by the name of " Blaan," and tended and cared for him for some time. At length he was sent to his uncle, Chattan, in Bute, who adopted and educated him for the priesthood, and shortly after his ordination he journeyed to Rome, and was consecrated Bishop by the occupant of St Peter's Chair. Returning to Scotland he settled in Perthshire, founding the sacred house of Dunblane, of which See he was the first bishop ; and after his demise his remains were conveyed to Kilchattan Bay, in Bute, the scene of his early life, to rest near the relics of his uncle and benefactor.

Not far from St Blane's Chapel there stands a vitrified Roman fort, showing that these ubiquitous conquerors had penetrated even here, and left the traces of their civilizing influences behind them. Indeed, the name " Bute " is said by some philologists to be a corruption of the Latin " budæ," the name applied by the Roman historians to the western isles of Scotland. The defective geography of the time probably led them to imagine that the whole of the west coast was protected by a continuous chain of

islands, extending from Orkney (" Ultima Thule ")
to Arran, inhabited by a savage and irreclaimable
people, upon whom the arts of Italy could
exercise no humanizing power. Bute, therefore,
seems to have been the spot chosen by them as
the extreme limit of the civilization of western
Scotland, and here they terminated their line of
defence.

All theories upon the origin of the fort of Dun-
na-Goil, regarding which no authentic records
exist, are but founded upon conjecture, and set
solely upon circumstantial evidence. The antiquity of Rothesay Castle, though wrapt in some
obscurity, is not so far removed from written
history ; and as the interest attached to it arises
from its connection with known events in the
annals of Scotland, the influence of inventive
romance is not so apparent.

The ancient Castle of Rothesay is peculiarly
situated. The bay takes a gigantic sweep inland
from the point of Bogany to that of Ardbeg ; and
at the very centre of this hemisphere, only a few
yards from the shore, this venerable pile has been
erected. Unlike most of the ancient Castles, it is
built upon low ground, and might be easily commanded from the heights. Its position, however,
has doubtless been chosen as affording an extensive view of the Firth of Clyde, though the
clustering dwellings which now surround it effectually interrupt the prospect. The building is
considerable in extent, though the various styles
of architecture and the methods of masonry

employed show that the original structure has been very much enlarged. Possibly the nucleus around which these additions have been made was the circular tower on the east side, which bears the greatest resemblance to the antique forts of remote times. And the derivation of the name of Rothesay, which authorities say is compounded from the Gaelic *Roth*, a circle, and *Suidh* a seat, give some countenance to the theory that the circular donjon was the earliest part of the building. The crow-stepped Flemish gables and circle-top windows of other portions belong to a period much nearer our own time.

The Castle has been of sufficient compass to contain within its walls an extensive court-yard and a private chapel. Though now entirely roofless, there are many traces left of foundations and razed walls which sufficiently indicate the importance and extent of the Castle. In many parts of the buildings the walls are over seven feet in thickness, and are composed mostly of square-hewn stones with rough rubble-work. The edifice is surrounded by a moat fifteen feet deep by about nine feet wide, which is supplied with water from Loch Fad, though probably in the earlier days of the Castle the waters of the bay have laved its walls.

The main doorway is the least imposing portion of the structure, though the sculptured arms above it, and the portcullis groove in the lintels still challenge the attention of the antiquary. The clustering ivy which luxuriates in every

portion of the Castle, clothing its rugged front
with vesture of perennial green, serves to enhance
the romantic effect of the whole scene, and to
awaken those memories of the past which are
ever associated with this "dainty plant that
creepeth o'er ruins old." And the past of Rothesay Castle is not uneventful.

It is supposed that the original building was
erected by Magnus Barefoot, King of Norway,
some time about the end of the 11th century.
This redoubtable sea-king had conquered the
Hebridean Isles, and, descending as far south as
Bute, he there established a post from which he
might menace the mainland of Scotland. And if
this tradition be correct, it is curious to note that
this Royal Castle of Rothesay was erected by an
alien and an invader, and must have stood for
many years as a sign of the subjection of the
natives to a foreign yoke. Yet those jovial fair-
haired Norwegians were no ascetics, but bold,
free-handed, and frank, as befitted the warriors
whose "march was o'er the mountain waves,"
whose "home was on the deep." And these old
walls, in their earliest days, must have witnessed
many a scene of "gamyn and glee," and resounded
upon festive occasions with "mirth and youthful
jollity." For we know the method of the Norwegian rover's life from the Saga of King Olaf—

> "The guests were loud, the ale was strong,
>   King Olaf feasted late and long ;
>   The hoary Scalds together sang,
>   O'erhead the smoky rafters rang."

And with some such rites as these was the baptism of Rothesay Castle accomplished in those distant times.

Some romantic theorists assert that the true meaning of Rothesay in Gaelic is " Wheel of Fortune," and state that this name was bestowed upon it in consequence of the rapid changes which took place in the possession of this ancient fortalice. The original appellation given to it by its Norwegian founders is now unknown ; but the study of its history sufficiently justifies this fanciful title, as shall now be related.

The topographical position of many of our Scottish Castles made them historical, even though they had no intrinsic claim upon the historian. The names of many of them are preserved, not so much in consequence of their importance as because they occupied debatable land, upon which opposing armies continually met to decide their contests. Such a position did Rothesay Castle occupy. Situated at the entrance to the estuary of the Clyde, and possessing a well-sheltered harbour and good post of observation, it was naturally one of the coveted spots which attracted the attention of the northern invaders. The Norwegians and Danes, who successively over-ran the coasts of Scotland, were not ignorant of the advantages possessed by the hold of this fort, and thus it happened that many a bloody fray took place beneath its walls. And so, for a hundred and fifty years after its erection the Castle changed hands frequently, until it came at length into the power of the Norwegians after a protracted siege.

The native Scots had not sufficient strength to dislodge them from this coign of vantage, and when Hako, the Dane, led his great Armada into the Firth of Clyde, he found in Rothesay a safe harbour for his fleet, and a strong fortress for his protection. Warily extending his conquests, he took possession of Arran and the Cumbraes, preparatory to making a descent upon the mainland; and gathering together the combined forces of Norway and Denmark, he landed on the Ayrshire coast immediately opposite Bute. But the young King, Alexander III., had already aroused the Scottish peoples to resistance, and, marching himself at the head of his army, he met the invaders at Largs, but a short distance from their point of landing.

The fortunes of war were not soon decided, as neither party gained palpable advantage over the other; and so the battle was renewed upon three successive days. But Neptune and Æolus, the gods of the Sea and the Wind, came to the aid of Britain, as they did three centuries later against the Spanish Armada of Philip II. The wild nor'-east wind sweeping down the Firth, and lashing the troubled waters into fury, drove the Danish ships from their anchorage, and dashed them helplessly upon the unfriendly shore. The noble barks, which had withstood the gales of many years, were powerless in the narrow, unknown channels in which they were drifting; and

the Danes found in their melancholy experience
that neither the winds nor the waves would obey
them.

The Scots were active in taking advantage of
this occasion; and they drove the too-confident
invaders ignominiously from their coasts. Hako
retired with difficulty, taking the remnant of his
army to Orkney; and there, lamenting the
flower of his warriors and his own near kinsmen
slain in this disastrous conflict, he finally expired,
the victim of grief and despair. Thus ended the
Battle of Largs, the last contest betwixt the Scots
and Danes upon our native soil. Nearly six
centuries after, the descendants of those warriors met in widely-diverse circumstances. Then
" mighty Nelson " led his fleet through the waters
of the Baltic to the very walls of Copenhagen, and
proved to the successors of the Vikings of old
that their rule over the ocean was at an end.
And if Hako mourned in defeat the brave army
which he left shattered and destroyed on the
shores of the Clyde, not less, even when crowned
with victory, should we—

> " Think of those who sleep
> Full many a fathom deep,
> By thy wild and stormy steep,
> Elsinore."

After the Battle of Largs, the Castle of Rothesay was garrisoned by the troops of King Alexander, and the Scots remained in possession of it
until the faint-hearted John Baliol surrendered

it to Edward of England, as an atonement
for his heinous crime of independence. But
the valour of King Robert the Bruce freed
Scotland from the presence of the English
soldiers for a time, and he regained the Castle.
Scottish politics became confused after his death;
and when Randolph, the Regent, died, affairs
reached a crisis. Edward Baliol, collecting a
scratch army in England, took advantage of the
prevailing confusion, and made a rapid descent
upon Scotland. His attempts were crowned with
success, however undeserved; and as the young
King, David Bruce, had been hastily conveyed to
Dumbarton Castle, as a place of security, the
invader followed him closely, and took the Castle
of Rothesay with ease. His army, however, was
not of sufficient strength to enable him to garrison
this stronghold, and it soon submitted to the
partizans of the King. And when, some fifty
years later, the troubled state of Scotland had
been somewhat allayed, the beauty of the surrounding country and the salubrity of the climate,
which had not been noticed in warlike times,
then attracted attention. Robert II., the first of
the long line of Stewart Kings, visited the Castle
upon several occasions, and latterly selected it as
his residence.

After his death his son John, who ascended the
throne under the title of Robert III., continued
to hold Rothesay in favour; so much so that
he conferred the title of Duke of Rothesay
upon his eldest son, making this an hereditary

title for the heir-apparent. Hence the Prince
of Wales, who is Duke of Cornwall, and was
Earl of Dublin in Ireland, is Duke of Rothesay
and Baron Renfrew in Scotland. The fate of the
first Duke of Rothesay could not be regarded
as a good augury by his contemporaries. The
mild King Robert III., unfitted by an accident in
early youth from mingling in the warlike employ-
ments of the time, was possessed of a mind more
inclined to religious melancholy and austerity
than chivalrous bravery. It was, therefore, with
deep regret and pain that he heard of the wild and
licentious character of his son, the new Duke of
Rothesay. The restraint imposed on this unhappy young man by the influence of his mother
had been withdrawn at her death ; and he had
given loose rein to his passions, and would abide
no rebuke. The King, his father, was weak
enough to allow his own brother, the wily Duke
of Albany, to poison his mind against Rothesay.
So great an influence did Albany gain over the
King that he finally obtained permission to con-
fine Rothesay in close ward.

The Duke of Albany lost no time in putting
this power into practice ; with the assistance of
an unprincipled retainer he seized his nephew and
conveyed him to his own Castle of Falkland,
where Rothesay was enclosed in one of the darkest
dungeons, and refused the ordinary necessaries
of life. Many strange stories are told regarding
this inhuman treatment. It is said that one of
the female servants assisted to keep him in life

by dropping meal into his prison-chamber through the crevices of the floor above ; whilst another bestowed upon him a portion of the provision which Nature had made for the support of her own children. Rothesay's unnatural uncle, having discovered the sources of this succour, ruthlessly put both of these ministering angels to death. When life became insupportable, the unhappy youth was relieved from his misery by welcome death, after enduring the most fearful torture of which the human frame is capable. His body was quietly conveyed to Lindores Abbey and buried there, and his ambitious uncle found himself, by his machinations, one step nearer to the throne. The title of Duke of Rothesay was transferred to his brother James, who afterwards ascended the throne as first of that name, and closed an unhappy life by a violent death.

After the murder of the first Duke of Rothesay, his father, King Robert, fearful that a similar fate might befall his only remaining son, resolved to send him to France for safety. But the ship in which the Duke sailed was captured by an English vessel, and the Prince was sent into captivity in London. The news of this fresh calamity fell with crushing weight upon the old King, and brought him, heart-broken, to his grave ; for, like Israel of old, he may have said, " If I am bereaved of my children, I *am* bereaved." And as the night of sorrow closed around him in his Castle of Rothesay, and he thought of one son murdered and another in

93

hopeless captivity, whilst the brother, to whom he had trusted all, had proved faithless and untrue, death must have seemed a glad release to him from the life-long trouble he had endured.

It must not be imagined that there are no pleasant episodes connected with Rothesay Castle. There is a story told of an unwilling visit paid to it by James V., which is not a little amusing. That merry monarch, whilst still " the Guidman of Ballengeich," had often gone in quest of amorous adventures, but at length he resolved to settle down to serious matrimony, and set forth, like Cœlebs, in search of a wife. An intimate connection had ever been maintained betwixt Scotland and France, and as a union with that country was most desirable, James naturally turned his thoughts in that direction. But the reformed doctrines had made many converts in Scotland, and the nobles looked with disfavour upon a project which might place them at the mercy of the ultra-Roman Court of France. James was self-willed, however, and would not be diverted from his purpose. He sailed from Leith, therefore, with the avowed intention of wedding a French Princess, despite remonstrances of his advisers.

The weather was propitious, and with " youth at the prow and pleasure at the helm," his noble bark sailed onwards. But the grim Scottish Barons performed the journey most unwillingly, and at length laying their heads together, they resolved to trick the King out of his purpose.

One night whilst he was asleep they persuaded the captain to put about ship and to run back to Scotland. Whilst their unconscious victim was peacefully dreaming of love and joy in France, his ship was speeding fast homewards and placing the rolling sea betwixt him and his hopes. Judge then of his surprise and indignation when he awoke to find that the distance between him and love was increasing rather than lessening, and that the power over his actions had been usurped by his officious advisers. He raged and stormed, and swore most likely (for at that time to " swear like a Scot " was a saying on the Continent), and vowed to punish the whole body of traitors who had dared to coerce him. Against the captain especially was his wrath turned, for the historian of the incident relates that " had not beine the earnest solisitatioun of monie in his favours he had hanged the skipper incontinent."

To vindicate his power he ordered them again to change their course, and selecting Bute as his resting-place, he remained for some time in the Castle of Rothesay, until preparation had been made to convey him to Stirling. Like all his race, this headstrong Prince became violent under opposition ; and as though influenced irresistibly by the magnet of love, he rested not until he had set out again to wed a damsel whom he had never seen. The unhappy Queen Magdalene, daughter of the King of France, whom he brought back to Scotland, survived her nuptials only forty days ; and shortly afterwards James journeyed again to France upon a similar errand, returning with Mary of Guise as his bride, the mother of the unfortunate Mary, Queen of Scots.

During the disturbed reign of Charles I., the Castle of Rothesay was garrisoned in the interests of the King by its hereditary custodian, Sir James Stewart of Bute ; but no serious engagement took place there, and the troops were despatched to aid the royal cause in other parts of the kingdom. When Cromwell entered Scotland he caused the soldiers of the Commonwealth to take possession of Rothesay Castle, probably anticipating that the resistance of the Highland Clans would be focussed there ; and as he did not care to leave a garrison so far from his main army, he instructed his men to destroy the strongest parts of the edifice. The command was faithfully obeyed by the Independents, to whom the demolition of Cathedral or Castle seems to have been alike palatable. And Rothesay, which had been a tower of strength for nearly six centuries, never again held its head aloft in proud defiance.

The old saying that " Time tries all," applies to Rothesay Castle, which was now drawing to the end of its existence as a royal residence. The Stewart line, the members of which had been its first patrons, had fallen upon evil days. Charles I. was beheaded ; Charles II. died without legitimate heir ; and the turbulent reign of the Duke of York (James VII.) had spread dismay amongst the majority of the Scottish nation. Many of the

Covenanting nobles had found refuge at the Court of William of Orange, and chief among them was the unfortunate Earl of Argyll, who, by a most iniquitous sentence, had been attainted and outlawed. The plots of William of Orange against his father-in-law, then styled "James II. and VII.," afforded opportunity for the malcontents. The growing feeling of dissatisfaction encouraged the expatriated noblemen to attempt a rising against the Government; and the joint-expeditions of the Duke of Monmouth and the Earl of Argyll were organised. It was proposed that the former should land on the southern shores of England while the latter made a diversion by invading the northern part of the kingdom. In June 1685, Monmouth landed in Dorset, and speedily drew a formidable following to his standard; but the rash encounter which he dared at Sedgemoor finally overthrew him, and awoke the vengeance of a ruthless government.

Argyll's expedition had no more fortunate issue. The leaders had disputed as to the proper point of attack; and in the multitude of counsellors there is danger. Argyll insisted upon landing in his own country, while some of the Lowland nobles more reasonably proposed to win over the landed proprietors in the south of Scotland by force or persuasion. A compromise was finally adopted whereby the first landing was arranged to take place in Argyll, but the attack to be directed against the rich counties bordering upon the Clyde. Landing in Cantyre, the little army was soon increased by the Campbell Clan ; and, taking possession of Rothesay Castle, they fortified it, storing the ammunition upon one of the small islands in the Kyles of Bute. But the irresolution of the Earl proved the destruction of the army. Urged by the confederated leaders to advance and give battle, he at last consented to move the troops into the Lennox country, but here, when in the presence of the enemy, his courage forsook him, and he declined to risk an encounter. There is often as much skill in avoiding a contest as in daring it ; but Argyll could neither lead an assault nor conduct a retreat, and his army was soon dispersed without having endured an engagement. He was himself taken as a fugitive, and as he had been sentenced to death in 1681, he was executed in 1685 without another trial, though he had again been a rebel— an instance of the vindictive rigour of the time.

Meanwhile the stores which Argyll had laid up near Rothesay were taken by the King's soldiers, and his brother, Lord Niel Campbell, whom he had left at the Castle, made his escape from the island of Bute, destroying the fortress ere he fled, and leaving little to the conquerors save the blackened and charred ruins which now remain. And thus, after a long and honourable career, this noble pile closed its history in no memorable conflict, nor amid the din of contending hosts, but during the tumult of a sham revolt the torch of the incendiary was applied to the structure in wanton malice by the hand of a Scottish nobleman. The third Marquess of Bute (1847-1900) did much to restore the outer portion of the Castle, the changes made by him being shown by the use of red sand-stone, so that they may be easily distinguished.

VIII

CASTLE FRAOCH-EILEAN, LOCH AWE

THE scenery of Loch Awe is deservedly held in remembrance by the tourist who has once witnessed its beauty. It is not easy to select from amongst the Scottish lakes that sheet of water which most fully exhibits the characteristics of Highland landscape ; but it will be found that those travellers whose experience of Scotland's lochs and hills is widest are inclined to ascribe a very high position to Loch Awe in comparison with wilder and more northern scenes. Embosomed amid "Heaven-kissing hills," and dotted with many islets crowned with verdure, this vast inland loch washes a shore-line which presents many varied aspects to the beholder. The glen in which it lies is formed by the overhanging hills of Argyllshire which rise precipitously all around, sometimes attaining so extreme an altitude that the extent of the loch is dwarfed beside them. Although nearly thirty miles in length, Loch Awe does not exceed two miles in breadth, and the frequent storms which come sweeping down from Glen Strae and the Pass of Brander keep the waters in such constant motion that it seems to be some gigantic river rather than a peaceful mountain-lake.

The isles which lie cradled in its bosom are rich in foliage, which contrasts with the bare, brown, heath-clad mountain summits, whose bold outline stands relieved against the sky, and in the midst of the overwhelming grandeur of the scene they assume fairy-like proportions which their actual extent does not justify. Far away north rises the peak of Ben Cruachan, whose summit is 3611 feet above the level of the sea. The springs which feed the tributary streams in this quarter mostly owe their origin to this mountain, and the valley which stretches from its base forms the bed of Loch Awe. The tradition which accounts for the origin and present position of the loch may be of special interest to the reader, and is not well-known.

In the times of remote antiquity, ere wizards, witches, and fairies had been scared from Scotland, the rich and fertile valley now covered by the waters of the loch, was in the possession of a brave and fearless woman, the daughter of a former chief who held the locality. For years she ruled the land which belonged to her wisely and well ; but by some hidden means the " uncanny folk " gained an ascendency over her, and wrought their wicked purposes upon her. She was laid under a spell which doomed her to death unless she performed a certain task with unfailing regularity. Her duty was a peculiar one. Midway up Ben Cruachan there was a tiny spring whose limpid waters had often solaced the chief's daughter and refreshed her followers upon

101

their return from the chase ; for in those days the toils and dangers of this sport did not terrify the softer sex. This spring she was enjoined to cover each night with a cabalistic stone whose potency should avert unheard of dangers from her. The unknown is always terrible ; and in dread of a peril which she could not understand, she did not fail to perform her nightly duty, though with fear and trembling.

At last a moment's weakness accomplished her destruction. Returning after a weary and fruitless chase one day, she was separated from her companions, and, footsore and "forfouchten," disappointed in mind and exhausted in body, she sank down at the base of Ben Cruachan, unable to reach her home. There are times when the most vigorous intellect must succumb to the influence of physical exhaustion, no matter how important the duties may be which lie before it, and then the overburdened spirit, weary of resistance, abandons the contest.

> "Is it not pitiful
> Our souls should be so bound about with flesh,
> Even when they leap and smite with wings and feet,
> The least pain plucks them back, puts out their eyes,
> Turns them to tears and words ? "

And so this Highland Diana, this mighty huntress, sank to rest beneath a beechen tree at the foot of the hill. She knew that the setting sun had its duty for her, but, reckless of consequences, she fell into a deep and troubled sleep.

102

She was destined to endure a rude awakening. Ere long there came the ceaseless drip-dripping of a running streamlet, which mingled pleasantly with her dreams, but soon increased to the murmur of the rill, the rush of the mountain-torrent, the thunder of the cascade ; and the *Cailleach Bhe'ir* awoke to find herself in the midst of a raging flood. The insignificant spring which she had despised had now become a foaming sea, and the fair and fertile vale, once her loved inheritance, was now the prey of the merciless waters. Regret became despair, and she plunged into the seething abyss, never more to return. And now Loch Awe stretches its waters, glistening in silver sheen, over this once fertile Vale of Tempe ; and the gentle undulations which arose upon the plain appear as crested islets, crowned with foliage, or fringed with sedge and dwarf willow.

One of the loveliest of these islands is that known as *Fraoch Eilean*, the Isle of Heather. On the mainland, immediately opposite to it, the mountain surfaces descend precipitously, forming the deep valley known as the Pass of Awe. Yet though exposed to the rude Borean blasts which sweep in fury down the loch from this spot, Fraoch-Eilean has ever maintained its fertile appearance. The verdant trees which cluster round the ruins of the ancient Castle effectually screen it from the view ; and few save those who care to explore the recesses of the wood are conscious of its existence. But the venturous spirit who threads the weedy maze by which it is encompassed will be repaid for his labour.

Though now roofless and uninhabitable the Castle, sometimes called Dunderawe, exhibits traces of its former strength, which plainly show that it was fitted to become the stronghold of a powerful Argyllshire Clan. And from the vantage ground afforded by the crumbling walls and tottering battlements the daring climber may obtain an enchanting view of the valley of Loch Awe. Northward the Pass appears to follow the trend of the basin of the loch, and, but for its elevation, would naturally have been a prolongation of it. The height of the hills which rise on either side causes this spot to become the scene of some of the grandest phenomena of storm and tempest. Their lofty crests, by intercepting the fleecy clouds which float in ether, bring frequent showers at unexpected moments upon the lowly vale, or, by attracting the dark-rolling thunder cloud, precipitate the atmospheric tumult, and draw down the ruddy levin-brand upon their elevated summits.

Southward, through the interlacing boughs, the silvery lake may be seen extending itself, with many a winding turn and creek, and encircling the sister isles of Innis-Hail, Eilean-taigert, and Innis-Connel, each claiming notice for some tale of long ago, inwoven with its history. To the east and west rise those peaks whose drainage, by stream and torrent, reaches the loch, and whose position compels the wild north wind

FRAOCH-EILEAN CASTLE

Valentine & Sons, Ltd.

frequently to rush with irresistible force down the
channel thus formed, and to lash the placid waters
of the lake into foam and fury. Fenced from the
storm by the trees which rustle in the blast, the
wayfarer may turn his gaze upon the scene which
is thus spread around, and feel that—

> " 'Tis pleasant from the loopholes of retreat
>   To peep at such a world."

Like many other ruins on the shores of the loch,
the Castle of Fraoch-Eilean has an unwritten
history. Tradition records that the island was
gifted to Sir Gilchrist Macnaughton by Alexander
III., who caused the first Castle to be built there
in 1267, and handed it over to the chief by making
him perpetual Castellan. The only duty imposed
upon him was the seldom-exercised one of pro-
viding entertainment for the King of Scotland
should he pass that way. But the journey to the
wilds of Argyllshire was not often attempted by
the Scottish rulers in early days ; for the state of
the roads and the manners of the inhabitants
made it neither pleasant nor safe for the King's
Majesty to venture within their bounds. And
when Robert Bruce made his presence known in
the locality, it was as an errant knight in search
of a kingdom ; and as the sworn foe of Macdougal
of Lorn, he could not receive the homage of the
lesser Chief Macnaughton. The keeping of the
Castle, therefore, became somewhat of a sinecure,
so far as kingly visits were concerned. Only

once is there record of special preparations having been made for a royal guest, and these ended in disappointment and failure.

During " Scotland's fule-time " in 1745, when the northern clans became insane upon the subject of government, and madly sought to place their King-Stork again upon the throne, the Macnaughtons were not exempt from the national frenzy. Prince Charlie, the gay inheritor alike of the vices and virtues of his race, was to pass near the shores of Loch Awe upon a semi-royal progress, and it became necessary that his Castellan should furnish his royal seat of Fraoch-Eilean, and provide such entertainment as befitted the heir of a line of kings. Doubtless the silent woods of the heath-clad isle resounded to the din and tumult which the unwonted occasion called forth and made necessary, and the hereditary cobwebs were swept from their places, lest they should offend the eye of Royalty. Horace describes a similar preparation for a feast in these terms :—.

" While all the hands were hard at work, and boys and girls ran here and there ;
    And brightly glowed the fires, which rolled their murky smoke to outer air."

But the ways of the Stewarts were not like the ways of ordinary mortals, and Prince Charlie suddenly altered his intention and passed the Castle heedlessly by. Now the boldest Macnaughton in that ancient and honourable clan would scarcely care to invite the royal presence to dignify the grey ruin which was once the seat of his chief.

Though there are few stories related of the Castle, the island itself is not bereft of tradition. By one of those curious coincidences which startle the student of folk-lore, it will be found that the ancient Greek fable of the Hesperides has its counterpart in a tale which has been handed down for many generations amongst the dwellers on the shores of this remote Highland loch. It may be possible to invent an explanatory theory to account for this fact; but as the romance alone make the frivolous tale endurable, the task would be a thankless one.

Once on a time there dwelt on the borders of Loch Awe a certain lovely "lady, the wonder of her kind," at whose feet knelt the bravest knights and the gayest courtiers of whom the locality could boast. To Sir Fraoch, however, did her heart incline; but with that caprice which so often works woe to womankind, she refused to bestow her hand upon him until he had accomplished some stupendous task which would place him above his rivals in knightly daring. The green isle, against whose shores the waters of the loch were fretting into foam, had long been famous as the natural orchard in which grew apples of gold fitted to charm the life of the possessor, and to confer unimagined blessings. But this precious fruit was jealously guarded by a huge serpent, the rival of Behemoth, whose very name carried fear and dread to the hearts

107

of the natives. With that folly and unreason which is sometimes found even in the tenderest bosom, the Lady of Loch Awe charged her knight as a true man and faithful lover to bring her some of these golden apples of fabled virtue, in defiance of the grisly monster in whose charge they were held.

Sir Fraoch thought not of the toil or danger, but only of the glorious reward which should be his, and at once addressed himself to his task. Entering his skiff he rowed rapidly towards the Isle of Heather, and daring wind and tide at last beached his tiny vessel. Drawing his sword from its sheath to be ready for any emergency he boldly leapt ashore, and looked around in vain for an opponent. The dreaded serpent seemed to him but a phantom of the imagination, since no trace of it was visible. Advancing through the wilderness of verdure which covered the isle, he sought to gain the spot where tradition had placed the auriferous tree.

> " His path was rugged and sore ;
> Through tangled juniper, beds of reeds,
> Through many a fen where the serpent feeds,
> And man never trod before."

But at length he won the coveted prize, and plucking some of the wished-for fruit he endeavoured to reach his boat. To his dismay he found his return prevented by the wily monster, who had suffered him to land upon this Circean isle that his prey might be more secure. Powerless are the emissaries of evil against the true-hearted knight (in fable at least), and after a deadly struggle Sir Fraoch escaped to his skiff, leaving the terror of the island vanquished and overthrown.

Faint from the fury of the fray in which he had been engaged, the knight rowed more slowly back to his lady's hall than he had set forth at early morn ; and, tempted by the beauty of the fruit he had won, he partook of the spoil thus dearly bought. Ere long he felt that sudden chill which creeps along the veins and paralyses the nerves, thus giving the first hint of poison ; and before he reached his destination he knew full surely that his hours were numbered. Yet not without a glow of triumph did he meet her for whom he had endured the extreme penalty, to lay at her feet the tokens of his victory. But the glazing eye and the interrupted speech told the tale too readily to her, and she soon saw that she had thrown from her the love and respect, nay, the life of her knight, to gratify an idle whim, and to indulge in wanton sport and wicked jest. The situation offered no escape for her save one ; and, as was the custom with mythological heroines when placed in similar circumstances, she tasted of the poisonous fruit, and then expired in her lover's arms.

Such is the flimsy tale still told by the credulous natives of Loch Aweside when accounting for the name of the island. A practical age, which believes only what it can understand, naturally rejects this imaginative fabrication, and finds a more likely origin of the name in the physical aspect of the scene. The Isle of Heather still deserves its title, though the years which have rolled over it have overthrown the proud dwelling which man had erected, and left the Castle desolate and ruined. The loch, the hill, the glen, remain as they have been from pre-historic times; but the men who loved them as the scenes of their early years now sleep within their shadow, or bear the memory of them wherever they may wander in distant lands or foreign shores.

" Not by the sunshine, with its golden glow,
  Nor the green earth, nor yet the laughing sky,
  Nor the fair flower-scents as they come and go,
  In the soft air, like music wandering by ;
  Oh ! not by these, the unfailing, are we taught
  How time and sorrow on our frames have wrought,
  But by the saddened eye, the darkened brow
  Of kindred aspect, and the long dim gaze
  Which tells us we are changed—how changed from
    other days ! "

The first Castle of Dunderawe, or Fraoch-Eilean, built in 1267, remained as the principal seat of the chiefs of Macnaughton for over three centuries ; but in 1596, Alexander Macnaughton erected the Castle, the ruins of which now remain. In early times this clan had large possessions, and " owned all the country between Loch Fyne and Loch Awe, parts of which were Glenira, Glen Shira and Glen Fyne." The chief had also Dhu Loch in Glen Shira, Macnaughton Castle in Lewis, and Dunnaghton Castle in Strathspey, so that his clansmen formed a very powerful clan. Alexander Macnaughton, who was knighted by James IV., fell with that monarch on the fatal field of Flodden. The devotion of the Clan to the Stewarts led to the forfeiture of their possessions in 1691 ; and the direct line of chieftainship terminated with John early in the 18th century. The succession then fell to the descendants of John, younger son of the hero of Flodden, who had settled in County Antrim, and become a Scoto-Irish Laird. In 1878, at a Meeting of the clan in Edinburgh, it was decided that the right to the chieftainship was then due to Sir Francis Edmund MacNaghten of Dunderawe, Bushmills, Antrim ; and the present chief is Sir Francis Alexander MacNaghten, seventh baronet, who resides at the residence of his late namesake. His uncle, the late Lord MacNaghten, in 1887, was made a Lord of Appeal, and officiated on the Committee for Privileges of the House of Lords. The ruined Castle shows the date " 1596," with the initials of " I.M." and " A.N." over the doorway, with the inscription, " Behold the End ; be not wiser than the Highest," and the clan motto, " I hope in God." The building, though a ruin, could easily be made habitable, and thus preserve the memory of a once-important clan, now dispersed throughout the world.

IX

MEGGERNIE CASTLE, GLEN LYON

MEGGERNIE CASTLE is the principal historic centre
of the beautiful valley of Glen Lyon. This glen is
the longest and one of the grandest in the Western
Highlands, extending in a westerly direction from
Fortingall to near Tyndrum, a distance of nearly
35 miles. It derives its name from the river Lyon,
which finds its way from its origin on the south
east side of Ben-a-Chastle, and is often a placid
stream, but sometimes during a winter spate a
raging torrent, expanding about midway in its
course into Loch Lyon, and flowing thence until
it becomes a tributary of the Tay, near Taymouth
Castle, its entire length being nearly 40 miles.
The narrow limits of the glen prevent the river
from ever having a broad surface, the distance
between the precipitous banks being only about
8 feet to 10 feet, and here the Lyon becomes
boisterous because of its confined course. But
the scenery in this quarter is of entrancing beauty,
and is thoroughly Highland in character. Where
Meggernie Castle stands the surrounding country
is in comparative solitude, and recalls the words
of the poet :—

> " Here have I found at last a place of rest
>   To hide me from the world."

MEGGERNIE CASTLE

It is not easy to reach the Castle from the outside, though the road up Glen Lyon to the Castle is in fairly good condition, and is carried through the locality right on to Logierait in the east. Several of the mountains in the neighbourhood of the glen rise to an altitude of over 3,500 feet, and are familiar to every devoted Scottish mountain-climber. The village of Fortingall is about 13 miles distant from Meggernie Castle, through a pleasant though wild district peculiarly typical of the Scottish Highlands.

In very early times the land on both sides of Glen Lyon as far south as Loch Awe, belonged to the MacGregor Clan, and there is every likelihood that the clansmen had a Keep of some kind on the site of Meggernie Castle, as this would command the whole district. The MacGregors claimed to be descended from Alpin, King of Scots, and were sometimes known by the cognomen of Clan Alpin or Mac Alpin. Their motto to this day asserts a lofty origin, as the Gaelic *S'rioghal Mo Dhream* signifies, " My Race is Royal." The statement has been made that a MacGregor chief built the Castle of Coalchuirn (sometimes spelled Kilchurn) on Loch Awe, but this is not well founded. The clan suffered misfortune at the hands of their two neighbours, the Campbells of Argyll and the Stewarts of Cardney. The MacGregors had been vassals of the Earl of Ross in the time of Alexander II., who reigned from 1214 till 1249, and the Earl bestowed upon them the lands of Glenorchay, at the head of Loch Awe which they had chosen as a residence, and which became their headquarters. The clan became a powerful one, and took a prominent share in the Battle of Bannockburn. But David II., the son of Robert Bruce, forgot his obligation to the Clan Gregor, and deprived them of Glenorchay, which he gave to the branch of the Campbells that had settled at Loch Awe, and the dispossessed clansmen had to retire to the Muir of Rannoch. The policy of the Campbells had long been one of lawless acquisition, and they drove the MacGregors out of Glen Lyon and seized upon their property.

The Stewart Kings were equally unjust to this harassed clan, for Robert II., who ruled from 1370 to 1390, confiscated the Keep at Meggernie, which the MacGregors had built and inhabited, and conferred it upon his illegitimate son, Sir John Stewart of Cardney. Thus, with the Campbells on the south of the glen and the Stewarts on the north, the poor clansmen were between two fires, and lost all their possessions in the district. The clan was dispersed and the clansmen became " broken men," dispersed through Perthshire, and long without an acknowledged chief. It is not necessary to pursue the history of this clan further, since it is here shown how they were driven out of Meggernie.

Though the exact date of the erection of the oldest existing part of Meggernie Castle has not been ascertained, there is a Charter in the " Register of the Great Seal," dated 4th March 1603, whereby James VI. confers upon Duncan Campbell of

Glen Lyon, certain lands which were united to make up the Barony of Glen Lyon, the chief house of the baron being named as " the Tower called Meggernie." The previous Keep seems to have been thatched, but Sir Duncan Campbell put slates on his tower, and it was finished much in the style it now shows. Additions have, of course, been made as the years went on, and there is now a fine modern mansion added to the old building and quite in keeping with it. The walls of the old Castle are five feet in thickness, and have evidently been erected for defensive purposes. There are four square towers, one at each corner, bracketed out from the walls, which give a quaint and ancient appearance to the structure, that is emphasised by the dormer windows with triangular tympanies. As was customary at the time of its erection, there are few windows in the walls, and some of these are only a little larger than old-fashioned arrow-slits. The Castle is five storeys in height.

Before leaving Sir Duncan Campbell of Glen Lyon, it may be as well to explain that he was not the first to evict the MacGregors, but he certainly carried on the heartless policy of his predecessors, and left it as a legacy to his descendants. So early as October 1488, the then "Duncane Campbell of Glenurchquha," entered into a contract with Robert Menzies, Laird of Weem, near Aberfeldy, by which they mutually bound themselves to protect and support each other against the MacGregors; and this arrangement was often renewed. Even so late as 1665, when Alexander Menzies of Castle Menzies, son of Duncan Menzies of Weem, was made first baronet, he was married to Margaret, eldest daughter of Sir John Campbell of Glenorchy ; and afterwards there were several marriages which linked the two families together. With such strong adversaries against them, it is no wonder that the ancient clan was dispersed and ruined.

" Glenorchay's proud mountains, Coalchuirn and her towers,
  Glenstrae and Glen Lyon no longer are ours ;
    We're landless, landless, landless, Gregarach."

In 1564, the Earl of Argyll obtained a Commission of Fire and Sword which was aimed at the extermination of the disbanded clan ; and long after that date the intermarriages of the Campbells of Argyll and the Menzies family kept alive the vendetta against the MacGregors. Then Captain Robert Campbell of Glen Lyon in 1695, having coveted the possession of Glencoe, then in the hands of a sept of the MacDonald Clan, put in execution that horrible incident known as the Massacre of Glencoe, which has branded his name with perpetual infamy. No doubt it was at Meggernie Castle—then called Glen Lyon—that he planned and carried through this execrable crime. The details of Campbell's treachery are well-known—how he was entertained by the Chief of the MacDonalds for a fort-

116

night, and fell upon the clansmen and slaughtered them:—

> "The hand that mingled in the meal,
> At midnight drew the felon steel,
> And gave the host's kind breast to feel
> Meed for his hospitality !
> The friendly heart which warmed that hand,
> At midnight armed it with a brand,
> That bade destruction's flames expand
> Their red and fearful blazonry."

In Thomas Talfourd's remarkable drama, " Glencoe ; or The Fate of the MacDonalds," the following lines occur in the speech of Lady MacDonald, reproaching Glen Lyon for his treachery:—

> " Glen Lyon,
> I pray you may have life stretched out beyond
> The common span of mortals, to endure
> The curse of Glencoe cleaving to your soul."

Glen Lyon survived, and did not expiate the fearful crime he had committed, for he was defended and even thanked by William III. for his deed of blackest treachery and ingratitude.

While the historical interest centres in Meggernie Castle, there is much to engage the attention of the visitor in the policies, and in the varied trees with which the place is decorated. This feature is almost entirely due to the devoted labours of James Menzies of Culdares, one of the most competent arboriculturists of his time. Culdares has been in the possession of a branch of the Menzies family from 1659 ; and it was in 1730-40 that the Laird carried out his great reform of the district by tree-planting. It is said that he was the first to make the larch popular. After passing the Bridge of Balgie, the road leads to the entrance to the policies of Meggernie Castle, which is approached by a splendid avenue of lime, beech, elm and spruce trees, the interlacing branches of which form a vernal arch of foliage beside the river Lyon. This avenue, which is nearly two miles in length, was entirely planted by Mr. Menzies, and has thriven remarkably. It circles around the Castle, which stands about 700 feet above sea-level. Authentic measurement of some of these trees are worth recording. One of the elm trees, measured in 1883, girths 19 feet 2 inches at one foot from the ground, and 16 feet 5 inches at five feet up the stem. The lime trees in the avenue are very picturesque, and have reached a fair development, one of them girthing 13 feet 3 inches at two feet from the ground. The beeches also a very satisfactory growth. Other notable trees are the larches and scots firs, some of these having attained considerable dimensions. All the country surrounding the Castle has been transformed since the time of James Menzies by judicious planting, and presents a scene of woodland splendour, though there are still portions susceptible of improvement.

The extensive estates of the Campbells of Breadalbane march with the policies of Meggernie, which have been held and greatly increased during several centuries. It used to be said that the Earl or Marquess could ride for a hundred miles over his own patrimonial domains. Meggernie remained in the Menzies family for centuries, but was acquired in 1884, by the late Mr. John Bullough, father of the present Sir George Bullough, 1st Baronet, who succeeded his father in 1891, and now resides at Kinloch Castle, Isle of Rhum, Inverness-shire. A few years ago Sir George disposed of Meggernie Castle and estate to Sir Ernest Salter Wills, 3rd Baronet, who succeeded his brother, the 2nd Baronet, in 1921, and makes Meggernie Castle, Glen Lyon, his Scottish residence. The Wills family have had a long and honourable connection with Bristol.

X

FERNIEHIRST CASTLE

THE lovely valley of the Tweed, and the whole stretch of the border-land through which it meanders, have been the theme of poet and painter from very remote times. The ever-varying shades of human character which the fluctuating current of events made dominant in that region, and the stirring scenes of which it was witness, awake the harp of the Border Minstrel, and called into existence the national historical ballads. And the situation of Tweed-side, upon the debatable ground betwixt England and Scotland, has caused each Tower and Keep to have its story of love or war, of jocund mirth or of unutterable woe. The hallowing influence of time and the growth of a higher form of human sympathy have conspired to render the stories of Border warfare interesting by force of contrast. And there is a flavour of romance about these bold Border Barons—the Free Lances of our country, who held the balance betwixt England and Scotland in their own hands, which links them with the Ritters of Germany or the Knights of France, rather than with the soldiers of a more prosaic country. Their mixed origin, which combined the boldness and daring of the

Southron with the "canniness" of the Scot, made them appear as a transitional race betwixt these two, and yet distant from either. And though their courage often bordered upon ferocity, and their liberty included an absence of all reverence for the Eighth Commandment, they are not the less interesting as studies of human nature.

The country in which they dwelt largely accounts for their peculiarities. The influence of scenery upon the formation of character has seldom been philosophically examined, yet there is much to be discovered in this line of investigation. The mysterious attraction which the snow-capped peaks of the Fatherland has for the Swiss emigrant whom Fate has transported to distant climes, has its parallel in the feeling with which the Borderer mourns his separation from the loved scenes of his youth, laments the inconstancy of fortune which has reft him from them, and hears in fancy reproaches of the departed spirits of his forefathers upbraiding him for his desertion. This forms the theme of many a Border ballad and song, and often awakens sad memories in impressionable hearts :—

" Their feeble voices from their stream they raise—
  ' Rash youth ! unmindful of thy early days,
  Why didst thou quit the humble peasant's lot ?
  Why didst thou leave the peasant's turf-built cot,
  The ancient graves where all thy fathers lie,
  And Teviot's stream that long has murmured by ? ' "

The verdant hills, the fertile meads, the whispering streams of his own native vale seem brighter and fairer when the memory comes back to him beneath the burning sky of a foreign land ; and the peace once enjoyed in the scenes of his infancy becomes still more dear, as it is less attainable in the ever-whirling race after riches. With something of this feeling did John Leyden write, when, from his natal spot, he mused upon the vagaries into which the pursuit of wealth had led him beneath the tropical sky :—

" By Cherical's dark wandering streams,
    Where cane-tufts shadow all the wild,
Sweet visions haunt my waking dreams
    Of Teviot, loved while still a child ;
    Of castled rocks, stupendous piled,
By Esk or Eden's classic wave,
    Where loves of youth and friendship smiled,
Uncursed by thee, vile yellow slave ! "

The Water of Jed, which rises, as Rowen Burn at an altitude of 1500 feet, on the western slope of Carlin Tooth, one of the Cheviot Hills, wanders in a varied course of about 22 miles, ere it falls into the Teviot near Mounteviot House, and then the conjoined rivers become tributary to the Tweed, and flow towards the North Sea. In its course the Jed passes through the ancient burgh of Jedburgh, and also is near to Ferniehirst Castle which is now to form our theme. Teviotdale, though ostensibly a separate valley, is really parallel with Tweedside, and has all the characteristics of that famous vale. It has been chosen as a proper and convenient site for a Castle to accommodate an important branch of the powerful Ker family, so as to be convenient when raids over the Border were contemplated.

The original Castle of Ferniehirst was destroyed, as is afterwards related, by the Earl of Sussex in 1570 ; but the exact date of the erection of the previous Castle has not been definitely discovered. Certainly there was a Castle of some kind here so early as 1445, for Thomas Ker of Smailholme and Ferniehirst is mentioned in a Charter of that date. He was the descendant of a branch of the family who settled near Jedburgh about the year 1330 ; and the Ferniehirst representatives claimed to be the lineal descendants of Ralph Ker, who were proprietors in the district about the middle of the 14th century, though a long dispute ensued between the children of two brothers as to which progenitor was the elder of the two. Andrew Ker of Ferniehirst, in 1509-11 acquired the Barony of Oxnam, and from him descended the later members of the family.

Early in the history of Scotland the town of Jedburgh, and the valley of the Jed, were a favourite resort of royalty, for the Castle of Jedburgh, upon whose site has been built the present County Prison, was the chosen home of David I. Here also his son Malcom IV. lived and died ; and was succeeded by William the Lion. Alexander II. resided frequently in Jedburgh

Castle. The story of Alexander III.'s connection with the Castle was a melancholy one.

Alexander III., who had paid frequent visits to Jedburgh Castle, was married to Joleta, daughter of the lordly De Coucy, Count of Breux, in the Abbey of Jedburgh, and celebrated his nuptials in the Castle by a grand ball. The family of De Coucy, thus united to the Scottish throne, was of Anglo-Norman descent, and held a high position in their native land for many years.

> "The fame of the fearless De Coucy
> Was boundless as the sea."

Indeed, so superior were the claims of this family to renown that their battle-cry evinced their contempt for ordinary titles, and gloried in their own name as superior to added rank—

> "*Je ne suis Roy, ni Prince aussi,*
> *Je suis le Seigneur de Coucy.*"

The wedding of Alexander III. with a daughter of this race was celebrated with becoming splendour. But the magnificence was marred by an untoward incident. Whilst the revels were at their highest an uninvited guest appeared in the shape of a grisly spectre, who mingled in hateful familiarity with the noble guests then present. So wretched a sight, so fatal an augury, could not escape remark and foreboding. The guests beheld with doubt and trembling the awe-inspiring vision, and feared to utter their apprehensive thoughts. As a quaint old writer has put it :—

" In the mid-revels the first ominous night
  Of their espousals, when the moon shone bright,
  With lighted tapers—the King and Queen leading
  The curious measures—Lords and Ladies treading
  The self-same strains—the King looks back by chance,
  And spies a strange intruder in the dance,
  Namely, a mere anatomy, quite bare,
  His naked limbs both without flesh and hair
  (As we depicture Death), who stalks about,
  Keeping true measure till the dance be out.
  The King, with all the rest, affrighted stand ;
  The spectre vanished, and the strict command
  Was given to break up revels ; each 'gan fear
  The other, and presage disaster near.
  If any ask, ' What did of this succeed ? '
  The King, soon after falling from his steed,
  Unhappily died ; after whose death ensuing
  Was to the land sedition, wreck, and ruin."

Apart from the superstition is undoubtedly the fact that Alexander III., so soon after his wedding, should have met a violent death. In less than a year from this time the King, riding by night on the perilous pathway betwixt Kinghorn and Burntisland, was thrown from his horse over the precipice which towers above the Firth of Forth, and killed instantaneously. And from this sad event arose the contest for the Scottish Crown which gave Edward I. of England an excuse for his fatal interference with the affairs of the nation. Few of the Kings of Scotland have been

more deeply lamented than Alexander III.,
possibly because few of them were so upright in
character and so morally pure as he ; and it was
not without foreboding that the statesmen of the
time looked into the future of their country. A
verse from an ancient ballad of the time expresses
this feeling in quaint language :—

> " Quhen Alysandre our Kyng wes dede,
> That Scotland led in luve and lee,
> Away wes sons of Ale and Brede,
> Of Wyne and Wax, of Gamyn and Gle ;
> Oure gold wes changey'd into lede ;
> Crist, born into virginite,
> Succour Scotland and remede
> That sted is in perplexite."

The political dilemma in which Scotland was
placed, and the ambitious designs of Edward,
made the Border-land the scene of continued incursions and retaliations, and the chiefs of the
various clans were compelled to erect strongholds
in their own defence. The power which they thus
attained made them less dependent upon either
party than they would otherwise have been ; and
they came to look upon the Marches as a separate
state, distinct from either Kingdom. A tacit
bond of union existed between the various septs
who inhabited the district, and they thus formed
an alliance for mutual defence. The Scotts and
the Armstrongs, the Johnstons and the Kers were
the Ishmaelites of Scotland, ever ready for a
foray either north or south of the Tweed.

Amongst these clans the Kers held a high position. For many years the head of the sept was Warden of the Middle Marches ; and as the ground over which his empire extended formed the natural communication between England and Scotland, the post was no sinecure. The Castle of Ferniehirst, near Jedburgh, which was held by Sir Thomas Ker from 1474 till his becoming a priest in 1481, and dying three years after, naturally occupied a prominent place in this long contest ; and for many years it was a centre around which conflict raged. Often has the courtyard rang with the warlike sound of spears and jacks, of boot and saddle, as the gay moss-troopers assembled within its walls, ready alike for feast or fray.

So important was Ferniehirst considered that, when the English under Surrey were engaged upon the storming of Jedburgh, it was deemed necessary to secure the Castle that the conquest of the locality might be complete. Lord Dacre was detailed for this service and sent with 800 men and several pieces of cannon to reduce the stronghold. He found the enterprise more difficult than he had imagined, for the walls of the Castle had been built to withstand a siege, and it was garrisoned by men who were fighting for life and liberty. Though ultimately captured by the English, it was not without great loss to the besiegers, and only the aid of the heavy ordnance made its defence impossible. The testimony of Surrey (no partial critic), to the courage of the

Borderers shows most clearly their aspect in war. Writing to Cardinal Wolsey, he says :—" I assure your Grace I found the Scots at this time the boldest men and the hottest that ever I saw any nation." Detailing his battle at Ferniehirst, he writes :—" They found hardy men that went nae back for theym, though after long skirmyshing and moche difficutie, gat for the ordynance within the house, and threw down the same."

But the Borderer, though conquered, never yields. Lord Dacre, after his fatiguing siege, and, contrary to the express command of Surrey, encamped beyond the lines of the English army. No longer anticipating resistance, an easy watch was kept ; and whilst the leaders were at dinner celebrating their victory, some of the Scottish troopers were hardy enough to approach the spot where the English horses were quartered, and turned them loose in the camp. The turmoil which the affrighted animals made terrified their masters, and the deepening twilight prevented them from ascertaining the true cause. The stampede which now ensued alarmed even the soldiers of Surrey, who believed that the horses, whose frantic gallop they heard in the darkness betokened the approach of a vast army to overthrow and utterly confound them. Nor was their error discovered before many of their steeds had fallen into the hands of the Scotsmen and became their lawful prey. The superstition of the age permitted Surrey's statement that the Devil was seen in a visible form six times during this

128

turbulent scene to pass unchallenged; and the
accusation of witchcraft formed an easy excuse
for the tremor of his own army. And though
victorious, he had to confess that he found the
inhabitants of the Scottish Border were of a
different character from the mixed army under
James IV., which his father had met and conquered at Flodden Field.

A time of reprisal at length arrived for the
Border Chiefs. After the disastrous Battle of
Pinkie in 1547, the English Army had again taken
possession of the country near the Cheviot Hills,
and garrisoned the town of Jedburgh. The French
General, Monsieur D'Essé, however, had led his
troops against them, and soon drove them from
this stronghold. Taking advantage of the diversion thus made in favour of Scotland, Ker of
Ferniehirst sought the assistance of the French
troops to regain his ancient homestead. To this
D'Essé consented, and despatched a reconnoitring
party under the command of some of his own
officers, whilst Ker followed with his main contingent. The Castle had been kept in garrison
by the English from the time of its previous
capture in 1523, and the rumour of disturbances
in the surrounding country kept them on the
alert. The advance guard of the French troops,
therefore, found that the narrow pass that leads
toward the Castle was defended by twenty-five
arquebusiers, who might serve as an outpost in
case of attack, and might warn the keepers of the
Castle of the approach of an enemy. The French-

men charged this picket and drove them in hot haste towards the fortress, pursuing them closely. They fired as they fled, endeavouring to keep their pursuers at bay; but ere they reached the gate ten out of the twenty-five were slain, and not one of them was without tokens of this bitter and close conflict.

The resistance which they had met only stimulated the attacking force to greater energy; and when Ker arrived on the scene, with the remainder of the troops, they at once set about an escalade. Throwing long poles instead of ladders against the walls, they boldly clambered up the escarpment; whilst many of them, infuriated by the blood already shed, made good their entrance by climbing up the rough-cast wall, heedless of the showers of missiles which the besieged rained incessantly upon them. Once on the battlements their task was comparatively light. They soon drove the English soldiers inside the donjon tower, the citadel of the Castle, and then, leaping from their elevation into the base-court below, they proceeded to attempt a breach in the wall of the inner works. Sheltering themselves from the stones that still poured down on their heads, they were not long in making an entrance. As the captain of the English forces saw his game played out, he offered to surrender if the lives of his troops and of himself were spared. But D'Essé would not listen to such terms of capitulation, and insisted upon an absolute surrender. Thinking himself safer with D'Essé than with the

Borderers, now all aflame for revenge, the captain consented ; but one of the Borderers, his sworn foe, came up and struck off his head at one blow.

The pent-up vengeance of the Scotsmen now had full sway, and they placed no restraint upon their passions. The unfortunate Englishmen had to endure the punishment due to the sins of their forefathers. It is even said that the prisoners that D'Essé had taken were brought forth that the Borderers might wreak their fury upon them, and fearful barbarities were practised upon their victims. The French General Beaugé, however, describes these as only fair retaliation for the conduct of their enemies towards themselves.

The term of the existence of Ferniehirst Castle was reached in 1570. The death of the Regent Moray had thrown political affairs into confusion, and Sir Thomas Ker of Ferniehirst and Sir Walter Scott of Buccleugh entered England with fire and sword, and joined the Earl of Westmoreland in a foray across the Border. Though successful in this enterprise they soon suffered retribution. Queen Elizabeth, enraged at the daring raid, ordered the Earl of Sussex and Lord Scrope to invade the Scottish territory and lay the Borders in ruins. These two noblemen at the head of a large army, entered the land of Teviotdale and laid waste the territory. The Scotts of Buccleugh, the Kers, and the Homes were the chief objects of their revenge ; and it is computed that they destroyed in this fatal conflict not less than fifty Castles, sacked and burned 300 villages, and finally took possession of Home Castle, which had been the centre of disaffection to English rule. The abode of so well-known a warrior as Ker of Ferniehirst was not likely to be spared in such a wholesale demolition ; and the troops which Sussex led against it left little save the bare and blackened walls.

The present edifice consists of these ruins, with some modern additions which render it habitable as a dwelling-house for the tenant of the farm. But its glory has long passed away ; and it stands now as a monument of that dim and shadowy past which was tenanted by beings whose boldness and daring are seldom met with in these latter days. The Age of Iron has given place to the Age of Electroplate, and we now plume ourselves upon the perfection of our shams, and indulge in congratulations over the success of our deceptions.

> " Now avardlie wisdom is deceit,
>   And falset haldin policie ;
> Richt few from guill can now debait,
>   So great is the hypocrisie.
> Some will speak fair and friendfullie,
>   For profit wald dissaive their brother ;
> Sae rife is infidelitie,
>   Ane kinsman skant may trew ane other."

Sir Thomas Ker of Ferniehirst, who died in 1484, left a daughter, Margaret, who married her kinsman, Thomas Ker of Smailholm, who thus came into Ferniehirst by marriage. The eldest son of this union was Sir Andrew Ker of Ferniehirst, whose death took place about 1545, when he was succeeded by his eldest surviving son, Sir John, who deceased in 1562. The next in succession was that Sir Thomas Ker of Ferniehirst, the adherent of Queen Mary, to whom reference has been made, and who died in 1586. His eldest son, Sir Andrew, was created first Lord Jedburgh in 1622, and there were three successive Barons Jedburgh, the fourth who bore the title, being Robert Ker of Crailing, the nephew of his predecessor, and the representative of the male-line of Ferniehirst. By a special contract it was arranged that failing direct issue the title and estate should fall to the Earl of Lothian. On the death of Robert fourth Lord Jedburgh without heirs, the Master of Newbattle, son of the Earl of Lothian, succeeded, and as ultimately he became second Marquess of Lothian on the death of his father in 1703, the present (1926) tenth Marquess includes among his titles that of Baron of Jedburgh.

XI

THREAVE CASTLE

THREAVE CASTLE, Kirkcudbrightshire, is a ruin connected with the famous Douglas family, and is a lofty stronghold on an island of the river Dee, less than two miles west of Castle Douglas. There is no landward approach to the Castle, and it can only be reached by wading through a ford on the eastern branch of the Dee, which will land the adventurous visitor at a short distance from the southern point of the island, and at a few yards from the ruin. On each side of the island the river is so deep that it can only be traversed by a boat ; and a wide ditch (formerly a march or moat) connected with the Dee, makes the access to Threave Castle still more difficult. The exact situation has been thus graphically described :—" The island, which is quite flat, extends about 500 paces northwards from the Castle, and is about half this distance in width, forming a fine pasture meadow of nearly 20 acres in extent. The river protects the Castle on the west, and on the other sides a strong wall with a sloping face and round towers still surrounds it, forming a courtyard on the south and east sides. The round tower at the south-east angle is entire, and is 9 feet 2 inches in internal diameter, and three storeys high, with three loop-holes in each storey." Though now in a ruinous condition, the plan of the Castle may yet be traced, and evidently it has been a structure of considerable strength, intended for defence.

There are many traditions connected with this interesting ruin, though some of them are not confirmed by credible history. It is supposed to have been built by Archibald Douglas, an illegitimate son of "the good Sir James Douglas," in the latter half of the 14th century. In 1369, this Archibald was appointed Lord of Galloway, holding large possessions in that quarter; and in 1385 he became third Earl of Douglas, and was known by the cognomen of " the Grim," because of his relentless nature. Threave Castle was erected by him on the site of a fortalice that had belonged to Alan, the last native Lord of Galloway; and in the time of the eighth Earl of Douglas (about 1450) it is recorded that there was accommodation within Threave Castle for a thousand men-at-arms. Ultimately, upon the fall of the Douglas family, it was forfeited to the Crown, and came into the possession of the Maxwells, Earls of Nithsdale, who were relations of the Earl of Douglas. Archibald the Grim died at Threave Castle in February 1401, and it was in 1455 that the Castle passed away from the Douglas family. This was largely because of a sad tragedy that took place there three years before, though the authenticity of the details have been seriously questioned.

135

One of the oldest families in Galloway was said to be the Maclellans of Bombie, who claimed the title of Lords of Galloway. They were certainly a powerful race in 1301, and controlled a large portion of the ground in the district. Pitscottie in his gossipy history tells how one of the family, known as " the Tutor of Bombie," had offended the Earl of Douglas in some undefined manner, and Douglas captured him, imprisoned him in Threave Castle, and afterwards hanged him on the battlements. It is stated that Sir Patrick Gray, brother-in-law of the Tutor, arrived at the gateway of the Castle with an order from the King—James II.—demanding the release of Maclellan, but the Earl disregarded this mandate, and proceeded with the murder. Meanwhile William, the eighth Earl, had been slain by the dagger of the King at Stirling Castle, in February 1451-2, and the Douglases were declared forfeited traitors, and their lands devastated by the Royal Army, and several of their Castles demolished.

The last stronghold retained by the ninth Earl of Douglas was Threave Castle, and James II. determined to lead his forces against it in person. He, therefore, marched into Galloway at the head of a numerous army, and made preparations to besiege the Castle. The story is told that a certain blacksmith, called M'Kim, seeing the weakness of the King's artillery, offered to make a special cannon that would destroy the place. The proposal was accepted, and M'Kim took his

THREAVE CASTLE

Valentine & Sons, Ltd.

assistants to the Three Thorns at Carlinwark, and there he speedily constructed the large cannon called " Mons Meg," which was first used in warfare against Threave Castle, and is still preserved at Edinburgh Castle. The story has been doubted, though the tradition yet survives in Douglasdale, and the place where the cannon was made is pointed out at Buchan's Croft. Two of the granite balls from Mons Meg were found in the wall of Threave Castle.

The Maclellans rose to great power in Kirkcudbright. Long after the siege of Threave Castle, one of the family, Robert, was created Lord Kirkcudbright in 1633, by Charles I., for his services to the King in Ireland ; and this title was held till the death of the eighth Lord in 1832, when it became dormant.

When Threave Castle was forfeited by the Earl of Douglas, it was conferred on the Maxwells, another prominent Border family, who were afterwards ennobled with the title of Earls of Nithsdale, and were made Keepers of Threave and Stewards of Kirkcudbright. In the time of the Civil War the then Earl of Nithsdale, at his own expense, held Threave Castle for Charles I., and armed, paid, and victualled 80 men-at-arms. He made a spirited defence as long as he could ; but at last the King, finding he could not assist him with reinforcements, sent him word to apply for the best terms he could obtain for himself and his garrison, and to resign the stronghold to the enemy. The Earl had to submit, and thus the

Castle passed temporarily out of his control. But the office of Keepers of Threave Castle was retained by the Earl and his successors, and they continued to receive the dues that had been contributed by every parish in Kirkcudbright for centuries, consisting of cattle for the sustenance of the Earl and his soldiers. Even in 1704, when the Earl of that time sold the estate of Threave, he continued to receive this perquisite, and remained Keeper of Threave Castle as his ancestors had been. At length the fifth Earl of Nithsdale took part in the Jacobite Rising of 1715, his chief opponent being the first Marquess of Annandale.

That nobleman was the head of the Johnstone Clan, one of the most powerful in the Border district, and an ardent supporter of George I., who had succeeded to the throne. As Lord-Lieutenant he had received intimation that Dumfries was to be attacked and captured by the Jacobites, so he set forth to defend the burgh. While Annandale was on his way thither he was surprised by a party of the rebels, numbering 200 horse, commanded by the Earls of Nithsdale, Winton, and Carnwath, Viscount Kenmure, and other noblemen and gentlemen, who, as he stated were "providentially prevented" from capturing him, and he reached Dumfries in safety, where measures were adopted for the defence of the place, which were successful.

Twice did the Jacobites attack Dumfries, but failed in their efforts and retired. The Rising was practically terminated by the Battles of

Sheriffmuir and Preston ; the leading Border noblemen were captured, and the fifth Earl of Nithsdale was attainted for treason, deprived of his title, and also of the office of Keeper of Threave Castle. In 1747, after the next Jacobite Rising, the Hereditary Jurisdictions were abolished, and thus the connection of the Maxwells with Threave Castle was definitely terminated. There is a romantic story told of the last Earl, which is thus narrated in the " Scots Peerage ":—

" William, fifth Earl of Nithsdale and fourteenth Lord Maxwell, born in 1676, was served heir to his father, ' Robert, Earl of Nithsdale, Lord Maxwell, Herries, Eskdale, and Carlyell,' 26th May 1696, and heir-male and tailzie to Robert, second Earl of Nithsdale, 19th May 1698. He joined the rising in favour of the Chevalier de St. George, and being taken prisoner at Preston in November 1715, was sent to the Tower of London. He pleaded guilty of high treason, 19th January, and was sentenced to death in Westminster Hall, 9th February 1716, and his honours were forfeited. His wife left Terregles in December to join him. Her coach was stopped at Grantham by snow, but she, though of delicate constitution, pushed on to London on horseback with her maid, Cecilia Evans, and her groom, their horses at times almost buried in drifts. On 13th February she gained access to the King and begged for her husband's life, in vain as she believed, though according to Lady Cowper, ' a reprieve for him was signed the very night of his escape on 23rd February (the day before that fixed for the execution).' Taking advantage of the free access to his room allowed to Nithsdale's friends, Lady Nithsdale, with her London landlady, Mrs. Mills and a Mrs. Morgan, was constantly in and out of it that day, and when at dusk she led him out in female dress, the guards, confused at all this coming and going of the women, let him pass, taking him for one of them. Having delivered him into the care of the maid, Evans, who took him to a friendly house known to Mrs. Mills, Lady Nithsdale returned to his room in the Tower, and after remaining a short time to disarm suspicion, she passed out with loud farewells at the door. Nithsdale was eventually hidden in the Venetian Embassy (without the Ambassador's knowledge) by one, Michel, a servant of the house, who, after a day or two, conveyed him, dressed in the Ambassador's livery, to Dover. Hence he crossed to France, and his wife, after a journey to Scotland to secure important papers, joined him at Lille before 25th September 1716. Henceforth the two lived, often in great poverty, at the Chevalier's Court at Rome, where Nithsdale, who was made a Knight of the Thistle by his prince, 31st December 1725, died on 20th March 1744.

" His wife was Winifred Herbert, daughter of William, third Lord and first Marquess of Powis, who had followed James II. into exile. The marriage, according to the contract, dated Paris, 2nd March 1699, was to be celebrated between

that date and the following Easter. Lady Nithsdale died at Rome in May 1749, ' very old and
in great esteem.' Her last years were made more
easy by money sent by her son when he got
possession of the family lands."

XII

DUNOON CASTLE

SCOTLAND is peculiarly favoured by the formation of her river system, as well as by the configuration of her coasts. So thoroughly is her coast-line indented, either by lochs or fiords, or by rivers and estuaries, that no part of the central portion of Scotland is far distant from the sea. On the eastern shore the Firths of Forth and Tay provide ready access to the ocean ; and though the Clyde is the only important river on the west coast, the vast fiords of Lochfyne and Loch Linnhe carry the shores of Scotland into the heart of the country. The intervention of the island of Ireland has protected the west coast of England from the encroaching ravages of the Atlantic Ocean ; and the east and west coast-lines of that portion of Great Britain do not therefore present the same contrast to each other as Scotland affords. But the north-western shores, exposed to the fury of the raging sea, and subjected to the denuding influence of the chief tidal river, have been worn into numerous bays and lochs, into myriad isles and peninsulas, which bestow a different character entirely upon the scenery.

Whilst the northern lochs might maintain a rude and migratory people, whose occupation as fishermen would prevent an indissoluble attachment to the soil, the true seat of civilization necessarily became fixed upon the fertile banks of the great western river, the Clyde, whose broad stream could carry the vessels of the early settlers far into the centre of Scotland. The very success of these hardy pioneers, and their increasing wealth, would inevitably bring in their wake the pirates and sea-rovers of less-favoured lands to live by rapine and pillage upon the fruits of native labour. The Clyde, as the main highway of ingress to central Scotland, became the battle-scene upon which all contests for supremacy between the possessors and the western invaders took place.

The very names of those adventurous spirits who thus strove to seize upon the most fertile part of Scotland, with varied fortunes, are both numerous and diversified. Caledonians, Picts, Scots, Romans, Irish, Norwegians have all held temporary possession of these shores and have left upon the land appropriate tokens of their sway. As time has rolled on these have subsided into the great past, and become but as shadowy memories :—

> " Name follows name
> For ever more,
> As swift waves shame
> Slow waves before."

The fierce warfare of olden days now attracts a new race of warriors ; and sceptical historians

demolish generations with the stroke of a pen.
Yet even the poet—least combative of men—
clings, despite the influence of reason, to what
some tell him are the dear delusions of youth.
To him the whole scenery of the Firth of Clyde
speaks eloquently of the Ossianic heroes who fell
" in the midst of their renown " :—

> " I behold thy towers, O Selma ! and the oaks of thy
>   shaded wall ;
>   Thy streams sound in my ears ; thy heroes gather around.
>   Fingal sits in the midst, and leans on the shield of
>   Trenmer ;
>   His spear stands against the wall ; he listens to the songs
>   of his Bards,
>   The deeds of his arm are heard, and the actions of the
>   King in his youth."

And as he pauses beneath the shade of Balclutha, or lingers by the shores of Comgall, he
may remember and fulfil the prophecy which con-
cludes the " War of Caros " :—

> " The sons of the feeble hereafter will lift the voice on
>   Cona,
>   And looking up to the rocks, say, ' Here Ossian dwelt.'
>   They shall admire the chiefs of old, and the race that
>   is no more,
>   When we ride on our clouds, Malvina, on the wings of
>   the roaring winds,
>   Our voices shall be heard in the desert ; and we shall
>   sing on the winds of the rocks."

Had there been no other attraction, the beauty
of the scenery of this part of Scotland might have

Valentine & Sons, Ltd.

DUNOON CASTLE

drawn these conquering hosts towards it. The devious way which the Clyde pursues, carries it through nearly every description of Scottish scenery. From its source in the distant Lead Hills until it loses itself in the Atlantic the river takes many a curious turn. Its way lies northward, westward, and then southward, and it thus encloses a portion of the most fertile Scottish districts. Leaving the mountainous spot where it originates, it passes through a pastoral country, which is succeeded by a mineral-bearing land, giving place to a great commercial centre, from which point its scenery frequently presents at one view all these characteristics. The development of trade and manufactures in this quarter has transformed the Clyde into the main pathway from Scotland to the western and southern parts of the world. The argosies of " Ormuz and of Ind " float peacefully upon her waters ; and the richly-freighted fleets of foreign nations sail tranquilly past the castled steeps and ancient fortalices which once frowned defiance to every foe.

> " How pleasing when war's dread alarms,
> The martial shout, the din of arms,
> The trumpet's dread-inspiring blast,
> In peaceful slumber sinks at last ;
> When men from strife enjoy release,
> And hail the happy days of peace."

The life of lawlessness, of terror, and of bloodshed which our ancestors endured may be fitly studied by examining the Castles and houses

K   145

they inhabited, and the towns they built. And though the ruthless hand of Time has frequently destroyed all save the faintest traces of these erections, yet there are few so utterly obliterated as to be silent upon their history. There are merely slight relics now remaining of the ancient Castle of Dunoon, yet these sufficiently record its story.

On a promontory upon the Argyllshire side of the Clyde, opposite to the Cloch Lighthouse, stood Dunoon Castle. As a post of observation the site has been admirably chosen, since it commands a good view of the Firth in all directions. The Renfrewshire coast on the southern shore turns southwards, forming the Bay of Inverkip, with Wemyss Point as its southmost extremity. Far away down the channel the islands of the Cumbraes may be seen dividing the waters, and forming, with Bute, which is barely discernible, the main thoroughfare for deep-sea vessels. The projection of the peak upon which the Castle stood brings into view the Cowal Shore, with the village of Innellan and the terminating height upon Toward Point. In the immediate neighbourhood of the Castle Hill may be found the sylvan retreat of " Morag's fairy glen," and the classic locality of Balgay (or Baughie) Burn.

Northward from the Castle, until the entrance to Holy Loch is reached, the shore is lined with a succession of villages and hamlets which are extended almost continuously. Dunoon, Kirn, Hunter's Quay, and Ardenadam are so intimately joined that it is difficult to discover their boundaries. On the opposite shore of the Holy Loch, quite invisible from Dunoon though historically associated with it, stands Kilmun, where for many years was the chief burial-place of the Argyll family.

The district of Cowal, in which Dunoon Castle stood, figures prominently in early history. Its position at the entrance to the narrower portion of the Firth of Clyde naturally attracted the notice alike of invaders and defenders, and the commanding situation of the promontory at Dunoon makes it probable that a warlike post was established here in pre-historic times. It cannot now be ascertained whence the Scots were originally derived ; but it is certain that they had an established kingdom before the period of the Roman invasion. From Strathclyde it is supposed that a number of them emigrated, and, landing on the north-eastern shores of Ireland, founded there a Scottish colony, bestowing the name of Scotia upon the country of their adoption. One of the warriors who led them in this campaign was called *Cairbrea-Riada*, and the portion of land awarded to him for his bravery was called *Dal-Riada*, the fields of Riada, and nearly corresponded in position and extent with the modern County Antrim.

In process of time the Scots in Ireland— known as Dalriads from the name of the founder of the colony, had increased in numbers so much that they had to extend their borders. The traditional accounts which their ancestors had left attracted their attention, and a large body of them returned to their original home on the Clyde, calling this revived district by the name of their Irish settlement, Dalriada. Thus there were two Scotias in existence, with a Dalriada in each. The leader of these wanderers was Fergus, son of Erc, a lineal descendant of Cairbrea-Riada, and the country which he selected for his new settlement was the land formerly held by his ancestors, which included all Argyllshire and far up the Clyde. Fergus was accompanied by his two brothers, Lorn and Angus, and they divided the land between them, expelling the Picts, who had over-run it after Riada's emigration. So far as can be discovered these brothers form a triumvirate for the government of the territory during their lives ; but their kingdom was divided by their children after their death.

Separate families selected different districts, although all were submissive to one central authority. The descendants of Lorn inhabited the tract of country still named after their founder, who was the eldest of the three brothers. The grandsons of Fergus—Gabrau and Comgall—chose respecectively the districts of Airgialias (Argyll) and Comgall (Cowal), while the children of Angus peopled the Islands of Jura and Islay. The Dalriadic Kings thus ruled over a very extensive territory, bounded on the south by the Clyde, on the north by Loch Linnhe, and on the east by the peaks of Drumalbin. Their capital was at Dunadd, near Crinan, and their coasts were defended by a series of forts which formed centres of civilization, and convenient rallying points in time of war. One of the most important of these is supposed to have been the original Castle of Dunoon.

The ancient name of this spot is said to be derived from *Dun-nain*, meaning the green hill. That this position would be selected as a point of defence is almost certain, for there are few places so well adapted by natural conditions to form a protective fort. And if the Dalriadic Kings founded a vitrified Castle here, it must have been about the year 503 A.D., although of that erection no trace now remains.

For 340 years these Scoto-Irish Kings ruled this quarter of the island, frequently encountering their warlike neighbours the Picts in battle, and maintaining, though not greatly extending their territories. At length Kenneth Mich Alpin, the last of the Dalriadic Kings, made good his claim to the throne of the Picts through right of his grandmother, Urguisa ; and he assumed the Crown and reigned over a united people. Removing his capital to Forteviot, in Perthshire, he directed defensive operations on the Clyde, the Forth, and the Tay, and sought to advance his kingdom south-eastwards to the fertile fields of the Lothians. In 859 A.D. Kenneth fell in battle, near Dundee.

The chief enemies of Scotland at this period were the Sea-Kings from Scandinavia and Denmark, who assailed the country on both sides. Finding their access to Scottish territory on the east coast curtailed by the vigilance and energy of Kenneth, they transferred their operations to the west, and strove to enter the land by the Firth of Clyde. Towards this spot, therefore, the defensive power of the Scots was directed ; and in these circumstance the importance of Dunoon as a post of observation would be great. But the successors of Kenneth were less skilful or less warlike than he ; and the Danes under Olaf, assembling a fleet at Dublin, sailed up the Clyde unopposed, and attacked and captured the ancient citadel of Dumbarton, returning past the helpless fort of Dunoon unopposed and triumphant.

All the Kings of Scotland since his time claim Kenneth I., as their ancestor, though long years passed before he found a valiant successor. Somerled, Thane of Argyll, assembled his fleet at the Mull of Kintyre in 1153, and sailed up to Renfrew in the absence of Malcolm IV., taking possession of both Dunoon Castle and Dumbarton Castle ; but when the young King returned from France in 1160 he took measures to recover Renfrew. Somerled was defeated and slain at Renfrew four years afterwards.

One hundred years later (1263) a great change took place. During the reign of Alexander II. (1214-1249) Haco, King of Norway, invaded Scotland, and captured the most important of the Isles of the Hebrides. The Scottish King was more of a diplomatist than a soldier, but as he found that politics were ineffectual with Haco, his ambition tempted him to lead an army against the invaders; leaving Dunoon as a defensive fort, he went forth to the conflict. As his fleet sailed through the Sound of Mull, King Alexander was attacked by a malignant fever, and death laid an icy hand upon him. He died on 8th July 1249, on the island of Kerrera, near Oban.

Haco of Norway, having heard of this expedition, hastened to oppose. Leaving Orkney with his fleet he sailed down through the isles which he called his own, and, with a kind of poetic irony, he chose Kerrera as the meeting-place of the Scottish fleet, to which many of the insurgent Norwegian nobles had joined themselves. The death of Alexander II. had discouraged the Scots, and deprived them of a leader. They retired from the contest, and Haco resumed his sway over the Hebrides, and reigned without interruption for the succeeding thirteen years. Meanwhile the new King of Scotland, Alexander III., though but a youth, decided to take up the policy of his father, and to support it by the sword, and thus win back the Hebrides. He incited the neighbouring lords on the islands and mainland who were well-affected towards him, to invade the Norwegian territory, and to sack, burn, and destroy every village whose inhabitants refused allegiance to him. The commission was faithfully fulfilled. From Jura to the Lewes these islands were filled with lamentations, the voice of the western Rachel weeping for her children.

This outrage could not be endured by the proud Norwegian spirit. Haco at once assembled a magnificent fleet, and set sail from Herlover on 7th July 1263, determined to avenge the blood of his subjects. As he proceeded his Armada received many augmentations, and when he reached Sanda Isle, at the south of the Mull of Kintyre, his fleet numbered a hundred sail, fully manned and equipped. Disposing of this powerful force he began operations against the coast of Argyll. One portion of the squadron attacked the Mull of Kintyre, whilst another beset and captured the Island of Bute, and the King himself entered the Firth of Clyde and sailed up unopposed to the shores of Arran, anchoring his fleet in Kilbrannan Sound.

The Scottish leaders, terrified at this prompt and successful invasion, endeavoured to secure peace by negotiation. They limited their demands, which had formerly included the whole of the Hebrides, to the cession of Arran, Bute and the Cumbraes, which barred the entrance to the Clyde. But Haco doubted their faith, and would have none of their treaties. Hoisting sail upon sixty of his ships, he penetrated to the head of Loch Long, throwing off as he proceeded marauding parties to ravage the coasts. The Cowal shore from Toward Point to Holy Loch was laid waste ; and the Castles of Rothesay and Dunoon were captured by the bold invaders. The hardy Norse sailors, undeterred by difficulty, landed at the north-eastern point of Loch Long (where Arrochar now stands), and making a "portage" they conveyed their boats over the hill to the waters of Loch Lomond, intending to seize upon Dumbarton Castle, and carrying fire and sword into these territories.

The Scots, thoroughly alarmed at the magnitude and success of the expedition, had assembled their forces on the southern and eastern shores of Renfrewshire and Ayrshire, from Kempoch Point to the Bay of Largs on the south bank of the Clyde; and the country was closely patrolled by the Scottish army so as to make a landing ineffectual. They feared to attack the Norwegian sailors upon the waters. But the God of the Winds benevolently interposed, and delivered the invaders into their hands. The portion of the fleet commanded by Haco was anchored in the channel between the Isle of Cumbrae and the mainland, but a fierce storm swept down from Loch Goil and drove the helpless vessels on the shore at Largs. The northern warriors, unable to maintain a position on the land, were hopelessly defeated. The discomfitted King, spiritless and heartbroken, recalled the shattered remnant of his fleet, and retired, downcast and overthrown, from the scene of his disgrace. And thus the reconquest of the Hebrides from Norway, which neither fraud nor force could accomplish, was effected by the adverse October gales which sweep down the Clyde from the lofty Argyllshire mountains. The unfortunate King of Norway retired into seclusion, and in 1266, the Battle of

Largs, after three years, brought about the formal cession of the Hebrides and the Isle of Man to Alexander III., and drove the Norsemen from Scotland. It has been stated that Haco died on board his vessel, and was carried a corpse to his kingdom, but this has not been confirmed. The Battle of Largs is commemorated in a pathetic poem by the late Professor John Stuart Blackie, in which the following verses occur :—

> " And at early burst of spring, Haco,
>   When the birds sang on the tree,
> They took the body of Haco
>   In a ship across the sea.
>
> Across the sea to Norway,
>   Where the sires make moan for thee—
> That the last of his race was Haco,
>   Who ruled the Western Sea.
>
> And they laid thee, Haco, Haco,
>   With thy sires on the Norway shore,
> And far from the Isles of the Sea, Haco,
>   That know thy name no more."

The peculiar circumstances whereby Dunoon Castle became a royal residence are worthy of notice. Malcolm III. (called *Ceannmor*, or Great Head, because he was the " Great Chief," not from any abnormal development of his skull), was the eldest son of Duncan I., and began his reign in 1057-8, on the death of his father. He found the kingdom in a turbulent and agitated condition. Fortunately he was surrounded by a trusty band of warriors upon whom he could depend, and Might in these days was Right. The mixed population upon the shores of the Firth of Clyde gave him much trouble, especially in the Island of Bute, which had been the headquarters of invasions by the Norsemen. The King deputed Walter, son of Fleance, to subjugate this territory, and rewarded his success by grants of the lands of Bute, and Cowal, and the baronies of Kyle and Renfrew. Dunoon Castle thus became one of Walter's possessions, and its convenient situation made him select it as the Seat of Government for the district. Alan, the son of Walter, was created High Steward of Scotland, and from him descended the race of Stewart Kings who ruled the kingdom for many years. Walter the sixth, High Steward, was married in 1315 to Marjorie, only daughter and child of Robert the Bruce by his first marriage, and their son, Robert, the then High Stewart, succeeded David II. as King of Scotland in 1370, and was thus the first of the Stewart Kings, with the title of Robert II.

The death of King Robert the Bruce in 1329 plunged the country, for which he had fought so nobly, into the extremity of despair. His son, David was only eight years old, and the dynasty of Bruce had no claim to superiority but the wisdom and bravery of its founder. The power with which he had repressed the incursions of the English, and the discretion whereby he had obviated the claims of others to the throne, were now alike powerless; and dissension and invasion became the order of the day. Edward Baliol, eldest son of King John Baliol, in 1332, made a compact with Edward III. of England, promising to render homage to that monarch for the Kingdom of Scotland in return for assistance in its conquest. This wretched agreement was fulfilled despite the patriotic efforts of the supporters of Bruce; and Baliol landed with an English army at Kinghorn, on 6th August 1332, and six days afterwards defeated the Scots at the Battle of Dupplin, near Perth. He was crowned as King of Scotland at Scone on 24th September in this year; but his heart failed him and he fled in haste about three months afterwards to England, where he died in 1363. The English army remained in Scotland after Dupplin, and were again victorious at Halidon Hill, near Berwick, in July 1333, where the Scottish nobles were dispersed, and had to flee for their lives. Amongst them was Robert, the young Stewart of Scotland, who was now nearest heir to the throne, and had to lurk in hidance in his ancestral Island of Bute.

Determined to extirpate the race of Bruce, Baliol attacked and captured Stewart's Castle of Dunoon, intending from it to menace the fortress of Dumbarton, which completely commanded the Clyde. But Robert Stewart, finding that the venality and cowardice of Baliol had alienated many of his adherents, took course with his relative, Sir Colin Campbell of Lochow, the nephew of Robert Bruce; and making a hasty descent upon Dunoon Castle, they surprised its defenders, and easily gained possession. This was the first reverse that Baliol had suffered and became the signal for a general revolt against him. The Brandanes of Bute, Robert's hereditary vassals, performed prodigies of valour in the assault, overwhelming Lyle, the governor, it is stated, with showers of stones. For their services on this occasion the Brandanes obtained perpetual exemption from the payment of multures ; whilst Sir Colin Campbell was made Hereditary Keeper of the Castle—an office which remained in the Argyll family as long as the Castle existed, and it became the frequent resort of the Stewart Kings.

Dunoon Castle figured in national history during an incident which need only here be referred to briefly. After the death of James V. in 1542, there was a contest between three persons as to the Regency during the infancy of Queen Mary. The Earl of Arran, as a near relative, became " Governor," having been supported by Cardinal Beaton ; but Arran was overthrown by the Queen-Mother, Mary of Guise, and the next opponent to her was the Earl of Lennox, also a relative. Lennox had spent some years at the Court of Henry VIII. of England, who still longed to gain possession of Scotland. Accordingly, in August 1544, Henry sent an invading fleet to the Clyde, who destroyed Arran's Castle of Brodick, and ravaged the neighbouring country. The ten English ships, full-freighted with their panoply of war, reached Dumbarton, then in charge of Stirling of Glorat, a servitor of Lennox, but to that Earl's surprise, Stirling threatened him with the Earl's own artillery, and the fleet had to retire discomfitted.

Sir Colin Campbell at Dunoon had word of this defeat, and received Arran at Dunoon, with a fusilade of guns; but Lennox, landing on the Cowal shore, with a troop of his followers, attacked Dunoon Castle and took it at the spear's point. Unable to leave a party in posesssion, Lennox was forced to return to the fleet, and sailing down to Kintyre he ravaged the district of the Campbells, and then went back to England to tell Henry that their project had failed. Dunoon Castle again fell to the charge of Sir Colin Campbell and his sucessors.

A different scene was enacted at Dunoon about twenty years after. In June 1563, Mary, Queen of Scots, who had sailed from Dumbarton Castle to France, had been married there, and had become a widow, was now in her native land, and planned an expedition so that she might make herself acquainted with her kingdom. Her half-sister (illegitimate daughter of James V.), was then Countess of Argyll, and she invited the Queen to visit her at Dunoon Castle, so that she might see life in the western Highlands. Queen Mary left Edinburgh, visited her birth-place at Linlithgow Palace, went thence to Glasgow where she remained for ten days, visiting Hamilton, Paisley, and other notable places in that neighbourhood. From there she went to Inveraray, where she spent some time in deer-hunting. As

in duty bound, she paid a visit to the ancient
Castle of Dunoon, one of the earliest palaces of
her race, and under the care of her sister she
spent the night there in mirth and banqueting.
A ballad of the period thus refers to the Queen's
visit :—

> " Now she's cast off her bonny shoon,
>   Made o' the gilded leather ;
> And she's put on her Highland brogues
>   To skip among the heather.
>
> And she's cast off her bonny gown,
>   Made of the silk and satin,
> And she's put on a tartan plaid,
>   To row amang the bracken."

Leaving Dunoon the Queen crossed the Clyde
into Ayrshire, proceeding as far south as Dumfries before she returned to Edinburgh. And with
that varied journey nearly all the happiness of
her life was completed.

There is little to record of the after-history of
Dunoon Castle save the story of an atrocious act
of cruelty carried out by the Campbells of Dunoon.
There had long been a feud between the Campbells and the Lamonts of Lamont and Castle Toward, and in 1646, by direction of the Marquess
of Argyll, the Campbells attacked Castle Toward,
which they plundered and demolished. Among
the documents in the custody of the present (1927)
Sir Norman Lamont, Bart., of Knockdow, there
is the complaint against the Marquess lodged by

159

Sir James Lamont, referring to this incident, in which the following passage occurs :—

" Ten dayes after the capitulations were ended, they carryed the said Sir James, his friends and vassals to a place called Dunnoone, about five miles from his principall garison. And there in the Churchyard they most cruelly murthered (without Assyse or order of law) on one tree thirty and six at one tyme of the chiefs and speciall gentlemen of that name, and before they were half-hanged they cut them down and threw them in by dozens in pitts prepared for the same, and many of thame striveing to ryse upon their feet were violently holden downe until that by throwing the earth in great quantity upon them they were stifled to death. And it is much to be remarked and taken notice of that the same tree upon which these thirty-six gentlemen were hanged, being shortly after cutt downe did immediately as it was in cutting spring forth blood, and notwithstanding the body of the tree was carryed away, yet did the root thereof continually cast forth blood for the space it continued in the ground, which was for severall yeares."

Whether it was the result of the Curse of the Lamonts or from some other cause, the Castle of Dunoon decayed from this period. It was used as a residence till 1670, but after that time all record of it ceases. The village which was growing up round it would doubtless be largely composed of the stones of the Castle ; for when

once the cold finger of Time brings decay upon
such an erection its demolition is speedy and complete. Now there are not so many stones remaining as to give an adequate idea of either the
form or extent of this stronghold ; and the green
grass waves luxuriantly over the foundations of
Dunoon Castle, telling silently, but eloquently, its
message of mutability to this generation.

XIII

ERCHLESS CASTLE

THE district of Beauly possesses a peculiar charm
for the Scottish tourist whose experience of the
scenery of Scotland has been confined to the
Lowlands. The northern portion of the kingdom
is so radically different in character from the
southern that one might readily imagine that the
Grampian Mountains formed the boundary of a
new State, or were the natural demarcation co-
inciding with the artificial dividing line between
two zones. The fertile vales of Tweeddale and
Clydesdale, with their inconsiderable mounts and
hills, give place, first of all to the varied uplands
and elevated plains of Perthshire, which are preparatory for the cloud-daring peaks of west
Aberdeenshire, and the rugged and barren moun--
tains of Caithness and Sutherland. Betwixt these
extremes of verdant slopes and heath-clad hills
the district of Beauly lies ; and whilst partaking
of the nature of each, it forms the connecting link
between the two dissimilar aspects of nature.

The varied country is here decidedly mountainous, and the waters which flow down the
sides of the hills are so concentrated and diverted
into the gloomy glens which lie between that
they assume the dignity of rivers. The inland

lochs which lie embossed among the hills find
their outlet to the sea through the straths formed
by the overhanging mountains; and though it
is difficult to trace a consecutive range of these,
the phenomena which they display are similar to
those of the Grampians. The water-shed of the
locality is east by north, and many of the rivers
join themselves together ere debouching into the
North Sea, the inward sweep of whose waters
has hollowed out the vast bay of the Moray
Firth.

Three inland lochs at different altitudes are
driven by the set of the land to seek the same
outlet. Loch Affrick, after gathering the drainage of Glen Grivie, flows into Loch Benevian
through the romantic Strath Affrick. Issuing
from the latter loch, the overflow takes the name
of River Glass, and assumes the proportion of a
considerable stream. Further north Loch Lingard
becomes tributary by pouring its waters through
Strath Cannich into the Glass; and beyond
Scuir na Lappish, Loch Morar's stream, rushing
through the depths of Strath Farrar, hastens also
to join the swiftly-flowing Glass, which becomes
known as the Beauly river after receiving this
accession. From Struan Inn, the point of con-
fluence of the Glass and Farrar, the traveller may
wander in any direction with the assurance of
meeting with lovely and picturesque scenery.
He may pursue the precarious path which leads
westward to the shores of Loch Morar, following
the devious course of the Farrar, whose waters

roll turbulently downwards to the ocean over rock and fell, forming myriad cascades of silvery brightness which sparkle in the summer sun, or dash impetuously down the strath, o'erladen with the spate of winter snows ; or, journeying south-westward, he may retrace the Glass through all its windings until he reaches the point where Cannich joins its stream. The road to the right will carry him to the still and silent shores of Loch Lingard, whose waters lie enclosed by mighty mountains and over-shadowed by lofty trees. But if he pursue the way which stretches before him he will ere long reach the hidden recesses where Loch Benevian and Loch Affrick form natural reservoirs to feed these rapid and overflowing rivers. Despite the volume of water which flows through the channel of the Affrick, the inequalities of the rocky way which it follows break it up into innumerable waterfalls of little altitude, but of great force and energy. And when Mamsoul and Beinattow, the presiding mountains which rule the Cannich and the Affrick, are capped with snow, and the wintry torrents are rushing down their precipitous sides, the picturesque effect which these rivers present is striking and impressive.

The fringe of the great Caledonian Forest, which once stretched from the Firth of Forth to the Banks o' Dee, here still retains a portion of its primeval grandeur, and gigantic birch trees and towering, pyramidal firs cast their sombre shadows over the restless stream which brawls below.

164

ERCHLESS CASTLE

" From the sources which well
In the tarn or the fell,
From its fountains
In the mountains,
Its rills and its gills,
 Through moss and through brake
It runs and it creeps
For a while till it sleeps
 In its own little lake.

. . . .

Here it comes sparkling,
And there it lies darkling,
Now smoking and frothing
Its tumult and wrath in,
Till in this rapid race on which it is bent
It reaches the place of its steep descent."

Amid such scenery thus imperfectly described
stands the old Castle of Erchless, the seat of the
head of the old Clan Chisholm. A short distance
from Struy Bridge, on the banks of the Beauly
formed by the conjoined rivers of Farrar and
Glass, and pleasantly situated upon a wooded
eminence overlooking the stream, this Castle
adds that element of human interest to the scene
without which it would be incomplete. The
many-gabled structure, with its quaint turrets
and hidden turnpike stairs, might well afford to
the student of architecture a compendious history
of his art. The original Castle, judging from its
plan, was erected early in the 14th century,
though there have been many alterations on the
structure since that time.

The oriel windows, elegant as they may be, formed no portion of the original building ; nor can one believe that the chief who laid the foundation stone in remote times ever crossed the threshold of his dwelling beneath a pillared portico. But these adjuncts, since they are so plainly *additions* and not *restorations*, add to the piquancy of the general effect. In any case it would be difficult to find another site for a Scottish Castle at once so picturesque and so commanding.

The Chisholms belonged originally to the Border Counties, the earliest noted in history being John de Chisholme, who is named in a Bull of 1254 by Pope Alexander IV. John's grandson, Sir John de Chisholme of Berwick, fought at Bannockburn in 1314, on the side of Robert the Bruce. About 1403, Alexander de Chisholme, of Chisholme, Roxburghshire, who was the son of Sir Robert, Constable of Urquhart Castle and Sheriff of Inverness, was married to Margaret, who is described as " the Lady of Erchless," and this seems to have been the earliest of the Chisholms of Erchless Castle. The lands in the possession of the family at this date were Strathglass and Ard, and later they came into the estate of Comar, which made them proprietors of a large part of Rossshire.

In 1685, when the Duke of York became James II. and VII., many of the Highland Clans adhered to his cause, as they were chiefly adherents of the Romish Church, and expected

the restoration of the ancient faith. The fatal
conflict at the Pass of Killiecrankie, where
Viscount Dundee fell in the hour of victory,
forced the Northern Clans to retire, pursued by
the Scottish Whigs and English Army. John
Chisholm garrisoned Erchless Castle to resist the
pursuers, but he had at length to surrender it to
General Livingstone (afterwards Viscount Teviot)
who was Commander-in-chief of the Scottish
forces of William of Orange.

With that blind devotion to the Stewart Cause
which is one of the problems of Scottish history
at the time, Roderick Chisholm, son of John,
took part in the Jacobite Rising of 1715, in
support of the Chevalier de St. George (James
VIII.) after his services had been foolishly refused by George I. The estates of Roderick were
forfeited, but he was afterwards pardoned in
1735, and the lands restored to him. This did
not prevent him from joining Prince Charles
Edward in 1745, and leading eighty of the Chisholms through the campaign till Culloden, where
thirty of them were killed and his son of the same
name also fell. The lands were not alienated at this
time, and have remained with his descendants
ever since in undisturbed possession.

Erchless Castle, though thus intimately associated with war, has also a traditional romance of
love, the story of which is still current in the
locality, though dates are lacking. About six
miles from the Castle, on the other side of the
Beauly River, stands the Castle of Beaufort, the

ancient seat of the Clan Fraser. It so happened
at one time that Fraser, the Lord of Lovat, had
an only daughter whose welfare was his chief
concern. Reared beneath the shelter of Beaufort Castle and encircled by the unremitting care
of her father and brethren, she grew up to womanhood. The young Chief of the Chisholms had
seen the maid and had fallen captive to her
charms ; but the two families were then at feud,
and though the lady reciprocated his affection no
marriage seemed possible. At length Chisholm
decided to win his bride at the point of the
sword ; and one moonlight night, accompanied
by a few of his faithful followers, he waylaid her
near some well-known trysting-place and bore
her away to his own territory. With commend-
able caution he refrained from carrying her to
Erchless Castle, where she would be first sought
for, but rather took her to a lonely isle in Loch
Bruirach where he deemed her safe from discovery.

Meanwhile the Frasers had found out the loss
of their young lady, and the baron rose up in
wrath and ordered a speedy pursuit :—

> " O fy ! gar ride, an' fy ! gar rin,
> An' hasteye, bring these faitours again,
> For she's be brent an' he's be slain."

The artifice of Chisholm in conveying his love to
the retreat he had chosen was of no avail. The
Frasers had mustered in force and the Chisholms
could not withstand them.

" From Beauly's wild and woodland glen
How proudly Lovat's banners soar ;
How fierce the plaided Highland clan
Rush onward with the braid claymore."

They soon discovered the spot which the youthful lover had chosen. What will not man endure when love and beauty is his reward ? But the odds against The Chisholm were fearful ; and when his lady clung to his arm and implored him to resign her again to her kindred rather than risk his life, her very entreaties impeded his swordsmanship. With his left arm supporting her whom he valued as dearer than life, he strove to beat back the weapons of his enemies ; and though his defence was a gallant one, of what avail was his prowess against so many ? Had he remained on the mainland some fleet horse might have borne him into the wilds of Glen Elchaig or the barren shelter of Mealfourvounie ; but the dark waters of the loch encircled him. Bearing up his precious charge he again essayed the combat, even though overborne by his assailants, but the moon was overcast by a flying scud which swept across the sky, and in the temporary darkness which was thus produced the fatal thrust which was aimed at his heart by one of her brethren was received by herself ! Sinking breathless, lifeless to the ground, the fair cause of this deadly tumult yielded up her breath, and lay before the speechless and agonized combatants in the chill embrace of Death ! Who shall dare intrude with officious description on such a scene as this, or strive with laboured words to explain the depth of such heart-misery ? Only the simple language of the ballad which describes a similar situation can express the profound emotions of such an incident :—

> " I wish I were where Helen lies !
>   Night and day on me she cries,
>   And I am weary of the skies
>   For her sake that died for me ! "

XIV

DUART CASTLE

THE tourist who takes shipping at Oban with the intention of passing through the Sound of Mull cannot fail to observe the picturesque ruins of Castle Duart, which stand on a promontory of the island of Mull, immediately opposite Lismore. The situation occupied by these remains exhibits the chief characteristics of Highland maritime scenery, and would be worthy of attention even were there no historical memories connected with it. The Point of Duart has been formed by the wash of the Atlantic Ocean rushing through the Sound of Mull, and the rugged peak which it exposes to the confined course of this current diverts its energy northwards to the indented shores of Loch Linnhe, to the coast of Morven, and to the islets around Lismore. The channel between this point and the nearest land is about four miles wide ; and as the Castle is exposed to all the fury of the northern gales which swoop down upon it from Loch Linnhe, the wildness of the surrounding scenery may be easily imagined. The hundred peaks of Argyllshire stand out boldly against the horizon, while the shore on either side of the Sound of Mull is dotted with the remains of ancient Keeps and

Castles, the relics of the stern feudal system which once obtained in the district, the deserted strongholds of some of the Highland Clans that are now scattered throughout the wide world. And as the rude rocks which line the shores tell the story to him who can read aright of volcanic upheavals and commotions which have altered the face of Nature in pre-historic times, so these silent ruins speak eloquently of fierce revolutions in the history of man, and, like enduring monuments, indicate the progress and development of civilization. They tell of times :—

" When sullen Ignorance her flag displayed,
  And Rapine and Revenge her voice obeyed."

But they also show by the very helplessness of their condition that the days of their years are fled, and their former glory has departed. The races which have compelled a subsistence from these barren hills, or wrested their means of support from the raging sea, have vanished from this scene, and left little behind them save the names which may be preserved in history, and the desolate ruins which become the wonder of succeeding generations :—

" All ruined and wild is their roofless abode,
  And lonely the dark raven's sheltering tree ;
  And travelled by few is the grass-covered road
  Where the hunter of deer and the warrior trode
  To his hills that encircle the sea."

DUART CASTLE

Valentine & Sons, Ltd.

Duart Castle

Amongst the Clans which formerly inhabited this quarter none was more famous than that of the Macleans, whose feudal stronghold was Castle Duart. By personal prowess they had extended their possessions, and by judicious intermarriages they had increased their power, until there were few amongst the western chiefs that could compete with them. And as every Highlander inherits the notion that *his* Clan was designed by Providence to lead all others, it was natural that the Macleans should be at feud with those who were not their vassals and inferiors. The situation of their Castle was peculiarly favourable for the development of their ambitions hopes, and they soon found that there were no "foemen worthy of their steel" in the whole island of Mull.

These marriage connections, however skilfully devised, sometimes brought the Macleans into serious difficulties. Their relations with the Clan Campbell, for instance, were at once put upon a war-footing by the brutal conduct of Lachlan Maclean towards his wife, a daughter of the Earl of Argyll, which true story is narrated further on in this notice as connected with the Lady's Rock, which stands about midway in the channel between Duart Point and Lismore.

It is impossible to give an accurate date for the erection of the oldest part of Duart Castle. There probably was an original Keep on the site of the present Castle, a portion of which, still in existence, has been adopted in the later erection. This part has high and massive walls, varying

173

from 10 to 15 feet thick, which enclose what is now the courtyard. The Castle was probably founded by Lauchlan Maclean, surnamed Lubanach, about the year 1366, in which year he married Margaret, daughter of MacDonald, first Lord of the Isles. As Maclean of Duart, he and his successors for a long time were heritable Keepers of many Castles in the district, and had many possessions both on the mainland and in the Western Isles. The first reference to the Castle in documents is dated 1392, but the building was not completely finished till the time of Hector Mor Maclean, about 1560, and this Chief also married Mary, daughter of Alexander Macdonald, then Lord of the Isles, whose seat was at Isla. From a comparison of the architecture of different parts of the Castle, it appears that the Great Tower was erected by this Hector Mor Maclean.

The MacDonalds had made common cause with the Macleans against the rising power of the Campbells of Argyll, but their alliance was short-lived. The Chief of the MacDonald's had formed an expedition along with Maclean of Duart, and they had ravaged some of the richest territories belonging to the Campbells. But the son of the Chief of the MacDonalds afterwards married a daughter of the second Earl of Argyll, and he thus became the enemy of Maclean. A curious complication arose later, when Sir Lachlan Mor Maclean sought to end the contest with the Campbells by wedding Lady Elizabeth

Campbell, another of the daughters of the second Earl of Argyll, and sister of the third Earl.

The ambition of Maclean was unbounded, and though his alliance with the House of Argyll ensured to him the peaceable possession of his heritage, he was not content with it. When Sir Donald MacDonald of Lochalsh sought to have himself proclaimed as Lord of the Isles, Maclean threw up his connection with his brother-in-law Argyll, and against the latter's advice, he stirred up an insurrection in the Hebrides. The powerful influence of Colin, third Earl of Argyll, whose first duty after his accession was to take up arms against his relative Maclean, at length quelled the turmoil. Maclean, however, seems never to have forgiven Argyll for his share in the affair, and determined to wreak his vengeance upon his own wife. History is not very clear as to the character of Lady Elizabeth ; for whilst one account makes her to appear almost in the light of a martyred saint, the other asserts that she had twice attempted to take away her husband's life. On thing is certain—that the misfortune of barrenness was magnified into a crime by the lawless Highland Chief, and he determined to effect her destruction.

The method which he adopted exhibited the refinement of savage cruelty. Off the coast of Mull, as already explained, there is still shown the bare and solitary rock which her lord determined should make her pathway to heaven. Fringed with sea-weed, and ever moist with the lapping waters which cover the surface entirely at flood-tide, this lone rock might well scare the high-born lady, whose brutal husband led her here to endure the agonies of a slow and torturing death. One may imagine the fearful forebodings of the Lady Elizabeth as the advancing waters by their resistless march bore her nearer and nearer to her doom. At length, when despair had all but seized her, she noticed a little boat upon the waters, whose occupants replied to her frantic signals of distress. They drew near, and to her infinite joy she beheld the faces of some of her own clansmen, whom Providence had sent to her rescue when in extremity. They bore her swiftly away to her brother's house, and restored her, weeping, to the shade of the paternal roof-tree.

The Campbells arose in a body to demand retribution, but the politic Earl did not care to press his brother-in-law too severely. The task of revenge fell therefore upon Sir John Campbell of Cawdor, whose courage kept pace with his impetuosity. Not long after, having heard that Maclean was in Edinburgh, Campbell hastened there, entered his lodgings, and slew him as he lay in bed, scorning to give him even the privilege of defence, since his intended murder of his wife had disgraced him as a Knight. As might have been foreseen, this rash deed at once drove the two clans to arms, and only the interposition of the Government prevented much useless bloodshed. Upon this strange story Thomas Campbell, the poet, founded his poem of " Glenara," which, though sacrificing facts for the sake of the poetry, is substantially correct :—

" ' I dreamed of my lady, I dreamed of her grief,
    I dreamed that her lord was a barbarous Chief ;
    On a rock of the ocean fair Ellen did seem—
    Glenara ! Glenara ! now read me my dream ! '

    In dust low the traitor has knelt on the ground ;
    And the desert revealed where the lady was found ;
    From a rock of the ocean that beauty is borne ;
    Now joy to the house of fair Ellen of Lorn ! "

Joanna Bailie made this story the subject of one of her " Plays of Passion," under the title of " A Family Legend," but used some poetic licence as to the details. The facts as recorded above are beyond dispute.

XV

TANTALLON CASTLE

THE ruins of the famous Castle of Tantallon
stand on the east coast of Haddingtonshire, about
three miles from the town of North Berwick. The
Castle occupied a noticeable promontory at the
mouth of the Firth of Forth, and has been
adequately protected on three sides by its position
on an elevated peninsula formed by precipitous
rocks which rise from the water. Only the landward portion needed to be fortified, as the
approach from the sea was quite impracticable
for an invader. On the inner or westward side
there was a deep rock-cut ditch, as well as lofty
walls nearly 50 feet high and 12 feet in thickness,
surmounted by battlements forming a straight
line, without the machicolations for artillery of
a later date. Within these walls is the large courtyard, which is about 500 feet long by 220 feet
wide, outside of which there is a deep ditch and
an elevated mound. On the westward side there
is another ditch and mound, so that the Castle
was perfectly protected on every side. Indeed,
it would be difficult to find a Castle in all Scotland so completely secured by natural formations
against an invading force. Even the entrance to
the Castle was by a draw-bridge over the ditch,

and a winding road which exposed intruders to
the arms and artillery of those defenders within
the Castle. No doubt the occupants in early
times were entitled to consider Tantallon Castle
as impregnable, being defended both by nature
and the devices of man. The fine description of
the Castle in its best days, given by Scott in
"Marmion," Canto V., is both poetical in form
and accurate in details, so far as one can judge
from the existing ruins :—

> "Tantallon vast ;
> Broad, massive, high, and stretching far,
> And held impregnable in war,
> On a projecting rock they rose,
> And round three sides the ocean flows,
> The fourth did battled walls enclose
> And double mound and fosse.
> By narrow draw-bridge, outworks strong
> Through studded gates, an entrance long,
> To the main court they cross.
> It was a wide and stately square ;
> Around were lodgings fit and fair,
> And towers of various form,
> Which on the court projected far,
> And broke its lines quadrangular.
> Here was square keep, there turret high,
> Or pinnacle that sought the sky,
> Whence oft the Warder could descry
> The gathering ocean-storm."

The exact date and the name of the builder of
Tantallon Castle are alike unknown, but it prob-
ably was erected about 1400, and possibly by
Robert, Duke of Albany, third son of Robert II.,

and Governor of Scotland while James I. was a
captive in England. It is certain that it was in
the possession of the Duke's eldest son, Murdoch,
second Duke of Albany, who succeeded his father
as Governor in 1420, and acted in 1424 at the
Coronation of James. Albany's Castles of Tantallon and Doune were forfeited to the Crown
after the conviction of himself and his two sons
of treason, and all three were beheaded in 1425
by the order of James I. These Castles remained
in the possession of successive Kings till 1479,
when Tantallon was granted by James III. to
Archibald Douglas, fifth Earl of Angus, known
in history by the sobriquet of " Bell-the-Cat."

An interesting historical event in connection
with Tantallon Castle occurred in 1528, which
involved Archibald, sixth Earl of Angus, in serious
trouble. Margaret Tudor, daughter of Henry VII.,
and widow of James IV., was married in 1514
to the Earl of Angus ; but the young King,
James V., resented being under the control of
his step-father, and escaped in 1528 from Falkland where he had been confined against his will.
Margaret had obtained a divorce from Angus in
1526, but two years afterwards he was forfeited
for treason along with his brother and uncle, and
he retired to Tantallon Castle, which he fortified
against the royal Army.

The King went in person to superintend the
siege of Tantallon, bringing against it all the
artillery he could obtain from Dunbar Castle.
But the stout walls of the Castle withstood all

TANTALLON CASTLE

the efforts of the King, and he had to raise the seige. The Castle, however, was rendered up to the Royalists by the Castellan, as Angus had made his escape to England. James V. at once set about improving the defences of Tantallon, causing masons to strengthen the walls and build up many of the windows. The work then done may still be traced in the ruins.

After the death of the King in 1542, the Earl of Angus was permitted to return from exile, and regained his former Castle, which he proceeded still further to fortify, until it became recognized as one of the strongest Castles in Scotland. Here the Earl remained till his death in 1556 at an advanced age, and was succeeded by his cousin, David Douglas, seventh Earl of Angus. The Castle remained in possession of this family for many years. The eleventh Earl was created Marquess of Douglas in 1633 by Charles I., and the third Marquess in 1703 was raised in the Peerage to the rank of Duke of Douglas. He died in 1761 without issue, when the ducal honours became extinct, and the Marquessate devolved on the Duke of Hamilton.

Long before the last-named date, however, Tantallon Castle had to pass many tribulations. The Covenanters had become a strong force in Scotland, and when the famous Assembly at Glasgow in 1638 passed a resolution abolishing Episcopacy, this was regarded as the signal for an armed revolt. At that time many of the leading Covenanters had been imprisoned as rebels in the dungeons on the Bass Rock, which rises abruptly from the sea at no great distance from Tantallon. In the following year, 1639, the conflict between the opposing forces became serious. General Leslie with a select company of a thousand musketeers attacked and captured Edinburgh Castle, and on the same day a bloodless victory gave them possession of Dumbarton Castle. Dalkeith was won by Monro with five hundred men, and they soon spread their conquests further. Strathaven Castle, belonging to the Marquess of Hamilton, also fell into their hands, as well as Brodick Castle, which was one of the seats of this nobleman.

A special attack was organized upon Tantallon Castle, the property of the Marquess of Douglas. The slogan by which the men were encouraged was designed to awaken their animosity. It ran thus :—

> " Ding doun Tantallon,
> Mak' a brig to the Bass,"

the purpose being to release the unfortunate Covenanters imprisoned there. The first part of the task was accomplished, but the second was impossible. Yet these intrepid soldiers, inflamed with religious zeal, carried out the demolition of Tantallon Castle which James V. had not done with the aid of his artillery. The strong walls were thrown down, and the remaining portions were garrisoned against the Royalist Army. This was the beginning of the destruction of the

Castle. Then in 1651, when Cromwell invaded Scotland and gained a victory at Dunbar, he sent General Monck (afterwards Lord Albemarle) to complete the overthrow of the ancient structure, and this he did most effectively. The ruins have been so long exposed without any attempt at repairs that they have become now irreparable.

The after-history of the Castle may be soon told. The place in all its disrepair still belonged to the Douglas family, but from them it was to pass away. In 1700, or thereby, the Duke of Douglas sold the ruined structure to Sir Hew Dalrymple, Bart., President of the Court of Session, with the title of Lord North Berwick. He was the third son of the first Earl of Stair, and was regarded as one of the best lawyers of his time. At his death in 1737 he was succeeded by a series of heirs to the baronetcy, and the title has been continued till the present day. Tantallon now (1927) belongs to Sir Hew Clifford Hamilton-Dalrymple, who is the ninth Baronet.

The story of Tantallon Castle shows that it has long been a prominent land-mark in the history of Scotland. Built by Murdoch, Duke of Albany, the grandson of Robert II., it was forfeited by his treason, and came into the possession of James I., thus becoming a Royal Castle. For centuries it was the residence of the Douglasses, Earls of Angus and Dukes of Douglas, and resisted a siege conducted by James V. against his stepfather. Then the Covenanters reduced it partly to ruins, and Cromwell and Monck completed the work of destruction. The Castle has stood in its present site for five centuries and a quarter, and is still attractive from its historical associations. And musing over this ruinous pile these lines seem appropriate :—

> " ' Why sitt'st thou by that ruined hall,
>   Thou aged carle so stern and grey ?
> Dost thou its former pride recall,
>   Or ponder how it passed away ?
>
> ' Know'st thou not me ? ' the deep voice cried,
>   ' So long enjoyed, so oft misused ?
> Alternate, in thy fickle pride,
>   Desired, neglected, and accused !
>
> ' Before my breath, like blazing flax,
>   Man and his marvels pass away ;
> And chasing empires wane and wax,
>   Are founded, flourish, and decay.
>
> ' Redeem mine hours—the space is brief—
>   While in my glass the sand-grains shiver ;
> And measureless for joy or grief
>   When Time and thou shalt part for ever ! ' "

XVI

HERMITAGE CASTLE

THE Castle of Hermitage, now a ruined structure, stands in the southern part of Roxburghshire, a few miles from Riccarton Junction, near Hermitage Water, which is formed by Twistlehope Burn and Braidley Burn, and becomes a tributary of Liddel River. It flows, therefore, through Liddesdale, and is not far from the Border between Scotland and England in the olden time. It seems probable that the site of the Castle was chosen because it lies between the two streams named, and these would not only form a protection from attack, but also furnish an ample supply of water for the ditches by which the Castle was surrounded. The whole district of Liddesdale was, in early times, in the possession of the De Soulis family; and it is said that Randolph de Soulis built a Castle in this district, but not on the site of the later Hermitage Castle, about the time of David I., who reigned from 1124 till 1153, and was the ninth and youngest son of Malcolm Caenmor and St Margaret, daughter of Eadward Atheling. It is possible that King David had met one of the De Soulis family at the Court of Henry I. of England, and may have brought him to Scotland when he succeeded his brother Alexander I. as ruler of that Kingdom. There is little doubt that the most of the Liddesdale country was in the possession of the De Soulis family about the 13th century.

The Castle of Hermitage was built on its present site by Nicohlas de Soulis, about 1240, and was made the excuse by Henry III. of England for an invasion of Scotland, on the plea that this stronghold was too near the Scottish Boundary, which was then formed by the Liddel River. So late as 1300, the Castle of Hermitage was regarded as one of the principal fortresses in the south-eastern part of Scotland. Very soon it came into the possession of William de Douglas, Knight of Liddesdale, who also held Roxburgh Castle, and was Keeper of Lochmaben Castle, and in 1332 was Warden of the Marches. Ten years afterwards (1342) he was specially favoured by David II., who sent him on an embassy to France. In 1346 he was taken prisoner by the English at Durham, and only released on the condition of becoming a vassal of Edward III. of England. But in 1353 the Lord of Hermitage Castle was murdered by his kinsman, and godson, William, Lord of Douglas, afterwards Earl. It has been stated, but without documentary proof, that the Castle of Hermitage was erected by Walter Comyn, fourth Earl of Menteith ; but there is little doubt that this was the main seat of the De Soulis family at a much earlier period.

Sir William de Douglas, the Knight of Liddesdale, was born about 1300, and was so brave and successful in war that he was styled by his contemporaries "the Flower of Chivalry." He was present at the disastrous battle of Halidon Hill, in 1333, and was taken prisoner by the English, and remained captive for two years. He became, after his liberation, one of the most strenuous supporters of the Scottish national party, and was active at the Siege of Perth in 1339, where he was wounded. His purpose was then to win back Teviotdale from the English, which he accomplished in 1342, when King David II. granted to him the Earldom of Atholl, which had been forfeited, and bestowed upon him many lands near Hermitage Castle, by which he became known as "the Knight of Liddesdale." He resigned the title of Earl of Atholl to the High Steward of Scotland in exchange for some of the lands in Liddesdale. He was then the largest proprietor of lands in the district; but his ambition and jealousy led to his downfall, and brought on the tragedy of Hermitage Castle.

At this time he was Custodian of Roxburgh Castle, though it was then in the possession of the English. Sir Alexander de Ramsay of Dalwolsy, ancestor of the present Earl of Dalhousie, was one of the most valorous Knights in the brilliant galaxy of warriors at the Court of David II. He had distinguished himself by bringing about the raising of the Siege of Dunbar; and in 1338 he captured the Castle of Roxburgh, and expelled the enemy. So pleased was the King with this exploit that he conferred at once upon Ramsay the office of Sheriff of Teviotdale, forgetting that the office was already held by the Knight of Liddesdale, and was thus deprived of it that it might be given to his rival. So he captured Ramsay while that unsuspecting Sheriff was presiding at a Court at Hawick ; carried him off to Hermitage Castle, and imprisoned him in one of the deepest dungeons. There he was confined without sustenance until he died of starvation ; his life having been prolonged by some grains of corn that fell from an upper chamber in the place where he was incarcerated. It is certain that Ramsay died at Hermitage Castle, and Andrew Wynton, the Chronicler, carefully remarks :—" Of his dethe wes grete pete. To tell you thare-off the manere it is bot sorow to tell here."

The Earl of Angus in 1470 appointed David Scott of Buccleuch to the office of Custodian of Hermitage Castle, and for many years the Scotts fulfilled this duty. In 1492, Archibald Douglas, fifth Earl of Angus, exchanged Liddesdale and Hermitage with Patrick Hepburn, third Lord Hales, who was created first Earl of Bothwell, for Bothwell Castle on the Clyde. Angus had married Mary Hepburn, daughter of the Earl of Bothwell, who thus became a son-in-law to Bothwell. The second Earl of Bothwell fell on the Field of Flodden, and the third Earl, his successor, died in 1556, leaving a son, afterwards the notorious James Hepburn, fourth Earl of Bothwell, whose marriage to Mary, Queen of Scots, led to

HERMITAGE CASTLE

his downfall. The sister of this Earl was married to John Stewart, Prior of Coldingham, a natural son of James V., and became the mother of Francis Stewart, another turbulent nobleman, who was created by James VI. the Earl of Bothwell of a new creation, but retaining the designation of fifth Earl though he retained his mother's name of Hepburn.

The story of the fourth Earl of Bothwell forms a prominent feature in the history of the reign of Queen Mary. While he lay wounded at Hermitage Castle in 1566, the Queen went from Jedburgh to see him, a distance of about 40 miles, and returned the same day, thus bringing on a severe attack of fever. This indiscreet action upon her part told against her when her marriage to Bothwell took place in May 1567, as it was supposed that she had consented to this unfortunate wedding. Bothwell escaped the vengeance of the Scottish nobles, fled to Kirkwall, and became a pirate. He landed in Norway, was sent to Denmark, and the King refused to surrender, but kept him in close confinement, first at Copenhagen, and afterwards at Malmö, and thence to Drangholm, where he died insane in 1578, having been imprisoned for over ten years.

The story of Francis Stewart or Hepburn, fifth and last Earl of Bothwell, was hardly less eventful and exciting than that of his predecessor. He has been described as " one of the most treacherous men of his time," always plotting and counterplotting against his relative James VI. After a very stormy career he went to France, was pursued thither, and forced to fly to Spain and Italy. He died at Naples in poverty and disgrace, in 1624, his title and possessions having been forfeited in 1592, after a daring attempt to carry off the King from Falkland Palace. His possessions in Liddesdale, including Hermitage Castle, were conferred upon Sir Walter Scott of Buccleuch, who was created, in 1606, as first Lord Scott of Buccleuch, from whom descended the Dukes of Buccleuch, holders of the title. The present Duke is the proprietor of Hermitage Castle.

XVII

STIRLING CASTLE

THERE are some Castles in Scotland which have become famous rather in consequence of their beauty than their strength ; but it will be found that those of them which are most memorable in history are noteworthy for both these elements. Edinburgh Castle, for instance, whilst long celebrated as the Maiden Fort which defied the invader, commands a prospect that alone would have made it worthy of remembrance In like manner the Castle of Stirling would have been noticeable for its picturesque situation, even had there been no important events connected with it. The beauty of its site attracted the notice of the Kings and Princes of early times as forming the position for a Royal residence, while its strength formed no mean recommendation as a protection for the Court in a lawless age. Hence Dumbarton Castle, Stirling Castle and Edinburgh Castle have at different times been the seats of Kingly power. Dumbarton was replaced by Stirling, then Perth, before the centre of government was settled at Edinburgh.

There are many derivations of the name of Stirling given by students of Place-names, though these are mostly variations of one idea. Its old

name of " Strila " is evidently compounded of
the Celtic words *strigh* (strife) and *laigh* (the
bending of the bow), and it has been alleged that
the name arose from the fact that the archery
butts were set up here at an early date. Its
second name was " Stryvelin," usually interpreted as " strife," and is poetically applied to the
meeting of the three waters—Forth, Allan and
Teith—near the town. The most reasonable
notion seems to be that which derives its origin
from *Ster* (a mountain) and *lin* (a river), since this
exactly describes the position of the town and
the Castle. And the fact that its alternative
title of " Snawdun," signifying " the fortified hill
on the river " gives additional weight to this
conjecture, and finds corroboration in the couplet
by old Sir David Lyndsay :—

" Adew ! fair Snawdun, with thy towris hie,
    Thy Chapell Royal, Park, and Tabyll Round."

No one can wonder that a Castle so beautifully
situated became a favourite residence with the
monarchs of Scotland.

The hill upon which the Castle is built, though
not in itself of any great height, towers so precipitously over the Carse of Stirling that it gains
an advantage, so far as stretch of vision is concerned over more lofty mountains. The stream
of the Forth, which is here a goodly river, flows
around the base of the eminence, and meanders
through the level country betwixt Stirling and
the sea, with many a graceful curve and winding

sweep. As seen from the Castle the view is exquisite. To the north-eastward stands the solitary peak of Abbey Craig, now crowned by the Wallace Monument, and overlooking the ever-memorable field of Bannockburn. Here, too, may be seen the ruins of Cambuskenneth Abbey, once a royal sepulchre ; while the dark purple of the Ochil Hills forms a dim receding background. Westward the wide carse of Stirling stretches far as the eye can reach, presenting an unbroken surface of fertile and variegated country, dotted with towns and villages in rich profusion. The majestic river winds with serpent-like and sinuous writhings through the green plain, casting abroad its gigantic folds, like some stupendous chain, whose argent gleaming reflects the rays of the sun with greater intensity because mellowed by the tint of the verdant and fruitful banks through which it pursues its course.

There are few prospects in " braid Scotland " more charming than this, and whilst the Castle was deemed important enough to be set aside as the dowry of the Scottish Queens, the lovely scene which lies before it did not escape the notice of the ancient ballad-singers. The river Forth here takes so many tortuous windings that in the space of six miles the stream measures twenty-four miles ; and these wimpling links are often celebrated in early Scottish song :—

> " Are these the Links o' Forth, she said,
>   Or are they Crooks o' Dee,

Or the bonnie wood o' Warroch-head
That I sae fain wad see ? "

In very distant times Stirling formed the
boundary of the great Nemus Caledoniæ, or Caledonian Forest, which was an insuperable barrier
against Roman invasion. And at this day the
ancient Seal of the Burgh of Stirling shows a
Forest, supposed to be this Scottish Wood, together with a Cross, explained as signifying the
great Cross set up at the Castle, and a Bridge
emblematical of the Bridge of Forth, both of
which erections were due to the Northumbian
invasion in 855, at which time the Castle changed
hands. Tradition asserts that from the Castle
the intelligent observer may descry thirteen
battle-fields, among which may be mentioned
Bannockburn, Sauchie Burn, Falkirk (twice),
Sheriffmuir, and Stirling Bridge. It is evident
that a locality such as this must be rich in
historic lore ; and the Castle of Stirling has been
the scene of many deeds of crime, of many
revelries and pageants, only equalled by Edinburgh, the Capital of Scotland. Some of these
incidents may be related, even though they are
not placed in chronological order.

The Castle of Stirling had been conferred
by James I. upon his English bride, Lady Joanna de Beaufort—the heroine of "The King's
Quhair"—as her dowry, and it was here that her
son, afterwards James II., was born in 1430,
being the younger twin-son of the King, the elder

of whom, Alexander, died in infancy. Some of the chroniclers state that the birth of the twins took place at Holyrood ; but possibly this may be an error caused by the anointing and crowning there of James II. in 1437, a year after his father's assassination at Perth. This may be doubtful ; but it is certain that the King (James II.), in February 1451-52, perpetrated at Stirling one of the blackest deeds of treachery which is recorded against the whole Stewart race to which he belonged.

From the time of King Robert the Bruce the family of Douglas, whose founder was the fellow-warrior of that King, had been rising into increased power. Honours were showered upon them by successive Monarchs—at first in gratitude but latterly in fear. For the dominion of the Douglases spread so widely, and drew within its scope so many warlike nobles that the Lanarkshire Earl might soon out-number the Crown in wealth, as in forces. As it was impossible, therefore, for the King to quarrel with so powerful a subject, he endeavoured to win the Earl over by making him Lieutenant-General of the Kingdom. But the possession of so important a post seems rather to have inflamed the ambition of the Earl than bound him to the King. So overbearing, indeed, had he become that the Monarch, whose favourite Douglas had been, was compelled to withdraw the Royal patronage, and to deprive the Earl of his post. The disappointed nobleman retired in chagrin to his Castle of Douglas and

meditated schemes of revenge against the King
and the Court party.

Nor was he long without opportunity of gratify-
ing his vindictive spirit. One after another of the
King's followers were attacked upon some pretext, sufficient in those times to justify sudden
reprisal; and the Monarch soon found that he
had made a dangerous enemy in the Earl of
Douglas. But it was not until he had openly
disregarded the King's mandate that he was
finally abandoned. The Earl had summoned
his vassals to meet him upon a special occasion.
Amongst those whom he had thus summoned was
M'Lellan, known as the Tutor of Bomby, in
Kirkcudbrightshire. This unfortunate man had
provoked the Earl by refusing to join with him
against the King; and Douglas had kidnapped
this daring vassal, and carried him off to the
Castle of Thrieve. The uncle of M'Lellan, Sir
Patrick Gray, Captain of the King's Guard—then
a favourite with the King—obtained a Royal
mandate ordering Douglas to release M'Lellan.

Sir Patrick set forth with this missive, but was
met by the Earl with every demonstration of
amity, inviting him to dinner, and protracting
the meal till his own evil purpose had been accomplished. Then he led Gray into the courtyard;
he pointed to a dead body lying there, and said:
" Sir Patrick, the letter which you bear comes
too late. There lies your sister's son, without his
head. To his body thou art welcome, an' it please
thee to mell with it."

" Nay," said Sir Patrick, " sen thou hast ta'en the head, make what thou wilt of the body ; for thou shalt answer shortly to the King for both." And mounting in hot haste, Gray sped to Edinburgh to report this outrage, pursued by the myrmidons of Douglas.

The recital of this new attack upon his kingly prerogative decided the King to adopt severe measures against the Earl of Douglas ; but he took a crafty method of doing so.

Having discovered that Douglas, who ruled in the south, had agreed with the Earl of Ross, who was all-powerful in the north, and the Earl of Crawford, whose influence spread throughout the east coast, to maintain each others quarrels, even against the King himself, his Majesty, fearful of the conspiracy, summoned his Parliament to Stirling to advise upon it. After deliberation, it was decided to bring Douglas to this conference, and to endeavour by argument to break this alliance. A safe conduct, under the hand and Seal of the King, was sent to him requesting his attendance. Trusting to the honour of his liege-lord, Douglas approached with but a few adherents, and even those were excluded from the precincts of the royal palace.

Alone, therefore, the Black Earl entered that portal through which he never more should pass. The King met him with accustomed cordiality, and, after supper, retired with him and a few of his counsellors to an inner apartment to discuss the affairs of State. Here James thought to persuade Douglas to abandon his league with the Earls Ross and Crawford ; but threat and persuasion were alike powerless upon him. Irritated beyond measure by this continued obstinacy, and well aware of the result of too great leniency towards him, the King at last drew his dagger, and exclaiming " By Heaven, if you will not break this league, I will," he stabbed the unfortunate Earl to the heart. The old enemy of Douglas, Sir Patrick Gray, with all the bitterness of his last grudge against him, was not slow to aid the King in his felon intent, and the body of the murdered nobleman was thrown from the window of that apartment in the Castle which is still called " the Douglas Room."

However disreputable the means employed, it is certain that the step which the King had taken ultimately compelled him to adopt repressive measures against the Scottish nobility, and finally to overcome and destroy the long-established feudal system. And, as a curious instance of historical retribution, it may be mentioned that the murder of James III. (son of James II.) at Sauchie Burn, was popularly attributed to the son of this same Sir Patrick Gray, the King's accomplice in his attack upon the Earl of Douglas.

Many additions were made to the Castle during the turbulent reign of James III., who made it his favourite residence. He built the large hall, now called the Parliament House, and erected the Chapel Royal, celebrated in song by the poets of the period, which was afterwards demolished by

James VI. to make way for a more pretentious structure. There is little doubt that the violent death of James III. was immediately caused by the treachery of the Castellane whom he had put in charge of Stirling, and who refused to open the gate to the King while in retreat.

During the reign of James V., Stirling was the scene of a very ludicrous scientific fiasco. The reputation which the King had gained on the Continent as a lover of literature and art had attracted many foreign adventurers to the Scottish shore. Poets, musicians, and alchemists flocked to the Court whose Monarch laid claim to a wide sympathy with the art of each professor ; and as the craze of the search after the " philosopher's stone " was not yet exploded, King James fell an easy prey to charlatanry and imposture. Chief among the alchemists that had gained an ascendancy over the King was an Italian monk, who so dazzled his dupe by unlimited promises that nothing was withheld from him. He was made Abbot of Tungland, and assigned apartments in the Castle that he might pursue his Rosicrucian studies unmolested.

That this monk was neither a Dowsterswivel nor a Subtle, may be surmised from the fact that he so far believed in his power as to experiment on himself. Having made aerial flight his study for a considerable time, he at last announced that he had solved the problem which had perplexed mankind till his day. He invited a large company to witness his triumph over gravitation ;

and having mounted the battlements of the Castle he boldly flung himself from the parapet. But he had miscalculated the attractive influence of our planet upon him. And so the astonished multitude, who expected to see him cleaving with mighty wings the blue empyreum, were shocked and dismayed to behold him falling like some ordinary mortal earthward, unable, even with the aid of all his familiar spirits, to escape the broken limb which the most illiterate lord might have as easily gained, without bravado.

One cannot but admire the pluck which led the Abbot to make this rash experiment, and the ingenuity with which he explained his failure. " Many of the feathers," he wrote, " whereof my wings were composed had been unwittingly taken from barnyard and dunghill fowls. Hence the earth had more influence upon them since they were unused to upward flight. Had they been eagles' feathers then the attraction of the heavens would have been as great as the attraction of the earth was in other conditions." There is no record of his ever having tried aviation afterwards.

For a considerable time the Castle of Stirling was selected as the place of Coronation for the Scottish rulers, and the fact of its being a favourite residence for royalty brought it into notice as the birth-place of a succession of monarchs, and it was also the scene of several tragedies connected with the royal family. Some of the latter incidents may be briefly noticed here.

Alexander I., who reigned from 1106 till 1124

STIRLING CASTLE

Valentine & Sons, Ltd.

is the first Scottish King who is recorded as having died at Stirling. William the Lion—1165-1214—died at Stirling in his 71st year. David, second son of Alexander III., born in 1273, died in Stirling Castle in 1281, aged 8 years, and as his elder brother Alexander died in his father's life-time, the succession fell to Margaret, "the Maid of Norway," whose death in 1290 brought about the trouble with the claimants, in which Edward I. of England interfered. While James I. was a prisoner in England, his uncle Robert, Duke of Albany, was Governor from 1388 till 1420, in which year he died at Stirling Castle. His son, Murdoch, became Governor, but when James I. returned to his kingdom in 1424, he accused Murdoch of treason, and caused him to be beheaded at Stirling Castle in the following year, together with his son, his nephew, and his father-in-law. James IV., in 1488, when he was only 16 years of age, was brought from Stirling Castle by the Lords, who had rebelled against his father, James III., and was present at the Battle of Sauchie Burn, near Stirling, where the King was assassinated. Alexander, Duke of Ross, sixth child of James IV., was born in Stirling Castle, and died there in 1515 in his second year. Prince James and Prince Arthur, sons of James V., both died in infancy at Stirling Castle, in 1541, thus leaving the succession to the Throne open to Mary, Queen of Scots, who was born in 1542, the year of her father's death. She was crowned in the Chapel at Stirling Castle in September 1543. The year 1571 witnessed a series of tragic incidents. John Hamilton, Archbishop of St Andrews, was accused as concerned in the murders of Henry Darnley and also the Regent Moray, and was hanged at Stirling Castle. The Regent Lennox, father of Darnley, was shot in a skirmish at Stirling; his successor, the Regent Mar, died at Stirling Castle in 1572. James VI. was baptized in the Chapel of Stirling Castle in 1566; and his beloved eldest son, Prince Henry, was born in the Castle in 1593, but died in 1612 in his 19th year, and thus the King was succeeded by his second son and fourth child, afterwards Charles I. These are all facts relating to the connection of the Royal Family with Stirling Castle.

The Union of the Crown in 1603, when the King and Court removed to London, had an important effect upon the whole of Scotland, and especially on Stirling Castle. The place fell out of notice for a considerable time, and until the great Marquess of Montrose restored the renown of Scottish chivalry its existence was placid and uneventful. The brilliant exploits of this famous commander brought renown to Scotland; and during the century which followed, the position of Stirling Castle as the key to the north by the east coast made it a scene of continued turmoil and strife. Stirling Castle was captured and held for a short time by the Covenanters. In 1651, after the defeat of General Leslie and the Covenanters at Dunbar by Cromwell, the fugitive

Scots made Stirling Castle their rallying-place. This led General Monck to besiege and reduce the Castle, and to carry off many of the national documents that had been brought from Edinburgh as less secure than Stirling. It was from the Castle in the same year that Charles II. set out upon his invasion of England, which was terminated by the fatal Battle of Worcester.

At the time of the Union of the Parliaments in 1707 Stirling was one of the four Castles that were specially described as the most important in Scotland . The first trial of its strength occurred in 1715, when Argyll on his way to Sheriffmuir was well-supported from the Castle. The next attempt on the Castle was in 1745-46, when the army under Prince Charles Edward was retreating northward. The leaders of the Highland forces promised the Stirling people would not be molested ; but this pledge was not respected by the Jacobites, and general plunder was the result. Preparations were made to besiege the Castle ; but the conflict at Falkirk, where the Prince was victorious, led to the prolongation of the siege (against the will of Prince Charlie) until the advance of the Duke of Cumberland's army compelled a retreat northward, which ended at Culloden. Since that time Stirling Castle has remained unassailed.

James VI. was the last Scottish Sovereign to live in residence at Stirling Castle. The Duke of of York (afterwards James VII. and II.) was here with his family for a short time in 1685, amongst them being the daughter who became Queen Anne. In September 1842, Queen Victoria and Prince Albert visited the place ; and in 1859, the Prince of Wales (afterwards Edward VII.) examined the historic Castle, so closely connected with the lives of his remote ancestors.

XVIII

ST ANDREWS CASTLE

THE situation of St Andrews Castle is exceedingly picturesque. The shore on each side of the ruins trends inwards, leaving a projecting headland, upon whose rocky summit stand the ruins of the Archiepiscopal Palace. The ceaseless beat of the wild North Sea has swept away the ancient landmarks upon either side, gradually leaving the foundation of the Castle to form an apex between two bays :—

"The peak on an aerial promontory,
Whose caverned base with the vexed surge is hoary."

If this spot be really the site of the original Castle of St Andrews, built by Bishop Roger in 1200, as there is little reason to doubt, it savours more of romance than of practical utility. For even though the encroachments of the sea have been great in this locality they cannot have so seriously altered the position of the Castle in little over seven centuries as to transform an inland fortress into a sea-washed ruin. And, however conducive to reflection in a recluse, it could not be altogether pleasant for men of the world, as many of the Prelates were, to hear the " hollow-sounding and mysterious main " dashing against the rock-bound coast, or watch it flinging its wintry spray defiantly upon the topmost battlement.

Whether for resistance by sea or land, no more commanding site could have been found along the coast than that on which the Castle stands. Its peninsular position would enable its possessor to sweep both the north and south coasts with ease ; while the approach from the land would be rendered difficult by the narrowness of the passage. Local tradition tells of subterranean caves hollowed beneath the foundations of the Castle, and represents the rock as honey-combed by the action of the waves ; and certainly there have been mysterious passages recently dis-covered which may have been formed by extend-ing such caves, though their utility has not been satisfactorily explained.

But the ruin which now crowns the rugged steep has not been reduced to its present state solely by the ravages of time or of the elements. The resistless surge of human passion and the fierce whirlwind of civil war have done more to render the Castle of St Andrews roofless and un-inhabitable than have the relentless storms of many centuries. And though first erected a dwelling for the men of peace, it was not long ere the warriors of Scotland discovered that the position which it occupied was too valuable to be sacrificed as a Parsonage ; even as they found that the site of Dunnottar Castle was too import-ant for a Parish Kirk. And thus it soon happened that the peaceful abode of the Bishops of St

Andrews became the residence of the fierce soldiery both of England and France, whose lawless presence drew down upon its innocent head the vengeance of their enemies. And the Castle, which might have existed as long as the Vatican at Rome, had it been left to its original possessors, did not continue for a century and a half without suffering almost total demolition. Arising again from its ashes under the benign influence of another Bishop, it re-asserted the proud position which it had formerly held, and remained intact for another hundred and fifty years. But the cloud of the Reformation had over-shadowed the dignity of the priesthood, and " their gilded domes and their princely halls " were now the abode of the leading spirits of the new birth.

Yet again was the ruined Castle rebuilt and made habitable, but it was now shorn of all its former greatness, and " Ichabod " was written on its ruins. And now, as if " unwilling to outlive the good that did it," or wilfully refusing shelter to the renegades from the faith of its founders, it stands bare and desolate, a barren relic of the glory that passeth away. Only a few yards from these ruins may be seen the burying ground where rest many of the Lords Spiritual, who once held sway within its halls, mingling their dust with that of the vassals whose toil supported them, and by whose labour they were maintained. And as we pass from these tombs by the ever-sounding sea to the melancholy ruin of former grandeur which the Castle presents, we feel :—

> " The sway
> Of the vast stream of ages bear away
> Our floating thoughts."

Here in the very birthplace of Scottish Christianity we find the cradle of the Reformation, and this grim ruin was the scene of many of the deeds of violence and of injustice and lawlessness that called aloud for a new upheaval of Society —the avatar of a Protestant Reformation. And now, as the moonlight breaks through the unglazed window apertures, or falls shimmering, clear and cold, upon the grass-grown courtyard, unroofed and open to the assaults of heaven, we cannot escape from the romance of the situation—

" I wandered through the wreck of days departed,
    Far by the desolated shore, when even
O'er the still sea and jagged islets darted
    The light of moonrise ; in the northern heaven,
    Among the clouds near the horizon driven,
The mountains lay, beneath one planet pale ;
    Around me broken tombs and columns riven
Looked vast in twilight, and the sorrowing gale
Waked in these ruins grey their everlasting wail ! "

The action of the water upon the free stone and shale forming the base of the Castle is apparent, though the extent of this influence is much exaggerated. Some local historians would have us believe that the angry surge has swept away towers and turrets, walls and battlements, but there is more fancy than fact in their statements. Yet there are many alterations in the

ST ANDREWS CASTLE

Valentine & Sons, Ltd.

formation of the Castle grounds plainly discernible. At some remote period the whole of the landward structure has been surrounded by a deep moat, presumably supplied with tidal water and furnished with lock-gates communicating with the sea. The *débris* of many years had accumulated within this fosse to such an extent that it was level with the ground. But some years ago excavations were made in the locality whereby the trench was quite cleaned out, and a more correct view of the fortifications thus obtained. Amongst other discoveries made, not the least interesting was that of the ancient Well in the courtyard, which has been cut out of the solid rock, and is more than twenty feet deep to the water surface. In the North Sea Tower on the north-west part of the courtyard, may be seen the Bottle Dungeon, a cavity quarried in the freestone, twenty-five feet deep, with an aperture forming the neck, seven feet in diameter and eight feet deep. Below this point the dungeon expands to nearly seventeen feet in diameter ; and as there are no visible means of entrance, it is supposed that the prisoners were incarcerated here by using rope and windlass to lower them into its loathsome depths. The imaginative inhabitants of this neighbourhood have peopled this fearful prison with many of the men familiar in history ; but the traditions connected with it are not very trustworthy. It is not likely that the place was used except for purposes of temporary confinement, and as an alternative to the rack or other form of torture. The whole plan of the Castle is now clearly visible, and as steps have been taken to preserve the ruins the ravages of time will no longer prevail to overthrow it. The vicissitudes through which it has passed, and which link it prominently with many notable events in Scottish story, entitle the Castle of St Andrews to the tender regard and veneration of the students alike of Church and of State History.

The exact date of the foundation of the Bishopric of St Andrews is not now discoverable, but it is known to have had a firmly established existence in the middle of the ninth century. For a considerable period the history of the Bishopric is but a succession of names and dates which, like the catalogue of the Pictish Kings, is now of little interest to us. Early in the twelfth century (about 1107) Bishop Turgot founded the Parish Kirk, and about fifty years after, Bishop Arnold, the possessor alike of larger views and increased revenue, began the erection of the splendid pile of St Andrews Cathedral, whose ruins still testify to its former magnificence. Having thus provided for the spiritual wants of their parishioners, it became advisable that the Bishops should look after their own temporal welfare; and so Bishop Roger laid the foundation of the Castle somewhere about the year 1200. Hitherto the holders of the Episcopal See had resided either in the ancient Monastery of the Culdees (now Kirkhill, where the foundations may be seen) or in the house of the Prior, which adjoined the Cathedral buildings. It no longer consorted with the dignity of so important a See that the Bishops should have nowhere to lay their heads, and as the Royal, as well as the Papal, favour had been bestowed upon them, they could well afford to indulge in a habitation for themselves.

Old Andro Wyntoun, Prior of St Serf's on Loch Leven, in his " Cronykil," records that Bishop Roger was son of the Earl of Leicester ; but to this statement exception may be taken, as it is not supported by other evidence. There certainly was a Roger de Bellomont who fought at the Battle of Hastings in 1066, and whose descendant was Earl of Leicester in 1128, but that Earl had no son called Roger. This is Wyntoun's account :—

> " This Rogere
> The Erle's son was of Laycestere.
> The Castell in his dayis he
> Founded and gart biggit be
> In Sanct Andrewys in that place
> Where now that Castel biggit was."

The undertaking, though considerable in those days, was but a trifle compared to the erection of the Cathedral which was then proceeding ; and it is extremely likely that the builders of the latter edifice were employed upon Bishop Roger's residence. The name of the architect of these two buildings has not been discovered. At that time Antwerp was the great school of masonry, and a travelling Guild of Masons may have begun the structure which took many years to complete.

By whomsoever devised and executed, the Castle was at length completed, and the Bishop would, no doubt, prepare with devout gratitude for his " house-warming." One may picture the venerable Bishop looking forward with hopeful eyes to a glorious future for the bield he had now " biggit," and prophesying of the halcyon days of universal peace which his firmly-founded Castle should never behold. Hope still looks forward, in defiance of history and human experience, for the brighter days that never come, and we delude ourselves by a faith in the future for which our past gives no warrant. And thus runs the world away ! —

" Golden days, where are you ?
    Pilgrims east and west
Cry, if we could find you
    We would pause and rest.
We would pause and rest a little
    From our dark and dreary ways,
Golden days, where are you ?
    Golden days ! "

Peace and prosperity were not long the heritage of the Castle of St Andrews, for in those stirring times the dignitaries of the Church were compelled to take an active part in the affairs of State. As St Andrews was the foremost See in Scotland, both because of its antiquity and extent, it was natural that the Bishop of so important a diocese should be frequently brought to the front. And as Glasgow bore the same relation to the west of Scotland as St Andrews did to the east, the

212

Bishops of these places were the leaders during the most turbulent times. Foremost among these patriots was Robert Wiseheart (Wishart), Bishop of Glasgow, in 1270, who was appointed one of the six Guardians of Scotland on the death of Alexander III. in 1286, though he supported Edward I. in 1290, but took up the cause of Robert Bruce in 1299, for which Edward imprisoned him. Afterwards he joined Wallace with the Scottish patriots, and officiated at the Coronation of Robert Bruce in 1306. His faithful ally was William Lamberton, Bishop of St Andrews in 1297, who supported Wallace, though he had sworn fealty to Edward. He was also present at the crowning of Bruce and was captured and put in prison by Edward.

It was during Bishop Lamberton's time that the building of the Cathedral was completed, and he also repaired the breaches in the walls of the Castle which Edward I. had caused after Wallace had escaped from it. Having had it put in repair for his occupancy, Edward I. and his Queen occupied the Castle from 14th March to 5th April 1303-4, together with the Prince of Wales (afterwards Edward II.), and to the Prince was committed by the King the stripping of the lead from the roof of the Cathedral to make ammunition for the siege of Stirling Castle. While Edward was in St Andrews Castle he received the homage of the leading Scottish nobles and clergy.

The Castle was held by the English till 1305, when it was captured and held by the Scots for a short period, but was regained from them in 1306, and remained an English fortress till 1314, the year of the Battle of Bannockburn. These frequent attacks must have seriously weakened the structure, for Bishop Lamberton, who died in 1328, found it necessary to spend his last years in the Priory instead of the Castle.

Hardly had Lamberton been gathered to his fathers ere the minions of Edward Balliol, son of King John Balliol, and a dependant on the bounty of the King of England, Edward III., seized upon the Castle, and forced the new Bishop, James de Bane, to fly for refuge to Holland, where he died in 1332, leaving the See unoccupied. Edward Balliol had invaded Scotland in this year, and won a victory at the Battle of Dupplin, and he placed a garrison in St Andrews Castle. The chief Scottish opponent of Balliol was Sir Andrew Moray of Bothwell, son of the companion-in-arms of Wallace, who was proclaimed Regent. Finding English soldiers in the Castle he attacked it and forced them away; but finding that he had not men to spare for garrisoning it he threw down some of the fortifications, and proceeded southward to expel the invaders from Scottish soil. This incident is thus recorded by Andro Wyntoun :—

> " Sir Andro Murray cast it doun,
> For there he fand a garrisoun
> Of English men intill that place,
> For the See than vacand was."

Ere another fifty years had gone the Bishopric

came into the hands of Walter Trail (1385-1401) a Prelate whose influence in the affairs of the kingdom entitled him to rank as a true patriot. During his term as Bishop the Castle was rebuilt and again made fit for an episcopal residence. Yet, by a curious fatality, the princely towers which he built became the prison-house of one of his dearest friends, shortly after his decease. In the story of Rothesay Castle in this volume, the sad tale of the murder of David, first Duke of Rothesay, son of Robert III., by his unscrupulous uncle, the Regent Albany, was narrated. Whilst this unfortunate Prince was supported by the counsel of his mother, Queen Annabella, of his father-in-law, Earl Douglas, and of his tutor, Bishop Trail, he withstood the insidious advances of his ambitious uncle ; but when death had removed all three of these counsellors, the craft of the statesman proved too much for the unsuspecting Prince. Rothesay was persuaded that after the death of the Bishop it was his duty to occupy the Castle till a successor was appointed. The young Duke made his way to Fife with a few followers, and was waylaid by the emissaries of Albany near Strathtyrum and thrown into prison at St Andrews Castle to await the instructions from his uncle. Ultimately he was taken to Falkland Palace, where he met the sad fate prepared for him. Thus the lordly dwelling which his old friend the Bishop had erected, and where he would have been an honoured guest, became the scene of his first imprisonment.

" What man that sees the ever-whirling wheels
  Of change the which all mortal things doth sway ;
But that thereby doth find, and plainly feels
  How mutability in them doth play
  Her cruel sports to many men's decay ? "

The Castle of St Andrews increased in importance as time rolled on, and soon had greatness
thrust upon it. Bishop Wardlaw had spent his
forty years within its walls ; and had done much
service to the world at large by founding the
University, building the Guard Bridge, and burning a few pestilent heretics " for the greater glory
of God." Bishop Kennedy had enjoyed his
quarter-of-a-century there, and signalized his
reign by erecting the College and Chapel of St
Salvator, founding the Greyfriars Monastery, and
endeavouring to introduce commerce to the city
by building a large vessel suitable for export
trade. But the vernal period of the Bishops had
arrived, and they were about to blossom into
Archbishops. Bishop Kennedy died in 1465, and
his half-brother, Patrick Graham, Bishop of
Brechin, succeeded him in the following year.
Bishop Wardlaw, in 1440, had appointed John de
Wemyss of Kilmany as Constable of St Andrews
Castle, so it had been kept in order during the
time of Bishop Kennedy. To his successor, Patrick
Graham, belongs the honour of being the first
Archbishop of St Andrews, but he did not take
up his residence at the Castle in 1466, going to
Rome for another purpose. In 1472 he returned

with Bulls from Pope Sixtus IV., constituting St Andrews the Metropolitan See of Scotland.

Despite the honour that Archbishop Graham had brought to this country his life was a miserable one. He had been impoverished by the bribes he had presented to the officials at Rome, who had assisted him, and in 1478 William Schevez, then Archdeacon, brought charges of heresy and simony against him, and he was deposed and imprisoned, first in the Monastery of Inchcolm, and afterwards in Loch Leven Castle, where he died, and was buried at St Serf's Isle. The ambitious Schevez succeeded as second Archbishop, and apparently resided at the Castle. Hardly had he been appointed than he dashed into a controversy with Robert Blacader, Archbishop of Glasgow, on a point of etiquette as to precedence. The dispute became so violent that it had to be submitted to His Holiness Pope Innocent VIII., who evidently gave the preference to St Andrews as the seat of the Primate. An ancient Chartulary, still in existence, throws a sinister light on this transaction. It shows that Schevez gave over the lands and Castle of Gloom, on the Devon, and the Bishopshire on the Lomond Hills to the then Earl of Argyll to bribe his support in the dispute with Glasgow. He thus proves himself as the mediæval ecclesiastic—solemn, precise, exacting—anything but profound, whose interest lay more in vestments and ceremonies than the welfare of the precious souls committed to his charge.

The Castle of St Andrews had now gained additional importance as the seat of the Primate, and the Archbishops took a prominent part in political affairs, and were recognized as statesmen. So far back as the time of William the Lion, the claim had been made, and since continued, that the King had the right of presentation to this Archbishopric. Hence, when the See of St Andrews became vacant through the death of James Stewart, second son of James III. (1497-1503), James IV., who bore the same name as his younger brother, exercised his right under peculiar circumstances. The King had then an illegitimate son, Alexander Stewart, born in 1493, but not of age to be made an Archbishop, so the See was left vacant till 1505, when he was nominated. In that year Stewart went abroad ; studied under Erasmus at Padua, 1508 ; returned to Scotland in 1509 for his installation ; was appointed Chancellor of Scotland, 1510 ; accompanied his father the King in 1513 to Flodden, and fell on the battlefield, in his twentieth year.

A very curious complication arose at Archbishop Stewart's death. The Queen-Regent (Margaret Tudor, sister of Henry VIII., and widow of James IV.), claimed the right of the Crown to appoint the new Archbishop, and was prepared to select the famous Bishop Elphinstone of Aberdeen, founder of Aberdeen (King's College) University, for the See of St Andrews ; but he died at Edinburgh in October 1514, before he could be installed. Meanwhile, in August 1514,

Queen Margaret had married Archibald Douglas, sixth Earl of Angus ; and to please her new husband she nominated the celebrated poet, Gawain Douglas, her uncle by marriage, to the Archbishopric. But the Chapter of St Andrews elected in preference John Hepburn, Prior of St Andrew, while the Pope recommended Andrew Forman, Bishop of Moray for the position. There were thus three claimants, proposed respectively by the Queen-Regent, the Chapter, and the Pope, representing the Crown, the Church, and the Papal power.

Gawain Douglas, the translator of Virgil, and one of the most learned and accomplished men of his time, made the first move by taking violent possession of St Andrews Castle, having the troops of Angus and the Queen-Regent to support him. The forces he had at his disposal were lulled into a false security by the ease of their conquest. Doubtless the new Archbishop, looking upon himself as the man in possession prepared to enjoy his " lordly pleasure-house " with as little apprehension of approaching danger as ever troubled the hero of his own exquisite poem :—

" King Hart into his comely Castel strang,
    Closed about with craft and meikle ure,
So seemly was he set his folk amang
    That he no doubt had of misadventure,
So proudly was he polished plain and pure,
    With Youth heid and his lusty levis greeve,
So fair, so fresh, so likely to endure,
    And also blyth as bird in summer schene."

219

But the dark-visaged Prior Hepburn meanwhile was not idle. Silently assembling the fierce Border Clans of the Hepburns and Homes, to whom he was related, he took the Castle by storm, and turned out its occupants in disgrace. Chagrined by his defeat, the Queen-Regent urged her husband, Angus, to besiege the Castle; but the bold Prior, like a true Churchman Militant, set the forces of the Crown at defiance. The combined efforts of the Royal troops and the Men of the Mearns were unavailing to conquer the hardy Borderers, and the unscrupulous Archbishop-elect for whom they fought.

Matters had thus reached a crisis, and it seemed as though Scotland were to be blessed with three Primates. The wily Bishop Forman, however, meddled less with arms than with men, and he soon gained over the Earl of Home to his cause by the old-fashioned method of bribery and corruption. Hepburn had no choice but to succumb to circumstances. He withdrew his soldiers from the Castle and resigned all claim to the Primacy on condition of receiving the Bishopric of Moray, from which See his opponent Forman had been promoted, together with a pension of three thousand crowns from the funds of the Archbishop of St Andrews, stipulating that no questions should be asked as to the revenues which he had uplifted whilst in possession of the See. And thus the presentees alike of the Queen-Regent and the Church were conquered by the favourite of the Pope.

The ambition of the Queen-Regent brought evil days upon her. When the Duke of Albany, grandson of James II., and heir-presumptive to the Throne, was appointed Governor of Scotland in 1515, he soon took vengeance upon those friends whom Margaret Tudor had favoured.

The relatives of the Earl of Angus, who were suspected, fell under Albany's displeasure, and first among them was Gawain Douglas. He was seized upon the pretext of some informality in his presentation to the post of Bishop of Dunkeld, was carried to St Andrews Castle and thrown into the Bottle Dungeon there in 1521, where the vagaries of Fortune would give him food for regretful reflection, in the darkness, upon the brief period when he was master in the Castle :—

> " But yesterday I did declare
>   How that the time was soft and fair,
>   Come in as fresh as peacock's feddar—
>   This day it stangis like ane eddar,
>   Concluding all in my contrair.
>
> Yesterday fair upsprang the flowers—
> This day they are all slain with showers ;
>   And fowlis in forest that sang clear,
>   Now weepis with ane dreary chere,
> Full cauld are baith their beds and bowers.
>
> So next to Summer Winter bein ;
> Next after comfort caris keen ;
>   Next to dark night the mirthful morrow ;
>   Next after joy aye comis sorrow ;
> So is this warld and aye has been ! "

By some obscure means Gawain Douglas escaped from St Andrews in 1521, and fled to England, where Henry VIII. was his patron ; but he died there in the following year, of the plague, aged forty-eight years.

Archbishop Forman died in 1522, and was succeeded by James Beaton, then Archbishop of Glasgow. Beaton was the son of John Beaton of Balfour, in Fife. He took his M.A. degree at St Andrews University in 1492 ; was Abbot of Dunfermline in 1504 ; Lord Treasurer, 1505-6 ; Chancellor, 1513 to 1526 ; one of the Regents during the minority of James V.; Bishop of Galloway and Archbishop of Glasgow, 1509 ; and Archbishop of St Andrews, 1523, continuing in that office till his death in 1539. He kept lordly state within the Castle, and was renowned for his hospitality, especially to French visitors to Scotland. Beaton assisted James V. to throw off the yoke of his step-father, the Earl of Angus, and in revenge Angus laid waste the Archbishop's Castle of St Andrews. Beaton, however, was a " building Prelate " even when in Glasgow, and he soon restored his Castle to its former magnificence. James V. was frequently entertained there, and it is possible that the King would have made the Castle the residence of his first Queen, Magdalen de Valois, in 1539, had he not built a special house in the Priory grounds for her reception. It was during the rule of Archbishop James Beaton that the persecution of the Scottish Protestants began, and in this work he was especially active, utilizing the dungeons in the Castle for the confinement of heretics. The Archbishop died in 1539, and was buried before the High Altar in the Cathedral of St Andrews.

The successor to James Beaton was his nephew, David Beaton, who was Archbishop from 1539 till 1546, when his death was violently accomplished. He was the third son of John Beaton, eldest brother of James Beaton, Archbishop of St Andrews, and was born in 1494; educated at St Andrews, Glasgow and Paris; Abbot of Arbroath, 1523; Bishop of Mirepoix, in Languedoc, 1537; Cardinal of St Stephen in Monte Coelio, by Pope Paul III., 1538; Co-Adjutor of St Andrews, 1538-39; Archbishop of St Andrews, 1539.

The character of Cardinal Beaton has puzzled many Scottish historians, their estimates being largely influenced by religious prejudices on one side or the other. To imagine that he was an empty and illiterate bigot is an open mistake. He was more of the time-server who could perceive where the necessity had arrived for him to bend to the blast, but who would strenuously hold fast that which he had until a better appeared. Yet, however opportunist his actions might be, he stoutly resisted the plans of Henry VIII. to conquer Scotland by capturing the infant Queen Mary. When the game lay between the wily Cardinal and bluff King Hal, it required skilful playing to come off victorious as Beaton did. He was sent by James V. to arrange the

King's marriage with Mary of Guise, which he accomplished successfully.

His uncle and predecessor, James Beaton, as already mentioned, had taken up a violent attitude against the Protestants, and the same policy was adopted and intensified by the Cardinal, and it ultimately led to his destruction. The methods adopted by him had made many enemies, but he pursued the persecution of the heretics, as he accounted them, as if it were a pious duty. The tragic incident of the Cardinal's assassination has been so often narratêd that it need not here be detailed. The dastardly deed took place on Saturday, 29th May 1546, when Kirkaldy of Grange gave admittance by the drawbridge to the Castle to Norman Leslie, Master of Rothes, John Leslie, his uncle, Peter Carmichael, James Melvil, and others to the number of sixteen, who sought out the Cardinal in his room, set upon him with swords and daggers, and violently bereft him of life. They then, it is said, showed the dead body at a window to the populace. The window usually shown to visitors was certainly not the spot of this exposure, as it was erected by Archbishop Hamilton, the Cardinal's successor.

Assassination is one of the most dangerous weapons that a struggling cause can adopt; and the deed, however convenient for themselves, was loudly blamed by the Protestant party. So far from rising into favour with their partizans, as the conspirators had hoped, they found themselves almost universally execrated. Thus Sir

David Lyndsay, no friend to the Cardinal, and a most undoubted and faithful Protestant, expresses his feelings :—

> " As for the Cardinal—I grant
>   He was the man we weel could want,
>   And we'll forget him soon !
>   And yet I think, the sooth to say,
>   Although the loon is well away,
>   The deed was foully done."

The assassins had taken possession of the Castle, which was well-provisioned, and expected that their sympathisers would have flocked to support them, and that they would hold this fort till Henry VIII. had sent troops to capture Scotland and end the Roman Catholic Church. In both expectations they were disappointed. Henry VIII., the indomitable champion of Protestantism, died on 28th January 1546-47, and on 30th March following, Francis I. of France, the hero of Romanism, " also died," so that both parties were deprived of their leaders. The Castilians, as they called themselves, found that even the Governor Arran had been the friend of the Cardinal, and they even sent an humble petition to him that he would apply to the Court at Rome for a Bull of Absolution to clear them of their crime. Well they knew that the message to Rome would occupy some time, and meanwhile the English troops might arrive to aid them. This was duplicity, but it was not worse than that of the Governor, who certainly sent a message to

P

Rome, as requested, but took up the interval before the answer was returned in frantic appeals to Francis I. to send skilful bombardiers to besiege St Andrews Castle. Evidently both parties were insincere. The Castilians, meanwhile, had received no inconsiderable additions to their numbers, amongst them the indomitable John Knox, who had written that he recorded the murder of the Cardinal "merrily," and who was yet to become a ruthless leader in the demolition of the Churches of Scotland.

The Governor Arran, who had returned to the Ancient Faith, found that his animated entreaties to the Court of France had been effectual. He had besieged the Castle for four months without victory; but at length the French soldiers and the artillery of Leon Strozzi reduced the Castle to such a ruinous condition that the Castilians capitulated in August 1547. And it is recorded by Lindsay of Pitscottie that, "the French captain entered and spoiled the Castle very vigorously; wherein they found great store of vivers, clothes, armour, silver, and plate, which, with the captives, they carried away in their galleys. The Governor, by the advice of the Council, demolished the Castle, lest it should be a receptacle of rebels." In the "Diurnal of Occurrents," it is stated that the captors "tuke the auld and young Lairds of Grange, Normand Leslie, the Laird of Pitmilly (Monypenny), Wm. Henry Balnevis, and John Knox, with mony utheris, to the number of sex score persones, and carryit thame

all away to France ; and tuke the spulzie of the
said Castell, quhilk was worth 100,000 pundis and
tuke doun the hous." It was this incident which
called forth the current verse of the time :—

> " Priests, content ye noo ;
> Priests, content ye noo ;
> For Norman and his companie
> Ha'e filled the galleys fou ! "

The French Commander, Leon Strozzi, had instructions to convey his Scottish prisoners to
Paris, and the King there decided that many of
the Castilians should be incarcerated in prisons at
the north of France, the ringleaders, including
John Knox, should be sent to the galleys and
chained to the oars. The bold spirits who had
put the Army of the Regent to defiance, were
now treated as malefactors, whose crimes were
only short of receiving the extreme penalty of
the law. John Knox was imprisoned at Paris in
1548, and released in the following year, He
went to Dieppe, Geneva, where he met Calvin,
and Frankfort-on-Maine, reaching Scotland in
1556, and resuming his position as a leader of the
Scottish Reformation. His death took place at
Edinburgh in 1571, when in his sixty-sixth year.

The successor of Cardinal Beaton as Archbishop
of St Andrews was John Hamilton, an illegitimate
son of James Douglas, first Earl of Arran, and
was born in 1511, was Abbot of Paisley, and afterwards Bishop of Dunkeld in 1546, and was translated to St Andrews in 1547 as Archbishop. The

first work which he undertook was the repairing of the ruinous Castle, and in this reconstruction he was probably assisted by the masons whom he had employed to complete the building of St Mary's College. When the Reformers had gained power in Scotland in 1559, Hamilton had to abandon the Castle, and from that time he was a fugitive until he was captured at Stirling in April 1571, accused of complicity in Darnley's murder, and hanged ignominiously.

The Castle came into the possession of the Protestants under the Regent Moray, and was used as a political prison by him and his successors as Regents, becoming, indeed, "the Bastile of Scotland." Though thus used as a secular prison, it was still a portion of the ecclesiastical property, and James VI. did not feel justified in annexing it without some process of law. This was not accomplished for many years, and the place had become partly ruinous from the repeated attacks made upon it by successive factions of the Scottish nobles. At length the King made a bargain with George Gledstanes, Episcopal Archbishop of St Andrews, as the representative of the ancient Prelates, and in July 1600 a charter gave the Castle to George, Earl of Dunbar, one of the King's favourites. This arrangement, however, did not last long, for when Episcopacy was fully established in 1612, the Castle was given back to Gledstanes, and the Earl compensated. The new Archbishops did not inhabit the Castle, but used it as an occasional prison, and the place soon became ruinous.

About 1650 the Castle passed into the hands of the Town Council, who shortly afterwards laid violent hands upon the masonry, and used it for repairing the Pier. There is thus little left even of Hamilton's restorations. One may fancy the shade of good old Bishop Roger addressing his successor, the Cardinal, in such lines as these of the old Scottish poet Robert Henryson :—

> " Thy kingdom and thy great empire,
>   Thy royalty nor rich array,
> Shall not endure at thy desire,
>   But as the wind will wend away.
> Thy gold and all thy goodis gay
>   When Fortune list, will from thee fall ;
> Sen thou sic sampills seest each day,
>   Obey and thank thy God for all ! "

XIX

DUNBAR CASTLE

THE situation of Edinburgh at but a short distance from the Firth of Forth, and therefore liable to invasion from the sea, has caused the whole length of the east coast of Scotland, from Berwick around to Leith, to be studded with Castle-towers and Keeps, at once the residences of the Court and the defence of the capital. The whole of the country from Edinburgh to the borderland betwixt England and Scotland had thus been erected into a cordon of forts, fitted to repel invasion and to preserve the capital inviolable from assault either from sea or land. And in former times, ere the Crown had attained the supremacy which it now possesses, the Castles soon became the means of overawing the independent Borderers, or were themselves the centres of revolt against the Throne, and the rallying points of the vassals of the rebellious Lords.

While the Castles on the line of the Border were intended to check the invasions of the English by land, the strong towers of Berwick, Fast, Dunbar, and Tantallon formed a chain of defence on the seaboard which might well discourage invasion from that quarter. The

magnitude as well as the strength of these
Keeps enabled their possessors to garrison an
army of very respectable dimensions, and their
proximity to one another rendered a junction of
their forces comparatively easy. And thus the
Lowlanders were prepared to resist their foreign
foes. Nor were their preparations uncalled for,
since their enemies were diverse and ubiquitous.
Now it might be :—

> " The Percy out of Northumberland,
>   And a vow to God made he,
> That he would hunt in the mountains
>   At Cheviot within days three,
> In the maugre of doughty Douglas,
>   And all that ever with him be."

Anon the defence had to be made against the sea-
rovers, when in that more dangerous time :—

> " Hither came from eastern shores
> The Jutes and Angles over the broad sea ;
> Fierce battle-smiths, and Britain sought,
> O'ercame the Welsh and gained the land."

In many cases the territorial defences proved
efficient, and the sacredness of the capital was
preserved. To the Castle of Dunbar some pro-
minence must be given, as the one post in the
country which effectually repelled the English
invader. Besides exhibiting the force of the
Scottish arms against the chosen warriors of
England, it has also a history intimately associated with the internecine turmoils in Scotland.

The position of Dunbar Castle topographically merits a word of description. The town of Berwick is exactly in meridian with Newburgh in Aberdeenshire, and between these two places the east coast of Scotland is hollowed out into a vast bay, extending at Kirkcaldy to about 45 miles inland from these two points. The influence of the wash of the waters of Forth and Tay must be allowed for when estimating the denuding force of the North Sea ; but the contour of the east coast will present peculiar appearances even to the least-skilled observer. One glance at the map of Scotland will satisfy anyone that the power of the North Sea over that country is not to be compared to the influence which the Atlantic has had upon the west coast. For while the North Sea has only transformed the coast line between Peterhead and Berwick into one great bay, the 2000 miles of raging Atlantic Ocean betwixt Skye and Labrador have hollowed the west coast into myriad outlandish forms, where only the stern endurance of the rocks has withstood the perpetual tempest which assails them.

The coast of Haddingtonshire has been doubly attacked—by the North Sea on one side, and by the rapid stream of the Forth on the other—so that it presents the appearance of an irregular triangle. About midway on the shore-line stands the ruined Castle of Dunbar, upon a rocky promontory around which the stormy North Sea breaks in foam. The influence of the strong Arctic current is visible here, as it is in the Bay of St Andrews ;

DUNBAR CASTLE

Valentine & Sons, Ltd

for the projection of Fifeness bears the same relation to St Andrews as St Abb's Head does to Dunbar. The resistless surge of the North Sea, dashing for centuries upon the slenderly-protected east coast, has thus gradually eaten its way inwards towards the heart of Scotland ; whilst the furious Atlantic Ocean, fiercely assaulting the barren and rocky coast-line on the west coast has won from the mainland many a green-crested islet, many a solitary peak, fitted alone to become the eyrie of the eagle or dauntless sea-birds.

The very position of Dunbar Castle shows that the encroachments of the sea in that quarter should not be disregarded. Its ruins now stand upon a rocky eminence, exposed to the fury of the wintry blast ; and the stormy sea, which has caverned and honeycombed the rock upon which it is raised, has left many chasms and tunnels in the cliff, regarding which a thousand wild legends are told. Though the exact date of the Castle, the ruins of which now remain, is not known, it must occupy the site of a much earlier Peel which would be in existence early in the 11th century. The first traces of this early structure are found in the records relating to William the Conqueror. In 1067, that monarch conferred the Earldom of Northumberland upon Robert Comyn, but he was so unpopular with his vassals that he and all his retainers were put to death in 1068 by the inhabitants of the district. Then Cospatrick (sometimes called " Gospatrick ") grandson of Malcolm II., King of Scotland, claimed the Earldom through his mother, who was a daughter of Uchtred, the Saxon Earl of Northumberland, but had ultimately to pay " a great sum of money " for it in 1067 to William the Conqueror. Soon afterwards Cospatrick quarrelled with William, and fled into Scotland with other northern leaders, finding refuge in 1072 with Malcolm III. (Ceanmor), whose wife, St Margaret, was a Saxon Princess. Malcolm conferred upon him " Dunbar with the adjacent lands in Lothian," and he thus became the first Earl of Dunbar. His death took place about 1089, and he was succeeded by his son, Cospatrick, second Earl of Dunbar, who was a benefactor to the Abbey of Kelso. Before his death in 1139, he had probably begun the erection of Dunbar Castle, as the oldest part of the ruins belong to about that period. This Earl was present at the foundation of Scone Abbey in 1115, and Holyrood Abbey in 1128, the former by Alexander I., and the latter by his brother and successor, David I., sons of Malcolm III. (Ceanmor).

The tourist who visits Dunbar expecting to find there the romantic ruins of some palatial structure will be grievously disappointed. The relics of its former greatness betray the fact that it has been constructed with an eye rather to strength than beauty ; and its position on the verge of the " many-sounding sea," whose billows lash its foundations, would seem to imply that its builders thought more of the preservation of their lives than the cultivation of the elegant arts. The peculiar

redstone of which the latest Castle has been built
is found still in the neighbourhood ; and there
are few traces now to be seen of Continental
mason craft about it. So that all the appearances
favour the supposition that it was called into
existence by the necessities of the time. Yet these
bare walls when draped with antique tapestries
and illuminated by cresset-torches would afford
in a rude age an illustration of how life may be
made endurable through the agency of judicious
luxury. And when beauty and valour combined
to grace the Castle in former days the lack of
mural decoration would not cause one pang to
the inmates :—

> " Schinand was the painted hall,
>   Wi' gladsome torches bricht ;
> For twenty gowden dames sat there,
>   An' ilk ane by a Knicht !
>   Wi' music cheer
>   To please the ear
>   Whom bewty pleased the sicht."

The ever-whirling wheels of Time have dealt
somewhat roughly with the building, and beams
and rafters, walls and battlements, have at length
experienced the doom of all things earthly. The
wild east wind now whistles desolately around the
roofless hall, and echoes down the untenanted
courtyard, sounding in the ear of the romantic
visitor as the whispering of elfin voices, or the
mystic murmuring of spirit tones, borne on the
balmy breezes of memory. The task now is to

translate these incoherent sounds into intelligible language, in fact :

> " To give to airy nothings
> A local habitation and a name."

Like many more of the Scottish Castles the date of the original Dunbar Castle is unknown, and many outrageous theories have been invented to account for its existence. The tradition of the locality ascribed its origin to the Picts, who at some remote period left the fertile hills and meads of their native Allemayne, and extravasated themselves upon the east coast of Scotland. Originally agriculturists, the necessities of their position forced them to learn to wield the sword as well as guide the ploughshare, for the savage aborigines did not resign their land without a fierce and protracted struggle. And if these eastern strangers did really build an early Keep on the site of the Castle (which may be reasonably doubted) they must have adopted the method of Nehemiah, " For the builders, every one had his sword girded by his side ; and so builded," thus carrying both the sword and trowel.

The mission of the Alemanni was essentially agricultural, and when they had established their colony in East Lothian they soon set about clearing the forest land and transforming the waste places into fertile fields. The Caledonians, like the Indians of North America, were content to leave their rude agriculture to their women and children, whilst they devoted their energies to the chase ; but the Picts had already learned all the humanising influence of agricultural pursuits, and knew something of the benefits derived from living in Society. Under their influence, therefore, the fringe of the great Caledonian Forest was reclaimed from its barren luxuriance ; and the desolate haunts of the wild boar and giant elk of Scotland were forced to yield subsistence to these pioneers of civilization. And now the traces of this influence may be seen in the agriculture of the district, whose fertility is unlimited even by the saline breezes which blow over two sides of East Lothian.

Although there is no proof that any part of the Castle of Dunbar was built by these hardy colonists, it is not unlikely that a Keep of some kind was erected by them near the coast, so as at once to protect their fields and to afford them means of escape by sea should Fortune frown upon them. And there could be no site chosen more fitted for this purpose upon the whole of the neighbouring coast. No competent Admiral would counsel an attack by sea ; and the subsequent history of Dunbar Castle showed that it could successfully resist an overwhelmingly land force, even under daring and skilled leaders.

When the union of the Picts and Scots took place under Kenneth I. (Macalpin) about 846 A.D., the lands and Castle of Lodonia (Lothian) fell into his hands. The title which the fort now received was " Dunbar," to account for which two theories are propounded. It is said that amongst the chieftains that followed Kenneth, one of the bravest was Bar, whose courageous bearing and ready sword had won the notice of the King. In acknowledgment of his services the Pictish fort was conferred upon him, and it was thenceforth known as " Dun-Bar," the Castle of Bar. Another theory holds that the title is purely topographical and descriptive, and, being interpreted, signifies " the fort on the height," which name it undoubtedly deserves. The debate, however, is a barren one, and hardly worthy of the labour that has been spent upon it. Indeed, authorities have not yet decided who the Picts were, and where they came from. Some theorists maintain that the Picts were Saxon invaders ; others declare that they were a sept of the ancient Caledonians who devoted themselves to agriculture. One thing at least is certain, that the two nations were united under one King in the person of Kenneth I. about 846 A.D., and it is at this period that the name of Dunbar first appears. It must be understood that the Pictish origin of Dunbar Castle is entirely traditional, though it seems not incredible. From Kenneth I. the whole long succession of Kings of Scotland and of Great Britain are descended.

That there was really a Castle on this spot over a thousand years ago is certainly true, however strange it may sound. And though it has long been in a ruinous state, the story of its chequered career is inwoven with the web of Scottish history, and its name is inseparably associated with some of the greater events which are now deemed memorable. The mist and obscurity which surround the record of its early days become cleared as we advance within the historic period ; and from the time at which Dunbar was erected into an Earldom it is not so difficult to follow its story. Yet the darker portion of that story should be known, since it makes much of the general history of Scotland intelligible.

The true Kingdom of Scotland was not really founded upon a secure basis before the time of Malcolm III. (Caenmor) about 200 years after Kenneth I. The union of Malcolm with St Margaret of England brought about a revolution in the manners and customs of the Scottish nation which more nearly assimilated them to their southern neighbours. The relics of Druidical religion had now disappeared, and the humanizing wave of Christianity, which had reached the remote shores of Norway, had also brought its influence to bear upon " Ultima Thule," the fabled last island on the verge of the world, over which Malcolm was King. And so, as the light dawned upon these " rude forefathers " of ours they began to see that man is neither absolutely self-existent, nor existent solely for self. Around the Castles and Towers of their leaders they congregated into little townships and petty estates, espousing the cause of their Lord without question, and laying the foundation of the feudal system which it took centuries to overthrow. The mere association thus together, with one distinct

239

aim, served to consolidate the Kingdom and make its independence more secure.

It is important to remember that the borders of England then extended much further north than they did in later times. The Forth was really the boundary of England instead of the Tweed ; and the Wall of Antoninus, which extended from the Forth to the Clyde, was more nearly the margin of the Southern Kingdom than the Cheviots. Indeed, the whole land betwixt the Forth and the Humber was continually changing masters, and the insecurity of the conquests of either party made it doubtful as to where the boundaries of the two kingdoms should be set. Thus, when David I. reigned, though then possessed of Lothian, the Scottish Crown had but an insecure hold upon Northumberland and York. The reign of his grandson, William the Lion, however, sufficiently settled the matter, for after his foolish escapade at Alnwick and Carlisle in 1174, when he was taken prisoner and carried to England and France, he was compelled to do homage to Henry II., not only for the territories betwixt the Humber and Tweed, but also for the whole Kingdom of Scotland ; thus establishing the unpatriotic usage of which Edward I. availed himself afterwards in his disputes with the Claimants to the Scottish Crown.

It will thus be seen that for a considerable time Dunbar was as much an English as a Scottish stronghold. And the indefiniteness of its nationality made it an object of envy to both parties.

So around this ancient Keep, which stood defiantly upon the brink of the Eastern Sea, there clustered many memories of former times, and many hopes for the future of Scotland which could never be fulfilled. The strength of the Castle, which rendered it almost impregnable, and the extent of the accommodation which it afforded, ever made it a coveted point in protracted warfare; and its possessor might easily sway the balance of fortune and decide the fate of either Kingdom. It was, therefore, important for the welfare of Scotland that the Castle of Dunbar should be in the hands of a true patriot. Unfortunately this was not always the case, and the history of the Castle alternates between treason and fidelity to the Scottish cause.

The incident by which Cospatrick, Earl of Dunbar, came to Lothian and was possessor of a Castle and a title has been already explained. When King John of England, in reprisal of a Scottish Border raid, marched into the land at the head of his army, and laid siege to the Castle of Dunbar, he was compelled to abandon his purpose, and leave the stronghold in the hands of its owner, Patrick, sixth Earl of Dunbar.

Unfortunately for Scotland's welfare some of the earls were not always faithful to Scotland. Patrick, eighth Earl, who liberated Alexander III. by surprising Edinburgh Castle, when held by the Comyns, became one of the Regents of Scotland after Alexander's death. His son, Patrick, ninth Earl, surnamed "Black Beard,"

was the first to be styled "Earl of March."
Unlike his father he swore fealty to Edward I.,
and was a faithful adherent of the English
interest. His wife, Marjory Comyn, daughter of
the Earl of Buchan, took up the cause of the other
party, and held the Castle of Dunbar for King
John Balliol until forced to surrender it to
Edward I. in 1296, who made the Earl two years
afterwards, "King's Lieutenant in Scotland."
Both he and his heir were present at the Battle
of Caerlaverock in 1300, when Edward's party
won the Castle. The tenth Earl of Dunbar and
March, Patrick, like his father, was devoted to
the King of England, and when Edward II. was
escaping after losing the Battle of Bannockburn,
in 1314, he sheltered the fugitive at Dunbar Castle,
and procured a fishing-boat to take him to England.

This tenth Earl was a "trimmer," and made
his peace with Robert Bruce when he saw that
Bruce was to be in the ascendant, and he was
made Scottish Governor of Berwick Castle, a
post which he held till the defeat of the Scots at
Halidon Hill in 1333 forced him to surrender.
While he was away, Dunbar was brought into
notice through the persistent bravery of his wife,
Agnes Randolph, daughter of the famous Thomas
Randolph, Earl of Moray, the comrade of Robert
Bruce, and also a grand-niece of Bruce, known in
history as "Black Agnes." The story has been
often told alike in prose histories and ballads, but
will bear repetition in connection with the Castle
of Dunbar.

After the death of Robert the Bruce in 1329, Scotland fell again into political difficulties which seemed even more dangerous than those from which that monarch had rescued her. His son and successor, afterwards David II., was a child of six years old, and a long minority was to be expected. For several years the country had suffered from military disquiet, first caused by Edward Balliol, and afterwards by Edward III., though the latter was a brother-in-law of King David. The English King had over-run Scotland, partly with the aid of Patrick, tenth Earl of Dunbar, who afterwards abandoned the support of the English in 1333. Before he returned to Dunbar Castle, the Countess, who had been left in charge of the place, had bravely defended the Castle against the English Army, and held it for upwards of five months, the date being 13th January 1337-8, till on 16th June 1338 the besiegers had to raise the Siege of Dunbar. The contemporary chronicler narrates the story thus :—

"The Castle of Dunbar, notwithstanding a heavy siege, held out manfully, and because the Countess of Dunbar, who was the principal guardian of the Castle, was sister of the Earl of Moray, then a prisoner at Nottingham, the English brought him down to Dunbar in April 1338, threatening that if the Countess did not surrender the Castle, they would put her brother to death ; to which she answered, ' If you do this I shall be heir to the Earldom of Moray,'' for her brother had no children. The English, however, did not wish to put the Earl to death, and sent him back to England to be detained in custody as before."

There is a curious incident in this siege which is not widely known. The English attacking party was under the command of William de Montacute, Earl of Salisbury. Finding that the methods of attack adopted by him were not proving successful, he descended to a little silent treachery. He had gained the ear of some of the servants in the Castle, who, with the knowledge of the Countess, had planned to give the Earl and a few followers admission at the great gate. Attended by some of his most daring knights, Salisbury approached the main entrance at midnight. As arranged, he found the drawbridge down and the portcullis raised, so that the entrance to the place was open to him. But one of his followers, more forward than the rest and eager to be noticed by the leader, pressed forward even before the Earl, and was the first to enter within the precincts. No sooner had he passed the sacred line than the portcullis descended between him and his companions, and the Earl with the remainder of his party had to beat a hasty retreat ere the rising drawbridge should entrap them and prevent their escape. Thus by one moment's precipitation the chance of capturing the English leader was lost, much to the chagrin of the Countess.

The protracted siege had naturally discouraged the soldiers within the Castle, and the provisions were growing scant when relief came to them from an unexpected quarter. The brave Sir Alexander Ramsay of Dalwolsey (Dalhousie), one of the foremost knights of the time (whose sad fate is related in the notice of " Hermitage Castle " in this volume), succeeded in breaking the blockade and carrying relief to the well-nigh exhausted garrison. Braving the restless surge and the still more merciless enemy, Ramsay found means of communication with the Castle by the sea-washed caverns beneath the rock of its foundation. Encouraged by this accession of strength, and relieved by the welcome stores which these adventurers had brought, the Scots determined upon breaking the siege by a vigorous sally. Selecting both the time and the men with the profound instinct that constitutes the successful general, Sir Alexander made a most daring raid upon the English forces, and so discouraged them that the valiant Earl of Salisbury, a man of vast experience in war, had at length to raise the siege, and beat a retreat within the English Border. And thus the prophecy of Black Agnes was fulfilled :—

" ' And do they come ? ' Black Agnes cried,
   ' Nor storm nor midnight stops our foes.
Well, then, the battle's chance be tried,
   The Thistle shall out-thorn the Rose ! ' "

Thus ended the Siege of Dunbar, and thus the hand of a feeble woman, when nerved by patriotism and armed with chosen Scottish valour, was sufficient to checkmate the plots and schemes which the English politicians had laid for the overthrow of Scotland.

It is sufficiently evident from the literature of the time that the English army expected that Dunbar would fall an easy prey into their hands. More as a jest than as a serious engagement did they begin the siege. There was, therefore, a little lugubrious humour in the songs which their minstrels sang in the camp before Dunbar ; and the laugh was latterly quite against them. One of these lays, preserved by Wyntoun, gives a glimpse of their elephantine humour :—

> " Of this assiege in their hethyng
>   The English oysid to make karping.
> ' I vow to God she makes great steer
>   The Scottish wenchie ploddiere.
>   Come I aire or I come I late,
>   I found Annot at the gate ! ' "

But when they returned to their own land, discomfitted, overthrown, and disgraced by the power and endurance of a weak woman, and the grim "heroes of a hundred fights," had to confess that they had found a superior in the Scottish heroine, well might they ponder on the text thus rendered by a modern poet :—

> " He has put down the mighty from their seat,
>   And has exalted them of low degree."

During the War of Independence in Scotland, no friends had been truer to each other in weal and woe, than Randolph, Earl of Moray, and the valiant Sir James Douglas. As companions-in-arms they had shared the toils of many a battlefield side by side, and though rivals for renown, each beheld the other's advancement without one pang of envy. But in the course of time an estrangement arose betwixt these two families after the demise of the leaders, and ere a hundred years had flown the descendants of Douglas and Randolph were deadly enemies. Doubtless this was largely owing to the rapid increase of power which the Douglases had gained on the Border, and which the Earl of Dunbar and March—descendants of Randolph on the female side—resented as an encroachment on their own territory. The middle marches of the Border were now under the control of the Douglas faction ; and the Earls of Dunbar and March were restricted to the eastern division of this part of the country by their neighbouring compatriots as rigidly as though they had been foreigners in the land.

The cause of the ultimate rupture betwixt these two powerful noblemen was peculiar. The unhappy King, Robert III., whose mind lay rather towards legislative reform than battlefields, was not competent to use the mailed hand that the times demanded ; and his brother. afterwards Regent. Duke of Albany, made the King his unwilling supporter. In the fulness of parental pride the King had made his son, the Duke of Rothesay, Governor of the Kingdom, but the levity of his conduct and the partial methods of his judgments soon estranged the nobility from him.

The deep-laid schemes of his uncle, the Duke of Albany, who coveted the Throne, were not unknown to him, but he affected to disdain duplicity.

The vacillating and weak-minded Robert III., wishful to obtain peace at any price, allowed his brother, the politic Duke of Albany, to carry out his ambitious plans. He made it known among the Scottish nobility that the Duke of Rothesay, the heir-apparent to the Crown, would require to be married, to maintain the succession, and the hand of the Duke would be assigned to the highest bidder. Foremost among the match-making nobles was George, eleventh Earl of Dunbar and March, who had a daughter Elizabeth of marriageable age; and it was intimated to him that if he could produce an adequate dowry his daughter might be prospective Queen. By some means the Earl fulfilled the conditions, and the Lady Elizabeth of Dunbar was declared to be the betrothed bride of the Duke of Rothesay.

The Earl of Douglas, however, had also a daughter of a suitable age for wedlock, and as his revenues vastly exceeded those of Dunbar, he saw a brilliant opportunity before him of ennobling his family by a connection with the Throne, and by the same stroke discomfitting his rival. The Duke of Albany astutely saw that whichever bride was chosen the result would be misfortune to his nephew, from the raising of one of two powerful enemies against him. Rothesay himself seems to have been indifferent, as he did not mean to be faithful to either bride, so he languidly acquiesced to whatever his uncle Albany proposed, and received the daughter of Douglas with as little regard as he would have bestowed upon the heiress of Dunbar. But the Earl of Dunbar and March could not bear the insult and contumely thus heaped upon him. Retiring from the Court to his Castle of Dunbar, he summoned his retainers around him, and prepared to open negotiations with the Court of England. Leaving Dunbar strongly garrisoned in the care of one of his near kinsmen, he journeyed himself to England expecting to receive the command of a contingent to invade Scotland.

No sooner had the Earl of Douglas heard of the preparations which the Earl of Dunbar and March had made than he assembled his own overwhelming band of followers and, marching straight to Dunbar Castle, invested it closely. This display of power so terrified the fainthearted Governor that he surrendered without striking a single blow. This completed the power of Douglas, since he had Dunbar, Bothwell, and Douglas Castles in his possession, which controlled all entrance to the south of Scotland. The succession of the Earls of Dunbar and March, thus rudely broken, was never thoroughly re-established.

For a considerable period the Castle changed hands frequently, as one or other of the Border Clans gained supremacy in the neighbourhood ; but its power of menacing the Capital was never forgotten. As a coveted stand-point for any ambitious Lord or successful Laird its history was a stormy one, though but imperfectly learned from authentic records. Now it was in possession of the Homes ; anon the Scotts won it ; and each of the more important Border Clans had this stronghold under their control and dared their rivals. Many strange scenes were enacted beneath the roof-tree of Dunbar, and many a deed of nameless violence, of clamant wrong, did the now dilapidated chambers witness :—

" Beneath those battlements, within those walls
  Power dwelt amid her passions ; in proud state
  Each robber chief upheld his armed halls,
  Doing his evil will, nor less elate
  Than mightier heroes of a longer date.
  What want these outlaws ; conquerors should have
  But History's purchased page to call them great ?
  A wider space, an ornamented grave ?
  Their hopes were not less warm ; their works were full
      as brave."

The most interesting episodes in the history of Dunbar Castle are those which relate to the connection of Mary, Queen of Scots, with this desolate ruin. After the ruthless murderers had perpetrated the outrage which they had long meditated, the very success of their plot found them unprepared for the results which followed. Their suspicion of the weak and vacillating Darnley on the one hand, and their well-grounded doubts of the faithfulness of the arch-traitor and hypocrite, Moray, perplexed the leaders of the assassination. The high-spirited manner in which the

Queen denounced their brutality led some of them to think that the safest way for them would be to fulfil the threat with which Ruthven quieted her, and " cut her into collops and throw her over the wall " ; the difficulty in which they were placed was a serious one. With Darnley at their head, and in the presence of the Queen, they had committed " murder most foul and most unnatural " by the assassination of Rizzio ; and the question arose as to what should be done with the Sovereign who was now in their hands.

The escape of the Queen with Darnley from Holyrood has been often narrated. The fugitives directed their way to Dunbar Castle. Her residence there, though short, was sufficient to strike terror into the hearts of the conspirators against the Throne ; and when she returned a few days afterwards to Musselburgh, it was to resume the power of which she had been so nearly deprived. Very different was her next visit to this sea-beaten tower.

However unworthy an object Darnley may have been, it is absolutely certain that Queen Mary loved him faithfully. His reckless conduct during the scene of the murder of Rizzio was easily pardoned by his affectionate wife upon the first intimation which she received of his penitence and contrition ; and thus the few days they spent at Dunbar Castle formed a brief but pleasant interlude in her chequered life. But soon afterwards the murder of Darnley changed the prospect of her whole future career, and all the years

she had yet to survive were shrouded in darkness
and despair :—

> " White as a white sail on a dusky sea
> When half the horizon's crowded, and half free,
> Fluttering between the dun wave and the sky
> Is hope's last gleam in man's extremity.
> Her anchor parts ! but still her snowy sail
> Attracts our eye amidst the rudest gale ;
> Though every wave she climbs divides us more,
> The heart still follows from the loneliest shore."

A new actor now appears on the scene.
The Earl of Bothwell, Lord High Admiral
of Scotland, Sheriff of Haddington, and Captain
of Dunbar Castle, had made himself extremely
busy in political affairs. His bold appearance
and invincible conduct quailed all his opponents,
and carried terror to the hearts of the conspirators,
who, with him, had brought about the murder of
Darnley, and whom he swayed as he wished.

Queen Mary had visited her infant son at
Stirling Castle, and on the morning of 24th April
1567 she left Linlithgow Palace for Holyrood,
with a small retinue ; and Bothwell, as High
Sheriff of East Lothian, had put himself at the
head of a thousand armed followers, and intercepted the Queen at Foulbriggs (now Fountain-
bridge), and carried her off forcibly to his Castle
of Dunbar, and, clasping the arm of the fair Queen
of Scots with his own rude mailed gauntlet, he
led his dejected captive within its walls. Picture
the misery of the poor Queen at this juncture :
her husband murdered by the agency of her

captor, her son secluded from her in a distant
fortress, and her own person in the power of a
reckless and unprincipled wretch, whose lawless
passions impelled him to unrestrained iniquity.
The dark story of her sojourn at Dunbar if fully
known would throw an entirely new light upon a
very dubious episode, which has been interpreted
to her discredit, without proof, by her antagonists.

As the Queen in her melancholy turret-chamber
at Dunbar gazed anxiously, hopelessly, over the
foam-besprent waters of the North Sea, the
memory of her own lovely canzonet might come
into her mind, and recall the pleasures of by-past
times, the milder woes of her early life :—

" The voice of my sad song
    With mournful sweetness guides
My piercing eye along
    The tract that death divides ;
      'Mid sharp and bitter sighs
      My youth's bright morning dies.

Can greater woes employ
    The scourge of ruthless Fate ?
Can any hope, when joy
    Forsakes my high estate ?
      My age and heart behold
      The shroud their love enfold.

O'er my life's early spring,
    And o'er its opening bloom,
My deadly sorrows fling
    The darkness of the tomb ;
      My star of hope is set
      In yearning and regret."

And as she heard the step of her hateful captor approaching her chamber would not her mind dwell upon those gentle and loving words which her murdered spouse had addressed to her in the full hey-day of youth and love ?

> " The turtle for her mate
>   More dule may not endure
> Than I do for her sake
>   Who has mine heart in cure,
> My heart, which shall be sure
>   With service to the deed
> Unto that lady pure,
>   The wale of woman heid.
>
> Yet no mirth till we meet
>   Shall cause me be content !
> But still my heart lament
>   In sorrowful silence sore
> Till that time she's present,
> Farewell, I say no more ! "
>   Quod *King Henry Stuart.*

The gay King Henry's farewell had been realised, and the Queen had to endure the insolence and the lawlessness of his cruel murderer. The Bride of France, the Queen of Scotland, was now the leman of an unprincipled Border Chief, whose meed was the gallows, had each man his due.

Ten days after her solitary confinement in Dunbar Castle, the Queen was bidden to accompany her captor (now raised to the rank of Duke of Orkney) to Edinburgh. She expected to be taken to Holyrood, but instead she was conveyed to Edinburgh Castle. Bothwell still thought that he was acting as a freeman, but he was really playing into the hands of the Associate Lords. He stealthily carried the Queen to Borthwick Castle, but he was soon followed by the Regent Moray's troops, who invested the place, but had not artillery to besiege it. He escaped by a secret passage, leaving the Queen to the mercy of the soldiers. She donned the costume of a cavalier, mounted a horse, and was making her way towards Edinburgh Castle, when her captor appeared, seized her reins, and led her once more to Dunbar Castle.

Queen Mary's association with this stronghold has been fully explained. It only now remains to say that it was at Dunbar where Bothwell devised the Battle of Carberry Hill which proved so fatal to the hapless Queen. The Regent's troops overcame Bothwell's scanty force, and Mary was captured, conveyed a prisoner to Edinburgh, and thence to incarceration in Loch Leven Castle. The Regent Moray, in December 1567, obtained an Act of Parliament directing the demolition of Dunbar Castle and the Fort on Inchkeith, which, however, was not immediately put in execution. Not until the army of Moray returned victoriously from Langside, in May 1568, did he set himself deliberately to destroy Dunbar Castle, as being a fitting emblem of his triumph over the Queen.

And now the site of this ancient fortress is left desolate and unlovely. The few stones which mark the spot where once it reared its head proudly are moss-covered and time-worn, and but for the interest that clings about them because of their eventful history, they might readily be passed unnoticed by the traveller. Yet memory and imagination alike conspire to recall and vivify the departed forms which once lived in joy and sorrow, in hope and despair, within these ruined walls :—

" Nae licht is schinand in the lodge, and nae porter keeps the door ;
Nae warder strides, wi' lustie spear, that dreirie lodge before ;
Nae harp is heard inurth the ha', and nae sang frae lady brave ;
But all is quiet as Eremit's howff, and stilliche as the grave."

The ruins of Dunbar Castle belong by heritage to the Earl of Home, as representing the Douglas family, to whom the structure belonged in early days.

XX

INVERARAY CASTLE

THE Highland Clans whose territories bordered upon the Lowlands occupied a position much more favourable for the spread of civilization amongst themselves than did the more northern septs. For, apart from the fact that the country wherein their lot was cast afforded more opportunity for the advance of progress by means of agriculture, the very proximity of a race at once so peaceful and industrious as the Lowland Scottish race would exercise a powerful influence upon them.

Among the Clans thus brought within the reach of civilization the Campbells have ever been eminent. Though their origin is wrapped in obscurity, there are few spots whose history may be more readily followed within the limits of historic time. Leaving out of notice the apocryphal tales which many of their bards relate, which would carry back their origin to a period anterior to the Deluge, it may be found that in the first half of the 12th century (November 1153), Somerled, the Thane of Argyll, who is supposed to have been of Norwegian origin, invaded Scotia in the reign of Malcolm IV., " the Maiden," and made his name terrible in the west of Scotland. By dint of energy and fearless daring, he over-ran the whole tract of country, now known as Argyllshire, and put to flight the savage aborigines. At length fate overtook him at Renfrew in 1165, and as he died unmarried he was not the direct progenitor of the Campbell Clan. He had been associated, however, with his two nephews, David and John MacHeth, great grandsons of Malcolm I. (died 1040), and they seem to have carried on the family. Whether Somerled was really the direct ancestor of the Campbells of Argyll is a dubious question, and one over which historians still wrangle. For with that national pride for which the Highlanders are proverbial, many disputants indignantly disclaim aught save a purely native origin. And their tale is not an improbable one.

A certain western warrior, whose deeds live now only in his name of Diarmid O'Duibhne, was in possession of the lands around Loch Awe early in the 11th century. And from him in the female line, so far as can be known, this ancient race has sprung—an idea somewhat corroborated by the fact that the family is still denominated in song *Siol Diarmid*, the race of Diarmid. The name Campbell was first introduced to the Clan by the marriage of Eva, daughter of Paul O'Duibhne, surnamed *Insporran* because he bore the King's bag, with Archibald Gillespie Campbell, the descendant possibly (like the Lyons of Glamis) of some Roman settler in Britain, whose proud title of Campo-Bello, though suited for the yellow Tiber, suffered contraction when he came within

the sphere of the Clyde. The lands of Loch Awe
were thus transferred to him, and he became the
direct founder of an unfailing race, great alike in
the Council and the Field. And even now Argyllshire is the spot :—

" Where Campbells, sprung of old O'Diubhne's race,
  Old as their hills, still rule their native place.
  No ancient chief could like the O'Duibhne wield
  The weighty war, or range the embattled field.
  Unmoving bear the shock of charging foes,
  Pierce throng'd battalions, or their ranks inclose."

The shadowy shapes of these early characters
fade into darkness before the fame of Sir Colin
Campbell of Loch Awe, who was knighted by
Alexander III. in 1280, one year before the King's
daughter, Margaret of Norway, was married to
King Eric of that country. This Sir Colin had
largely increased the possessions of his Clan in
Loch Awe district, as well as gaining a great
reputation as a warrior, and so he came to be
distinguished as *Cailean Mor*, Colin the Great (not
MacCallum Mor, which means son of *Malcolm* the
Great, quite a different name). From this great
Chief the numerous Campbell descendants are
styled MacCailean Mor till this day. It was the
fate of Colin the Great to be slain in a conflict
with his powerful neighbour MacDougall, Lord
of Lorn, which took place at the String of
Cowal in Argyllshire. This Lord of Lorn
was descended from Somerled, Thane of Argyll,
to whom reference has been made as ancestor

also of Campbell of Loch Awe (originally spelled "Lochow"), and thus a feud was begun between the two families which lasted for many years.

Sir Niel Campbell, eldest son of Colin the Great, was knighted by Alexander III. in 1286, and was afterwards concerned in the appointment of a successor to the Scottish Throne, after the death of Margaret, the Maid of Norway, in 1290, which left a vacancy. When Edward I. of England came as Over-lord to Scotland in 1296, he persuaded Sir Niel to swear fealty to him, and also induced Sir Niel's three brothers, Sir Dugald, Arthur and Duncan to join the English ruler. But these four Campbells did not adhere to their oath to Edward I., for as the star of Robert Bruce rose in the ascendant they all joined the Scottish claimant, and remained his faithful supporters during all the King's varied career. So highly did King Robert appreciate Sir Niel that he gave him his sister, Lady Mary Bruce, as his wife, who thus became ancestress of the Argyll family connected with Royalty. The King also bestowed upon him and his son, Sir John of Moulin, all the lands which had been forfeited for treason by David de Strathbogie. As Sir John fell at the Battle of Halidon Hill, without heirs, the title and estates reverted back to the Crown. Sir Niel died in 1316 and was succeeded by his eldest son, Colin.

Sir Colin Campbell of Lochow, received the Governorship of Dunoon Castle as a reward for his prowess in aiding the Steward of Scotland in regaining it from the English, and this post remained in the family until the edifice had fallen into ruins. He died in 1340, and was succeeded by his son Sir Archibald of Lochow, and afterwards by his grandson, Sir Duncan of Lochow. The honour of having built the first Inveraray Castle and completed it is shared by Sir Duncan and his son, Sir Colin.

By the middle of the 15th century the Campbells had been noted as munificent Castle-builders. The various heads of branches of the families sprung from Lochow vied with each other in erecting each one a more beautiful structure than his near relative. Thus Sir Colin Campbell built Inveraray Castle about 1450, as well as his own Castle of Kilchurn on Loch Awe, the Tower of Strathfillan, and the enclosing walls of the Isle of Tay. The Chapel at Finlarig was also erected by him, while Colin, the Laird of Balloch, built the Castle there which was afterwards known as Taymouth Castle. Sir Duncan, known as " Black Duncan," erected the Castle of Finlarig and Lochdochart (now a ruin), as well as the " great house of Barcaldine." The Campbells by this time had been making acquaintance with Continental civilization, and cultivated Latin, French and Italian poetry and literature, as well as painting and architecture. Meanwhile they had not neglected their patriotic devotion to the land of their birth, but still remained true and loyal Scotsmen.

When Prince James of Scotland was despatched

by his alarmed father, Robert III., to France for safety, after the murder of his elder brother, the Duke of Rothesay, the emissaries of Henry IV. of England captured him off Flamborough Head, and bore their prize joyfully to the Court at London. Here he was detained for eighteen years —1406-1424—and was only liberated on the bond of some of the leading nobles and gentry of Scotland promising to pay the ransom of their King, which was set down at forty thousand pounds.

Amongst the list of noblemen there appears the name of Sir Duncan Campbell, under the title of Lord of Argyll; and as a proof of the rapid advance of the Clan we may notice that the income at which he is rated (1500 marks) was not excelled by any of the Scottish nobility, and only equalled by the Lord of Dalkeith. This proves as conclusively as possible that the heads of the Clan Campbell had not frittered away their substance in futile and harmful war, but had devoted much of their attention to the culture of their lands, since those wild hills, once barren and unproductive, could at that time rival the fertile fields of Lothian and Tweeddale.

Nor did the Prince, when he ascended the throne as James I. of Scotland, forget the Highland Chief who had thus pledged himself to procure the liberation of his native Prince. Sir Duncan was raised by James II. to the dignity of a Lord of Parliament, and assumed the title of Lord Campbell of Argyll. In the Privy Council he held a prominent place, and was nominated Justiciar of the County in which his possessions were situated. The connection with the Crown which the Campbells enjoyed already was rendered still more intimate by his espousal, first of Mariota Stewart, daughter of the Regent Albany, and afterwards of Margaret Stewart, daughter of an illegitimate son of Robert III. It will thus be seen that Lord Campbell was a man of mark in his generation, and one well-fitted to hand down his name to posterity. But perhaps the crowning effort of his life was the transference of the seat of his Clan, which had been located at Loch Awe for centuries, from their hereditary rendezvous to the shores of Loch Fyne.

It is no easy task to persuade an ignorant and unreasoning race to leave the homestead about which all their associations of memory linger, to abandon the glories which cluster around the ancestral pile, renowned alike in song and story, and to transfer their affections, with their Lares and Penates, to new and unfamiliar scenes. But the Lord of Argyll proved himself equal to the difficulty, and as the new abode of the head of the Clan gradually rose in all its magnificence before the astonished Campbells their regret for the past became hope for the future. Of the mansion of Lochow there are no remains which could afford data for a comparison, but it may be safely concluded that it could not compare with the Castle of Inveraray, either in size, position, or grandeur. And though the chances and changes of time

have laid the latter structure low, and supplied
its place by a more modern erection, the relics
which even yet remain indicate somewhat of its
former greatness. An imaginative Scottish historian thus compares the first and the present
Castles of Inveraray :—

" If we may believe a curious old print, the
present unsightly pile, with its clumsy bulk and
tawdry decorations, must have displaced a predecessor which, in the beautiful variety of turrets
and decorated chimneys crowning the massive
cluster of square and round towers built into
each other at different ages below, probably excelled Glamis, and the finest specimens of this
peculiar architecture in the north."

The reasons which would influence Lord Campbell in deciding upon a removal from Loch Awe
to Loch Fyne may be readily understood. Situated upon an inland Loch, and hemmed in by hills,
whose towering peaks defied the advance of an
army, the ancient house of Loch Awe was secure
from attack. But a clan whose strength is ever
increasing soon finds that the bulwarks which
were convenient for purposes of defence become
absolute barriers to their own progress. The
inland loch is soon explored, and its shores
speedily subjugated ; and the resistless conquerors are athirst for new worlds to encounter.
The politic leader who can " discern the signs of
the times," will look around for an outlet for the
enthusiasm of his followers, lest it grow too much
for him to command. And as Lord Campbell

seems to have been a shrewd student of mankind, he judged wisely in carrying his clansmen to the shores of an open firth which communicated directly with the Atlantic Ocean, and thus laid a whole world under tribute to the daring and adventurous soul who cared to try his fortunes on the great waters.

Nor would the picturesque situation of the new Castle be wholly without its effect. The existing Castle, which is built but a short distance from the site of the original structure, sufficiently shows the prospect as it would appear to the denizens of the older edifice. And the glorious scene that spreads itself before the view from this standpoint is not seriously altered by the fact that you look upon it now through the apertures of a pseudo-Gothic window-frame, whose affected uncouthness may become a disturbing element to the sensitive soul; whilst Lord Campbell viewed the same scene from his Scottish-Baronial tower-light with greater joy than yours. For to him the panorama thus disclosed must have seemed almost a discovery, a new Eden brought within the reach of his kinsfolk.

Yonder before you lies Loch Fyne, which, by the peculiar bend it takes might deceive you into the idea that it was a peaceful inland lake, but that the rising and falling tides, with their loads of saline weeds, sufficiently show that it is but a minute portion of the illimitable ocean. The river Aray, which bestows its name upon the

Castle and township, flows down from the heights above Loch Awe close beside the building, whilst the Shiray, taking its rise in the mountains farther north, sweeps down more rapidly towards the Loch, thus forming a kind of peninsula between the rivers. From the town of Inveraray the shore circles inwards as a crescent-like bay, at the southern horn of which stands the little county town, whose importance is more derived than personal. The houses are few and not particularly elegant, and thus they add to the imposing effect of the Castle, which is essentially the point in the scene. The structure is of comparatively recent date, having been erected during the latter half of the 18th century near the spot whereon the original Castle stood.

The wooded hill of Duniquoich stands forth in solitary grandeur from the lesser eminences around, and brings the Castle, which lies at its base, into bold relief against the dark background thus provided. Had the stone used been either the white granite of the North of Scotland, or the marble of Italy, the effect would have been too dazzling by contrast ; but the dull colour of the greenish slate of which it is built harmonizes exquisitely with the foliage that surrounds it. The building is quadrangular, with massive towers rising from the foundations at the corners, and a square pavilion with rectangular flanking-towers over-topping the whole. Though somewhat pretensious in its style, the desired effect is produced,

for you cannot escape from the Castle if your eyes
once turn in its direction. The design has been
attributed to the famous William Adam, the
father of the two famous architects, Robert and
John Adam, who enjoyed a European reputation.
The Castle of Inveraray was begun by the third
Duke of Argyll (born 1682, died 1761) in 1744,
and William Adam died in 1748, the work of com-
pleting the design having been committed to
Robert Morris, a famous English architect, and
finished about the time of the Duke's death.

The feud which had existed between the
Campbells of Loch Awe and the Lords of Lorne
since the time when the " Great Colin " was
slain, was finally tranquillized by the all-powerful
influence of Love ; and the sovereignty of the
Campbells over Lorne was obtained by the no
less potency of gold. Colin Campbell, grandson of
Sir Duncan, first Lord Campbell, had won the
heart of the eldest daughter of John Stewart,
third Lord of Lorne and Innermeath, for the
ancient possessors of this district, the Mac-
Dougalls, had failed to provide male heirs to
inherit their dignities, and these had passed into
the hands of the Stewarts. In 1465, the marriage
of Colin, Lord Campbell took place, and the title
of Lord Lorne was added to his other dignities,
and Castle Gloom—afterwards named Castle
Campbell—near Dollar, became his by right.
He was created first Earl of Argyll in 1457, and
filled many important positions at the Court, as
Ambassador frequently, and Lord High Chancellor

of Scotland in 1482. His death took place in 1493, when he was succeeded by his eldest son, Archibald, the second Earl, who fell in command of the vanguard at the Battle of Flodden.

This second Earl worked more faithfully for the advancement of his family than for the welfare of the kingdom. He had taken part with his father in the struggle betwixt James III. and Prince James (afterwards James IV.) which ended in the violent death of the former at Sauchieburn ; and was duly rewarded by the new King. The Governorship of the Castle of Tarbert, and command of the King's lands in Knapdale and Kintyre, gave him control of the Campbell lands in that district of Ayrshire. As disputes had arisen as to the division of the spoil among the conspirators who had fought for James IV., the Earl of Argyll and the Earl of Lennox fell to quarrelling together. Ultimately this dispute was settled by the marriage of Argyll to Elizabeth, daughter of Lennox. It is possible that the very efforts of the parents to prevent this union only served to intensify the passion of the enamoured pair, for, as the old song says :—

> " There is no striving
>   To cross his intent,
> There is no contriving
>   His plots to prevent ;
> But if once the message greet him
>   That his true love doth stay,
> If Death should come and greet him,
>   Love will find out the way."

Their love was finally crowned with success, and the union of the two powerful families of Argyll and Lennox, whose lands were contiguous, placed the shores of the Clyde from Glasgow to the sea, and the mountains, fields, and valleys of the Levenax and Loch Awe beneath the rule of two competent and friendly leaders. The storm between Scotland and England, which had been gathering for many years, at length burst on the fatal field of Flodden, and brought woe and tribulation over the whole land.

Few Scotsmen care to dwell even now on the story of Flodden, for it requires all the lustre of Bannockburn to counterbalance its disgrace. The absolute incompetence of the King for the post of leader, which he would not resign, despite their entreaties, to more experienced hands, brought about the climax of the disaster. It must have been with feelings of amazement and dread that veteran warriors like Angus and Huntly saw the troops of England dashing unopposed over the narrow bridge at Twisel, and ranging themselves without hindrance immediately opposite their own army on the field of Flodden. The obstinacy and self-confidence of the Stewart race was again to bring calamity on the Scottish nation.

The order of battle may be briefly explained. The troops on either side were divided into four companies. Surrey opposed the King, and was supported by Lord Thomas Howard and his brother, Sir Edmund, on the right, and Lord Stanley on the left, while Lord Dacre commanded

a reserve of horse. The King had two companies
on his left, led by Crawford and Montrose, and
Huntly and Home, whilst his right was composed
of the West Highlanders under Argyll and Lennox, and the reserve was under the charge of
Bothwell. The left wing under Huntly and Home
was the first to encounter the English troops, and
their victory was easy ; but when the rude Highlanders under Argyll mingled in the fray, their
ignorance of civilized warfare proved their ruin.
Unused to depend upon aught save personal
prowess, the bold mountaineers rushed precipi-
tately forward upon the steady and immovable
spearmen under Stanley. With unquenchable
ardour the clansmen fought, each man a hero ;
but their independent valour was misspent :—

> " For on the left, unseen the while,
> Stanley broke Lennox and Argyll ;
> Though there the western mountaineer,
> Rushed with bare bosom on the spear,
> And flung the feeble targe aside
> And with both hands the broadsword plied,
> 'Twas vain."

The prodigies of valour then performed shall never
be adequately recited. In such a case mere personal valour is often of no avail against firm
discipline and brute force. And this was the fortune of the right wing at Flodden. As the smoke
of the battle rolled away from the field, and the
English spearmen looked round for their foes,
behold ! they were not :

" Like the leaves of the forest when summer is green,
    That host with its banners at sunset was seen ;
    Like the leaves of the forest when autumn has blown,
    That host on the morrow lay withered and strewn."

The brave leaders, fellow-champions and companions-in-arms, had not spared themselves amid the general carnage, but the time was gone. From that dread onslaught the Earls of Argyll and Lennox returned no more, and such glory as gilds the soldier's tomb is theirs by right of conquest. The romantic mind cannot refrain from turning to that woeful scene by the banks of the Till, when :—

" Mony were the mudie men
    Lay gasping on the green ;
    And mony were the fair ladies
    Lay lemanless at hame."

The death of the Second Earl of Argyll at Flodden, however mournful as an incident of war, had the happy effect of bringing the claims of the family more prominently into notice. The Earl had a family of four sons and seven daughters ; and it was the lot of one of these sons to become the ancestor of another line of Campbells now represented by the Earl Cawdor. The story is a romantic one.

Sir John Campbell of Lorne, third son of the second Earl of Argyll, whilst wandering with a band of his clansmen in the vicinity of Cawdor Castle, Nairnshire, had the good fortune to encounter the heiress of Sir John Calder, Thane of that Ilk, then a young girl, with no protector near save her nurse. There was no feud betwixt the Campbells and the Calders at this time, so it may be supposed that the opportunity of " reiving " a wealthy heiress was too great a temptation for Sir John Campbell to resist. The youthful Muriella was seized and borne away with speed from her ancestral domain by one portion of the band, whilst another party lingered behind to form a rearguard in case of pursuit. By an inexcusable neglect they had overlooked the capture of the nurse, and she managed to escape to Calder Castle and to raise an alarm. Then there was hurry and turmoil over the loss of the young maiden :—

> " It's fy gar ride, and fy gar rin,
> And haste ye bring these traitors again,"

and soon a powerful party started in pursuit of the kidnappers who had stolen away the Chieftain's daughter.

Ere they had gone far they overtook the Campbells, and startled them while halting around their camp-fire, flattering themselves upon the ease with which they had gained their prize. The sudden descent of the Calders at once put an end to their self-gratulation, and they found it necessary to defend at once their captive and their lives. They had determined in any case to secure the heiress of Calder (now spelled " Cawdor "), and the ruse by which they accomplished this

272

INVERARAY CASTLE

feat has been seldom paralleled for bravery.
Campbell of Lorne, mounted on his steed, and
bearing the young Muriella in his arms before
him, retreated rapidly, with a few chosen followers, on the road to Inveraray. His uncle,
Campbell of Inverliver, seeing the swift approach
of the Calders, ordered his seven sons to throw
over a large camp-kettle which had been in use,
and to gather around it in battle-array so as to
deceive the Calders into the belief that their young
lady-heiress was beneath it. Impelled by their
duty both to father and chief the brave clansmen
did as required, and the stratagem succeeded.
Never doubting for a moment that Muriella was
below the utensil thus strangely transformed into
a citadel, the pursuers dismounted and attacked
the small body of Campbells on all sides. Undis-
mayed by the onslaught, even though hopeless
of relief, the brave Campbell clansmen made a
gallant defence, and though they knew that
certain death awaited them they resolved to sell
their lives dearly. Their opponents, however,
were too powerful for them, and one after the
other fell, never to rise more.

With a shout of victory the Calders rushed
forward to release their imprisoned lady ; but
their exultation was changed into chagrin and
disappointment when they found that their
wished-for prize was fled, and saw that the
strategy of the Campbells had duped them into
a fatal and irretrievable blunder. Now they discovered that whilst engaged in this fierce struggle,

s

and, as they thought, on the point of obtaining a victory, their young heiress was being borne away swiftly in the arms of her captors, through the wilds of Inverness-shire and Ross-shire, and was speeding away in frantic haste to the distant Castle of Inveraray. Pursuit was hopeless, and they were forced to leave her to her fate.

And that fate was a peculiar one. Sir John Campbell, who had thus taken her as a spoil in war, carefully tended her through girlhood to budding prime, and at length married her, thus bringing the rich heritage of Cawdor into the Campbell family. A curious story is told regarding this Muriella, which exhibits some of the queer morality of the time. When the nurse was set upon at Cawdor she well knew what the result of the attack would be. To prevent the substitution of a changeling for the true heiress, she determined to put an indelible mark upon her. Seizing the child's hand, she bit off one of the joints of her little finger, thus brutally maiming for life her foster-child. And though when Muriella became heiress there was no doubt of her identity ever suggested, it may readily be supposed that had she died in infancy the Campbells would have stretched their morality so as to secure the inheritancy to which she was entitled. Nor was the nurse's work altogether a piece of wanton cruelty, for, to judge from their own words, the Campbells would not have hesitated to serve a stranger as heiress had aught befallen Muriella in her early years. The only mark which Nature had bestowed upon her was her auburn hair; and when some one suggested to Campbell of Auchinbreck that their toil would be mis-spent should she die in infancy, his reply was :—

"She can never die so long as a red-haired lassie can be found on either side of Loch Awe."

But fate spared the clan from this imposition, and Sir John of Lorne married the golden-haired beauty, whom he had reft, as if she had been a Sabine maid, from her home ; and he forgave the missing joint in view of her fortune. Another of the romantic incidents in the life of this Sir John Campbell is narrated in the article on Castle Duart, within this volume.

The system of family feuds was then in full force, and the absolute obedience with which the clansmen executed the commands of their Chiefs perpetuated these hereditary quarrels. There were not those wanting who whispered that the Argyll family secretly encouraged the disaffection of the Isles that they might increase their own possessions through the folly of their dupes. The position which the Earl occupied as Sheriff of Argyll and Justice-General of Scotland gave him a powerful hold over the ignorant and lawless tribes in his own neighbourhood. The third Earl died in March 1529, having married a daughter of the Earl of Huntly, the leader of the Catholics in the north ; but Argyll's son, the fourth Earl, was the first prominent Scottish nobleman who supported the Protestant religion. Two of his sons succeeded to the Earldom. Archibald became fifth Earl, and was an ardent supporter of Mary, Queen of Scots, and even commanded a section of her army at Langside. Though twice married, he left no issue, and was succeeded by his half-brother, Colin, sixth Earl, who had not a very distinguished career.

It is not possible within reasonable space to give details of the nobles of Argyll up till the present day ; so a brief notice is all that is neces-sary, as their lives may be read in the national history of Scotland. Archibald, the seventh Earl, served as an officer in the Spanish Army of Philip III. when the States of Holland were captured. Archibald, eighth Earl, was a very notable figure in Scottish affairs during the seven-teenth century. He was Commander-in-Chief of the Covenanters. In 1641 he had been raised in the Peerage by Charles I. to the rank of Marquess of Argyll ; but in 1645 he was defeated by his valiant rival, the great Marquess of Montrose, at the battles of Inverlochy and Kilsyth. His insincerity was shown when at Charles II.'s Coro-nation in January 1650–51 at Scone, he placed the Crown on the King's head, and shortly after-wards he assisted at the Proclamation of Crom-well as Protector in Scotland. When Charles II. was restored to the throne in 1660 Argyll went to London thinking to ingratiate himself with the King ; but he was sternly repulsed, accused of treason, tried, and executed at Edinburgh in May 1661.

Archibald, ninth Earl of Argyll, son of the foregoing nobleman, had a similar fate. The original title and estates had been restored to him, but he was of a turbulent nature, and, having resisted the Test Act, he was tried for treason, and condemned to death in 1681, the date being left to the King's discretion. Argyll was imprisoned in Edinburgh Castle, from which place he escaped. Returning to this country, he endeavoured to organize a rebellion in favour of the Duke of Monmouth, but failed in the project, was captured and executed without another trial upon the decision of 1681 at Edinburgh in 1685, his title and estates being forfeited. His eldest son, Archibald, succeeded, and had his father's forfeited estates and titles restored, thus becoming tenth Earl of Argyll.

With this Archibald the fortunes of the Campbell family revived. He joined the Convention of Estates and took part in the movement in favour of William of Orange and Mary, joining that Prince at the Hague, and bringing him to England as William III. For his numerous services he was created first Duke of Argyll in 1701, and thus introduced the ducal title. His son and successor, John, second Duke of Argyll, was the famous statesman and military leader whom Pope thus eulogized :—

" Argyll, the State's whole thunder born to wield,
  And shake alike the Senate and the Field."

It was the second Duke who arrested the Jacobite

Rising of 1715 by his famous victory at Sheriff-muir, after which he was appointed Field-Marshal of all His Majesty's Forces. He died in 1743, and as he had no male issue he was succeeded by his brother, Archibald, who became third Duke of Argyll, and was Lord Justice-General, Lord Clerk Register, and Keeper of the Great Seal. He also died without male succession, and the fourth Duke of Argyll was the cousin of his predecessor. It is not necessary to trace the family further in detail, save in this condensed manner :—

John, fourth Duke, cousin of third Duke, died 1722.

John, fifth Duke, son, 1723–1806.

George William, sixth Duke, son, 1766–1839, no issue.

John Douglas, seventh Duke, brother, 1777–1847.

George Douglas, eighth Duke, son, 1823–1900.

John Douglas Sutherland, ninth Duke, son, 1845–1914, known for many years as Marquess of Lorne before he succeeded his father in 1900 ; was married in 1871 to H.R.H. Princess Louise-Caroline-Alberta, daughter of Her Majesty Queen Victoria, who survived the Duke of Argyll. As there was no family, he was succeeded by his nephew, Sir Niall Diarmid Campbell, tenth Duke of Argyll, born 1872, son of Lord Archibald Campbell, second son of the eighth Duke, whose death in 1913 made Sir Niall in 1914 nearest in succession to the title.

The varied story of the Campbells of Argyll and of their connection with Inveraray Castle is here completed, and it will be seen that nearly all of them were high-souled Scottish patriots. And the song of Argyll has ever been like this :—

" 'Tis not for the land of my sires to give birth
  Unto bosoms that shrink when their trial is nigh ;
Away ! we will bear over ocean and earth
  A name and a spirit that never will die.
My course to the winds, to the stars I resign ;
But my soul's quenchless fire, O my country, is
    thine."

XXI

FOWLIS CASTLE—CARSE OF GOWRIE

EACH of the great rivers of Scotland—Clyde,
Tweed, Forth, Tay, Dee and Spey—has special
characteristics and attractions. The Clyde takes
its rise in an agricultural district, but completes
its course by passing through a dense population.
The Tweed is a placid river, flowing gently amid
a pastoral country, and past castles full of historical associations. It seems ever to be murmuring :—

> " With many a curve my banks I fret,
>   By many a field and fallow,
> And many a fairy foreland set
>   With willow-weed and mallow."

The Forth, with numerous curves and windings,
though never a turbulent stream, is replete with
fragments of Scottish history, from Stirling even
to Edinburgh and Leith. The Dee, rising in the
distant Grampians, may thus be appropriately
described :—

> " I come from haunts of coot and hern,
>   I make a sudden sally,
> And sparkle out among the fern
>   To bicker down a valley.

280

> By thirty hills I hurry down,
>   Or slip between the ridges,
> By twenty thorps, a little town,
>   And half a hundred bridges."

It begins near the Royal Castle of Balmoral, and terminates in the Royal City of Aberdeen. The Spey is reckoned the most rapid river in Scotland, and passes through typical Highland scenery :—

> " I chatter over stony ways,
>   In little sharps and trebles,
> I bubble into eddying bays,
>   I babble on the peebles."

The valley of the Tay, from the source of that river in the west to its debouchment at Dundee, in peculiarly rich in historic memoirs. Taking its rise in the remote borderland between Perthshire and Argyllshire, the Tay flows through a country which exhibits many of the varieties of Scottish river-scenery, from the wild and wooded glen to the fair and fertile Carse, and displays within its course the mountain torrent, the silent tarn, the rugged cascade, and the broad-bosomed, silvery loch. As its pathway lies through the very heart of Scotland, and amid some of its grandest scenes, the multitudinous contrasts which it thus shows are not inexplicable.

The rising hill-lands of Perthshire rapidly encroach upon the magnitude of the Grampians ; and though the country is so broken up by plateaus that it does not seem extremely elevated, still the peaks which are thrown up here and there

281

to a respectable altitude indicate with sufficient clearness that the locality is in the immediate vicinity of a vast mountain range. The volcanic forces whose energy formed the Grampians years ago are visible here also ; and the scattered bens of Perthshire, thus heaved up by Titanic skill, have exercised a powerful influence in the development of Scottish landscape.

The hills have drawn towards them the thunderous clouds, whose intercepted showers have become the sources of countless mountain-streams. The valleys have collected these into vast lochs, themselves the reservoirs of mighty rivers, which dash impetuously through their rocky beds to join the fathomless sea. And thus, by Strath and Carse, by Clachan and City, the Tay pursues its majestic course towards the ocean. Stretching over half the breadth of Scotland, the stream leaves the uplands and moors of Western Perthshire, and, winding its devious way through gloomy shades and by sunny leas, finally becomes a navigable river, flowing through a pastoral country on its way to the North Sea. The lower reaches of the Tay being not only richer but also more accessible than the remoter portions of the valley, are therefore intimately connected with the history of the country, and even now exhibit traces of the fierce contests which took place in the locality betwixt the myriad invaders of the soil and the aborigines. Betwixt the City of Perth and the sea-coast the whole stretch of country on each side of the Tay is dotted with Towers and

Keeps, with ancient fortresses and modern mansions, which show unmistakably the progress of civilization in Scotland.

No Tayside family has been longer or more honourably connected with the Gowrie district than that of the Grays of Gray. The lands they possessed were in themselves fertile, and by their proximity to the town of Dundee a ready market was found for their agricultural produce. Hence their importance to the locality may be understood. Three seats are now associated with their name—Fowlis Castle, Gray House, and Kinfauns Castle, the first of these being the most ancient.

The Castle of Fowlis occupies a commanding position upon an elevated table-land at some distance to the north of the river bank, and is skilfully placed so as to resist an attack. The approach from the roadway near which it is situated might easily be defended, and the steep ascents of the Den of Fowlis on the one side, and the brae on the other, would render assault from these quarters extremely difficult. With such recommendations in times of war, it was not without its attractions in " piping times of peace." The view from the upper windows is very lovely. Looking southward the spectator has presented to his vision a succession of fertile fields, which descend from the altitude on which the Castle is erected by easy gradations until they reach the brink of the river. Far beyond the silvery stream, which extends its broad expanse at this point to the greatest width (nearly three miles) of all its course, the dim outline of the Fifeshire coast may be seen, from the ancient spires of St Andrews to the still more ancient Tower of Abernethy, with all the intermediate monuments of progress, the ruins of Lindores Abbey, and the palatial mansions of Newport-on-Tay.

Westward on the north side of the river lies the famous Carse of Gowrie, extending its green and fruitful glade far as the eye can reach, and dotted with innumerable points of historic interest—Invergowrie, Errol, Kinfauns, and many others—which awaken recollections of Scotland's days of chivalry. And through the verdant slopes which line each bank the path of the Tay may be traced by the gleaming streak of reflected light which glistens in the sunshine and marks its meanderings. Eastward the towers and spires of the ancient City of Dundee may be seen, now pleasantly situated upon the eminences that in former days shut her in from the world, but which the irresistible tide of progress has brought within her boundaries. The towering mount which overhangs the burgh, and which Dundonians proudly denominate " the Law," stands forth in stern majesty, closing the view in that direction. Further northward the Sidlaw Hills show their summits above the rising ground, and around towards the margin of the Carse the sharply defined range of mountains, of which King's Seat and Dunsinnan are the most noticeable peaks, serve to limit the view.

It will be seen that from the spot occupied by

Fowlis Castle the deep valley lying between the spur of the Sidlaw Hills on which it is built, and the " blue Lomonds " in Fife, which show their faint outlines in the hazy distance, is quite commanded, and lies like a panorama at the feet of the beholder. And there are not many spots in Scotland which exhibit so much richly varied landscape at one glance of the eye. The woods of Camperdown and the orchards of Errol, the green waving fields of Gowrie, and the cultivated mounds of Newburgh and Balmerino, the glistening river, and the mystic and far-distant ocean—

> " All form a scene
> Where musing Solitude might love to lift
> Her soul above the sphere of earthliness,
> Where Silence undisturbed might watch alone."

Nor need the glamour of the scene be limited only to those portions of it which are at one view perceptible. By ascending the beautiful acclivity to the north of the Castle the lovely vale of Strathmartine may be seen stretching to the very base of the Sidlaws. Beyond the Lomonds on the south lies the peaceful Loch Leven, the lake of Romance and Chivalry ; and hidden by the range which terminates with the Hill of Kinnoul, on the western side, the ancient City of Perth sits queen-like by the rapid-flowing Tay.

Here, in the centre of this scene of surpassing loveliness, fraught with the memory of noble deeds of daring, the ancient Castle of Fowlis once reared its turrets. The portion of the Castle still remaining gives but a very imperfect notion of its former extent. Probably this only formed one wing, and in an old plan, made in 1696, " the Lady's Tower " encloses an internal staircase which runs from basement to top-rafters, and was on one side of a quadrangular building, the other erections being designed for the accommodation of the servants. A carved stone from the Castle was found built into a modern house, and bearing the date " 1640," which suggests that this portion, at least, was erected by Andrew, eighth Lord Gray, who succeeded to the title and estate in 1612, and 1663 was the date of his death. The earlier Castle, of which nothing now remains, belonged to a much earlier period.

The origin of the name of Fowlis is much disputed. One theory is that it is derived from the title of a Norman-French knight who had settled in Kent some time previous to the Conquest in 1066, and who stoutly resisted the invasion of England by William of Normandy. Having aroused the vengeance of the Conqueror, he was compelled to flee to the north ; and throwing himself upon the generosity of Malcolm Ceanmòr, he found his confidence in that monarch was not misplaced. The Knight of Feuilles (leaves) was welcomed by the King in his Palace of Hurley-Hawkin, near Fowlis Castle, and Malcolm bestowed upon him the lands adjoining his own dwelling, which have since borne the name of the stranger knight. It is more probable that the name is a corruption of the Gaelic *Foil-es*, signifying a deep valley, such as the Den of Fowlis.

The fanciful tradition as to King Malcolm's generosity is directly contradicted by the genealogy of the Gray family prepared by Sir Bernard Burke, Ulster King of Arms. He claims that the family is descended from a common progenitor of the ducal houses of Suffolk and Kent, the baronial houses of Gray and Warwick, and the houses of Dorset, Tankerville, and Stamford. This ancestor, Anschetit de Croy, one of the companions-in-arms of William the Conqueror, who gave him large grants of land in the County of Oxford and elsewhere. From this person there descended Sir Andrew Gray of Chillingham, Northumberland County, and who had so faithfully aided Robert the Bruce in his claim for the Crown of Scotland that in 1306 the King conferred upon him the Manor of Longforgan, Perth County, other lands in Forfarshire, and the lands of Browfield and Broxmouth, Haddingtonshire. The lands of Fowlis did not come into the Gray family till the end of the fifteenth century.

The following statements are founded upon veritable documents. In 1180 the church and lands of Fowlis belonged to William of Maule, who is said to have received them from King David I. as a reward for his bravery at the Battle of the Standard in 1138. He purposed founding a family of Maules of Fowlis, but he had no son, and as one of his daughters married Roger of Mortimer, Sheriff of Perthshire, the estate and Castle fell to their share. Though so intimately connected with the history of Gowrie, there are few records found of the family, save that they were known as Lords of Aberdour, and that the possession of the Castle of Fowlis descended in direct line for several generations. It seems probable that the Mortimers were descended from Roger, second Baron of Wigmore, who aided Edward II. in his flight after Bannockburn, and received from Edward III. the empty title of Earl of March, which became extinct with the fifth earl in 1424. The Mortimers of Fowlis continued till the death of another Roger, who left only one daughter, Janet, who married Sir Andrew Gray of Broxmouth in 1397, thus bringing the Grays of Fowlis into existence.

The first of the new race was directly descended from the companion-in-arms of Robert Bruce already mentioned. He was created a Lord of Parliament, with the title of Lord Gray of Gray and Fowlis, 1437 ; by his wife, Janet Mortimer, he had one son and six daughters ; and by his second wife, Elizabeth Buchanan, he had four sons and one daughter. At his death in 1449-50 he was succeeded by his eldest son, Andrew, second Lord Gray. This nobleman became a man of mark in history, as Scotland was then in a perturbed state through the death of Robert III. in 1406, and the capture of his son James I. in that year, and his long imprisonment for 18 years in England. While still Master of Gray during his father's life-time the second Lord

FOWLIS CASTLE

Gray was chosen as one of the noblemen who were sent as pledges for the ransom of King James. For three years—1424–1427—he was kept a prisoner in England. After his return he rose rapidly in the favour of James I.

When Charles VII. of France, whose kingdom had been ravaged by the English army, sought to form a matrimonial alliance with Scotland for defensive purposes, he suggested the marriage of the Dauphin with the Princess Margaret, eldest daughter of James I., the Master of Gray was sent as one of the Commissioners to effect this union, which took place in June 1436; and after the death of Charles VII. in 1461 he was succeeded by the son of this marriage as Louis XI. After his father's death in 1449–50 the Master of Gray became Lord Gray, was appointed Ambassador to England, and in 1452 made a pilgrimage to Canterbury. After his return to Scotland he was received into the Royal Household, and obtained a license from James II. on any part of the estate which he might select. The Castle of Fowlis by this time had become too small for the accommodation of the numerous Gray family; and Lord Gray selected a site on the plateau near the river, a little south-west of the Foulis Castle. The second Lord Gray died in 1469, and it is likely that he had begun the new Castle before that, but it was not completed in his time. The successor was his grandson, Alexander, third Lord Gray, who increased his influence by two judicious marriages, connecting him with the Keiths,

Earls Marischal, and the Earl of Atholl, and was appointed Justice-General of Scotland. At his death in 1514 he left a numerous family. His eldest son, Patrick, became fourth Lord Gray, after he had reached the age of manhood.

It was the lot of this Lord Gray to see the completion of the Castle, probably during his father's life-time. He had been married to Lady Jane Gordon, daughter of the Earl of Huntly ; and as the Castle had not then been named, he devised the designation of " Castle Huntly," which it still bears. This Castle was sold in 1614 by Andrew Gray, eighth Lord Gray, to the first Earl of Kinghorne, when the name was changed to " Castle-Lyon " after that Earl's family. It remained in the possession of the Lyons, Earls of Strathmore and Kinghorne until 1776, when it was sold to Mr George Paterson. He was married to the Hon. Anne Gray, and he resumed the old name of Castle Huntly, bestowed on it by her ancestors. This splendid baronial pile still (1927) belongs to the Patersons.

The new Castle Huntly became, of course, the principal residence of the Lords Gray for a long period, and it is not necessary to deal with each of them. It is interesting, however, that the desertion of Fowlis Castle, according to a local current superstition, was followed by a total change in the policy of successive Lords Gray. It has been pointed out that loyalty to the reigning monarchy had been habitual with them, but that was changed shortly before they left the ancestral Castle. The Lord Gray of the time introduced a system of double-dealing in public affairs. Though an intimate friend of James III., he conspired to remove him from the throne; and he took part with the Prince (afterwards James IV.) at Sauchie Burn, where the King was assassinated. One of his successors, though a Reformer, sought to promote the appointment of Cardinal Beaton as Regent after the death of James V.; but he was not even true to him, for he signed a bond, which was found in St Andrews Castle, by which Lord Gray bound himself to hand over certain Scottish Castles to the English invaders under the Protector Somerset.

The acme of treachery was reached by the Master of Gray, who was known by that designation till 1609, when he became sixth Baron Gray. His early years were spent in France during the young Queen Mary's residence there, and he was in close touch with the Guises and other French friends of the Queen. He betrayed Mary's secrets to the Scottish Privy Council and the Governor Arran; concluded an agreement with Elizabeth and James to the exclusion of Mary from the throne, while acting as Ambassador to England; and formally protested against the condemnation of Mary, but secretly advised her assassination. He was exiled from Scotland for impeding the marriage of the King with Anne of Denmark in 1587, but returned shortly after, and joined with the traitor Francis Stewart Hepburn, who attempted in 1592 to capture the

King at Falkland. Gray ultimately escaped the punishment of death for treason, but was exiled to France, where in 1612 he died.

Through the marriage in 1763 of the Hon. Jane Gray to Francis, Earl of Moray, the proprietorship of Fowlis Castle would have passed to that family; but after Cromwell's invasion the fines he levied on the Royalists told so heavily upon the Gray family that the Castle and grounds had to be sold in 1669 to Sir William Murray of Ochtertyre, Baronet. The family of the Murrays of Ochtertyre could claim a very respectable antiquity. The first of the name died in 1476, and the third holder of the title is enumerated amongst the slain on Flodden Field. It will thus be seen that the new inhabitants of Fowlis were not mere "new rich" people, elevated to unwonted dignity by successful speculation, but had been connected with Perthshire for a considerable period. Originally the family name had been "Moray," and they claimed descent from Sir David Moray of Tullibardine, one of the ancestors of the Atholl family; but that Sir William who purchased Fowlis Castle changed the spelling of the surname to "Murray." He was created a Baronet of Nova Scotia, and was succeeded by his son, Sir Patrick, who largely added to the family possessions. By prudence and economy he had amassed a considerable fortune, which he expended in acquiring land. There were not wanting those who whispered that his employment by King William III. to subsidise the Highland Chieftains had been one of his most profitable speculations. Though in possession of several seats, he selected Fowlis Castle as his residence, and beneath its roof-tree his eleven children were born. He reached the patriarchal age of 80 years, and was succeeded in 1735 by his eldest son, William.

This nobleman had made an unfortunate matrimonial alliance with a daughter of Hugh, eleventh Lord Lovat, which involved him in the troubles of the 1715 Jacobite Rising; and though he escaped immediate punishment, his prospects of success under the Hanoverian Government were completely blighted. The parsimony of his father, who had at least the sense to choose the successful party, had plunged Sir William into debt; and though he only survived his parent four years, that could not be a happy period. His widow died at Fowlis Castle in 1771, having reached the age of 81 years, during which she had been intimately connected with the two great Jacobite Risings of 1715 and 1745, and had buried her husband and her son, had witnessed the marriage of her grandson, and the birth of her great-grandson, each of whom held the title of "Murray of Ochtertyre." She had herself borne nineteen children, several of whom now sleep with her in the old Kirk of Fowlis beside the Castle.

With her death a considerable alteration took place in the dignity of Fowlis Castle. Her grandson, Sir William, had married one of the daughters of the unfortunate Earl of Cromartie, who endured sentence of death for his concern in the Jacobite Risings. The matrimonial alliances which the family had lately made had developed an increase of the thirsted-for position which often accompanies wealth ; and Sir William, no longer content with Fowlis Castle, set about building the House of Ochtertyre, which soon eclipsed by its magnificence the older structure. The Castle was thus abandoned, and the seat of the family was transferred to its territorial locality near Crieff. His son, Sir Patrick, afterwards sixth Baronet, was born at Ochtertyre, and the Murrays have resided there since about 1770. The present (1927) holder of the title is Captain Sir William Keith Murray of Ochtertyre, who, on the death of his father in 1921, became ninth Baronet.

And so the Castle of Fowlis, with all its honourable memories and dishonourable recollections, falls out of the regard of existing dilletantism.

> " 'Tis thus the mighty falls.
> There is the moral of all human tales ;
> 'Tis but the same rehearsal of the past,
> First freedom, and then glory—when that fails,
> Wealth, vice, corruption—barbarism at last,
> And History, with all her volumes vast,
> Hath but one page."

XXII

MAINS CASTLE—FORFARSHIRE

THOUGH the great events in Scottish history have usually occurred in connection with the principal rivers, because, as a rule, the largest cities were constructed upon the chief water-ways, yet many memorable incidents took place upon inconsiderable streams. Bannockburn is a mere rivulet; Sauchie Burn, where James III. was assassinated, is even less important; and the Till near Flodden Field is an unimportant tributary of the Tweed. There were, nevertheless, historical characters and events connected with all these streamlets; and that is particularly striking with reference to Mains Castle, Forfarshire, which is near Dundee, and was recently acquired, with the lands, by a wealthy citizen, and presented to the city as the site of a public park.

Fintry, or (as it is more generally called) Mains Castle occupies a pleasant situation upon the south side of the tributary stream known as Gelly Burn, which flows into the Dichty River through the Den of Mains. The Dichty rises in the Sidlaw Hills, and flows through the Howe of Strathmartine to join the sea at Monifieth. Its course is more fantastic than imposing, and nowhere does it attain dimensions entitling it to a higher dignity than that of a rivulet. Though it receives the drainage of the Strath, the burns which are its tributaries are so much the creation of the rainy season that frequently its rugged bed is nearly dry, and Dichty, like

> " Kedron at our feet its scanty waters
> Distils from stone to stone with gentle motion."

The many reservoirs which the commercial enterprise of the locality has formed upon its banks assist greatly in bringing about this result ; and the stream which in remote times may have run red with the gore of our heroic forefathers, now combines with chloride of lime and soda-ash to aid the progress of civilization by peacefully bleaching yarns upon its verdant banks.

Yet though thus in itself so inconsiderable, this little Dichty river flows through a historic country. The Lairds of Auchterhouse, of Strathmartine, of Claverhouse, and of Fintry have figured prominently in general as well as county history. And if the Dichty cannot boast of any of the glorious battle-fields of Scotland, it has not been without its influence in the development of the varied fortunes of the Scottish nation. The land through which it meanders is now highly cultivated ; the people who inhabit its valley study the arts which " make for peace " ; and only those who examine the occult causes at work to produce history can have any idea of the power exercised upon the outer world by the quiescent attractions of its streamlet. The

MAINS CASTLE

Castles which have been built near its course have been erected rather as rural retreats than as strongholds, and thus exhibit the home-life of those who have passed their time amid busier scenes. But this aspect of existence is not without instruction to the student of humanity.

The Gelly Burn, which flows past the Castle, is never of any great volume, and is unworthy of attention until it reaches the site of that building ; but here the ground suddenly alters. The level banks rise upon each side of the stream with precipitate abruptness to a height of about 50 feet above the water, and the pastoral verdure which to this point had fringed its surface is intermingled with oak, beech, and elm trees for the remainder of its course. This marked topographical contrast is chiefly noticeable from the bridge which leads across Gelly Burn to the Castle. Westward the scene presents little to attract the eye of the beholder, showing merely an uninteresting burn wandering between its grassy banks ; but eastward the sudden declivity, the darksome foliage, and the half-concealed thread of rippling water far below, give to the spot the salient characteristics of a miniature glen or deep defile. The left bank is crowned by the ancient graveyard of Mains, and was formerly the site of the old kirk of the district ; whilst immediately opposite to it stand the picturesque ruins of Mains or Fintry Castle.

Originally this building has been of considerable extent, and the style of the masonry and the elegance of the design show that it has been erected in a civilized period, and by a wealthy proprietor. The large square tower, with dressed corner-stones, which forms the distinctive feature in castle-architecture of the sixteenth century, is of unusually spacious dimensions, and is still (1927) in good preservation. The outer west wall, enclosing the courtyard, and having the main entrance gateway, has suffered severely by the hand of Time, and gives evidence by the misplaced lintels of some of the window embrasures of an injudicious attempt at restoration. A very elegant ornamented window may be seen near the door. Above the gateway a circular turret has risen, the lower portion of which is visible, and in the projecting base may be seen the orifice through which the keepers of the Castle could defend the doorway without exposing themselves to attack. Turrets have probably been erected also at the corners of the north wall ; and it is likely that the courtyard had an entry from the south as well as from the west side.

It is not now possible to tell with accuracy how high this outer wall rose, for the finished masonwork of the tower does not afford any absolute indication of this. Doubtless the northern and eastern portions of the Castle were reserved for the apartments of the residents, whilst the southern part of the building was devoted to the accommodation of the menials and retainers, and the western served for purposes of defence. The most striking view of the Castle is to be obtained

from the western side, although the height of the
tower and the low elevation of the remains of the
outer wall give the building rather " a lean and
hungry look."

Strange tales are told by the credulous natives
as to the age of these ruins, and even some grave
historians have been sufficiently deceived by
their pertinacity to assert that the Castle was
built in 1311. It is almost needless to say that
the style of the architecture conclusively proves
that the Castle belongs to a much later date ; and
though there *may* have been a Fort of some kind
on the site at that time, it certainly was not that
one whose ruins now remain. And even the
indirect evidence thus afforded is supplemented
by the dates still to be found on the building.
The keystone of the western gateway bears the
date " 1562," and the lintel of a door in the east
portion which opens into the courtyard has a
carved Latin motto with the further date of
" 1582," so that it may be concluded that the
Castle was begun and finished between these
years. With this clue it is easy to trace the
history of the building. Before examining details
it might be advisable to narrate the earlier history of the locality.

It is supposed that the Earls of Angus in olden
times had a residence somewhere in the Strath of
Dichty, although its exact site has never been
determined. This notion is founded upon the
fact that in all ancient documents which refer to
the lands these are described in Latin as " Strath-

Dichty Comitis," and in Scottish as "Earl's Stradichty." It is well to remember that the County of Angus, or Forfarshire, formed one of the ancient kingdoms into which Pictish Scotland —north of Forth and Clyde—and extended from the Tay on the south, the Isla on the west, the North Esk on the north, and the North Sea on the east. When the kingdom was consolidated under the Celtic Kings, about 1005 A.D., in the time of Malcolm II., the various divisions were ruled by Mormaers, and that name was maintained till the reign of Alexander I., 1106 till 1124 being the date of his occupancy of the throne. The Mormaers, however, began to be superseded by Earls, a dignity borrowed from England.

The first Earl of Angus recorded was Gillebride or Gilchrist, whose father, of the same name and title, fought under David I. in 1138 at the Battle of the Standard. The fifth Earl in succession was Malcolm, who died in 1242, leaving no son, but an only daughter, who was Matilda, Countess of Angus in her own right. Her first husband was John Comyn, titular Earl of Angus, who died in 1242 in France ; in the following year the Countess married Sir Gilbert Umfraville, a powerful Northumberland Baron, who became a prominent figure in Scotland as Earl of Angus until his death in 1245, while the Countess died in the succeeding year. The Earls that bore the name Umfraville may be briefly noticed, especially as they were anti-patriotic to Scotland, one of them being appointed Governor of Dundee during the

War of Independence. The third Earl of this line died in 1325, and was a marked man because of his support of Edward II. after Bannockburn.

In 1329 Robert the Bruce conferred the Earldom upon Sir John Stewart of Boncle, who was descended from his own original — the High Steward of Scotland. This was the first Stewart, Earl of Angus, and these continued in succession from 1329 until 1402, the date of the death of the second Earl. His widow, the Countess Margaret, had a son by William, Earl of Douglas, while she stayed with him (her brother-in-law) at Tantallon Castle, about 1376, and this son, George Douglas, became the first Douglas, Earl of Angus. From this line the titles of "Earl of Angus and Marquess of Angus," as well as Duke of Douglas, were continued till the death in 1761 of the first Duke of Douglas.

During all this long period the Earls of Angus seem to have controlled the whole district of Strath-Dichty ; and occasionally there are records of donations from the property to the Monastery of Arbroath, and other numerous philanthropic objects, from the lands of Strath-Dichty. Whether there was a Keep or Castle for the successive Earls at or near the site of Mains Castle cannot be absolutely asserted, though it is extremely probable. In any case, these researches show that Strath-Dichty as a title stretches far back into remote times. Even the present (1927) Earl of Strathmore is described in his Patent of Nobility as " Baron Glamis,

Tannadyce, Sidlaw, and Stradichtie," and that was when the new mills were opened. Besides, it is extremely likely that Earls of Douglas should have a castle near "Lumbtithen, which was a jointure house of the Scottish Queens at the place near Dundee, now known as Lunlathen, of which one part belonged to the Earl of Angus." No trace of a very early Castle has been found in the vicinity. Fortunately the history of the existing ruins can be settled historically.

In proof of the proprietary interest of the Earl of Angus in Strathdichty, the following documents are authentic and valuable. By a Sasine dated "14 April 1425, proceeding upon a Precept of William Douglas, Earl of Angus, the lands of Kirktoun of Strathdighty, in the Regality of Kirrymuir," are apportioned to "Thomas Clerk, Burgess of Dundee." A Bond by the Earl of Angus, signed 20th January 1444, obliges that nobleman to receive "James Scrimzeour, his cousin, to be the tenant in the said lands." On the 6th of March 1450, "Thomas Clerk executed an assignation to John Scrimzeour, son of James Scrimzeour of Dudhope, of the foresaid lands," and they remained in the family for a considerable time. Matilda, the sister of this John Scrimzeour, was married to John Graham of Balargus, and thus indirectly brought the latter family to the locality.

The son of this marriage obtained a Charter under the Great Seal of an Annual Rent out of the lands of Kirktoun of Strathdichty, dated 14th

March 1529-30. He purchased the estate of
Claverhouse in the immediate neighbourhood,
which afterwards gave his heirs their territorial
title, one of them being the famous John Graham
of Claverhouse, Viscount Dundee. The marriage
of John Graham of Balargus with a daughter of
the house of Beaton of Balfour, and his connection with the family of Graham, afterwards Dukes
of Montrose. gave him some importance in the
county. He derived his descent from that
branch of the Grahams which had settled at
Fintry in Stirlingshire ; and when Sir David
Graham, the head of that sept, had converted the
" Annual Rent " of Kirktoun and the lands of
Lumlethan (now Linlathen) into a safe proprietary, it is probable that he began to build the
edifice, the ruins of which remain, and called it
by the name of " Fintry Castle " in remembrance
of the estate from which his family had come.

The acquisition of the lands of Claverhouse had
the effect of bringing two families of the name of
Graham into Strathdichty—the branch which
retained the designation of Graham of Fintry and
resided in the Castle of Mains, and the heirs of
John Graham of Balargus, who adopted the title
of Claverhouse from their new estate. It is likely
that the first John Graham of Claverhouse built
a residential Castle upon his estate, which lies
a little to the west of Mains Castle, on the other
side of the Dichty, although there is now no trace
of it remaining ; and nothing marks the supposed
site which it may have occupied save a quasi-

Gothic structure in form of a dove-cot, erected from the ruins of the original Castle in 1850, near the ancient village of Trottick, and visible from the main road to Baldovan. But the inhabitants of the Castle of Mains or Fintry still retained their territorial title, and thus the latter erection became associated with the elder portion of the family. The double connection of this branch of the Grahams is not generally known. Genealogical writing is not always attractive to the reader, though this will serve to show how closely the Grahams have been associated with Forfarshire for a very long period.

William, Lord Graham of Kincardine, had as his second wife the Lady Mary Stewart, second daughter of Robert III., who was a much married lady. In 1397 she married George Douglas, first Earl of Angus of that family. Her second husband was Sir James Kennedy of Dunure, in Ayrshire. Sir William Graham was her third husband, and after his decease she wedded Sir William Edmonston of Duntreath. There were several things to attract her to Strathdichty. The jointure-house of her mother, Queen Annabella Drummond, was there. Her first husband, Earl of Angus, was the superior of all the property, and so she persuaded her third husband, William, Lord Graham, to take up a residence in that district. Lady Mary's eldest son was Sir Robert Graham of Strathcarron and Fintry. Sir Robert's second wife was a daughter of the Earl of Angus, thus forming another tie with Strath-

dichty. By her he became ancestor of the
Grahams of Claverhouse. His great-grandson first
assumed the latter territorial title, and was contemporary with that Sir David Graham who
built Mains Castle.

Although there are no very notable acts recorded of Sir David Graham, there is ample
evidence that his interests had been largely
transferred from Stirlingshire and Dumbarton-
shire to the district of Angus. The fate of Sir
David Graham, the builder of Mains Castle, was
a strange one. Throughout the alternations of
the religious professions of the Scottish nobility
during the reign of Mary, the Grahams of Fintry
remained steadfastly attached to the Romish
Church. They thus retained the friendship of
many of the northern nobles who still adhered
to the old religion, and were frequently engaged
in the conspiracies which foreign ecclesiastics
encouraged for its establishment in Scotland.
But after the Reformation faith had gained a
footing in Scotland—largely because of bribes of
the confiscated Church lands—this tampering
with superior forces brought retribution upon
them. The story of the conspiracy known to
history as " the Spanish Blanks " gives a melancholy interest to Mains Castle.

Had King James VI. been suffered to decide
for himself in religious matters his conduct makes
it probable that he would have chosen rather the
Romish than the Protestant form of worship.
But his early years were directed by those who

had risen into power entirely because of their opposition to Romanism, and whilst his mother, Queen Mary, lived, he dared not disobey them. During her long confinement in England, however, his support of the new religion had rendered it almost impossible for him to retract ; and as the great body of the people had by this time been incited to oppose the old Church, he found it impossible to withstand them. Some of the more powerful nobles in the north had still maintained their respect for the Church of their fathers, and nursed a spirit of discontent amongst themselves secretly.

In 1592 these secret communings had at last developed into a definite plot. The Earls of Huntly, Errol, and Angus, with the Lairds of Auchindoun and Fintry, had organized a distinct plan of procedure, and a prominent Roman Catholic, Dr. George Kerr, brother of the Abbot of Newbattle, was employed as their agent. It was their intention to summon His Most Catholic Majesty of Spain to aid them in reconverting Scotland ; and these nobles had signed a number of blank sheets of paper, which Kerr was to carry with him to Spain, and to have completed by writing the terms of their treaty over the signatures. From this peculiarity in the method adopted the plot was afterwards known as " the Spanish Blanks." The vigilance of one of the Protestant clergymen, however, defeated this project, and Kerr was apprehended on board the vessel that was to convey him to Spain, with the

Spanish Blanks in his possession. Having been put to the torture, Kerr confessed the whole conspiracy, implicating some of the most powerful noblemen in Scotland. The plan was a very bold one. The King of Spain was to land an army of thirty thousand men upon the west coast of Scotland, and, when joined by the insurgent Lords, purposed to divide his army, sending fifteen thousand of his soldiers over the Border, and subjugating Scotland with the remainder.

The action taken by King James makes it probable that he sympathised with this project. It was with extreme unwillingness that he proceeded against the nobles ; and though the Council had imprisoned the Earl of Angus, who had fallen into their hands, he contrived to escape from Edinburgh Castle—a feat which would have been impossible but for the connivance of his custodians. Compelled to take measures against the rebels, James led his army victoriously to the north, and skilfully succeeded in evading an engagement. Before setting out on this expedition, however, he deemed it necessary to vindicate himself from the charge of sympathy with the rebels, and he did so by apprehending Graham of Fintry, bringing him to trial, and procuring his execution at the Cross of Edinburgh. The Lord of Mains Castle was beheaded in 1593, and thus made the scapegoat for the sins of nobler traitors whom the King could not dismiss from his Court.

From this period the Grahams of Fintry seldom

appear in history, and the minor branch of the family which had settled at Claverhouse soon overtopped them. John Graham of Fintry married a daughter of James Scrymgeoure, second Viscount of Dudhope, and probably took part in the Parliamentarian Wars with Charles I. But the fame of John Graham of Claverhouse, Viscount of Dundee, in the following reign has quite overshadowed any distinction which he may have gained.

The family of the Grahams of Fintry retained the lands until early in the nineteenth century. The last holder of them was that Robert Graham of Fintry who was the friend of Robert Burns, and to whom the poet addressed two of his poetical epistles. Having fallen upon evil days, Robert Graham sold the lands of Fintry to David Erskine, W.S., Edinburgh, indirectly the ancestor of the last recently deceased Erskine of Linlathen. But Graham made the curious stipulation that his descendants should retain the territorial title of " Graham of Fintry," and that the older name of Lumlathen (now Linlathen) should be resumed for the estate. That condition has since been faithfully followed. The Grahams went to the Cape of Good Hope in a military capacity during the Kaffir Wars, and they founded the settlement of " Grahamstown," near Port Alfred, in South Africa, and married into some of the wealthy Boer families, and the name is thus preserved.

The estate of Linlathen, at least that part including the ruins of Mains Castle, were sold by the last Erskine of Linlathen to a wealthy Dundee citizen, Sir James Caird, Bart., LL.D., in 1913, and the whole of the purchase was handed over by Sir James to the Town Council, to be used as a public recreation ground to be called " Caird Park." The grounds have been laid out as a golf course, an artificial pond with cascades, and other appropriate purposes. It was opened to the public when completed in November 1923 by Mrs Marryat, half-sister of the late Sir James Caird, Bart, the generous donor.

XXIII

BOTHWELL CASTLE

The ancient Castle of Bothwell occupies a position more picturesque in its surroundings than the majority of strongholds of early times. In the days when men had to fight for the defence of their possessions it was usual for the lord of the land to select a point difficult of access—some lonely peak, some sea-beaten rock, or loch-encircled isle—as the spot most suitable for the erection of his fastness, so that it might afford him a secure retreat from his foes should Fortune turn against him. Hence, the most powerful in appearance of the Castles of Scotland are those which frown from the bleak summits of the barren hills of the north, or face the rude blasts which assail the storm-lashed coasts of Ayrshire or East Lothian; which overlook from their precipitous cliffs the profound depths of Loch Ness, like Castle Urquhart, or rest on some tiny islet in the midst of a billowy lake—

" A priceless gem, set in a silver sea."

like Lochleven Castle. But Bothwell Castle presents none of these characteristics. The scenery which surrounds it is essentially woodland and pastoral, and the quiet which reigns in the vicinity seems somewhat out of keeping with the massive towers and buttresses, which speak of inharmonious war in the midst of peaceful repose.

The Clyde, flowing around the domain of Bothwell, forms here a winding link, and wanders placidly betwixt verdant banks crowned with varied foliage. From one point of view the source and exit of the water are alike invisible, and the overhanging boughs of the trees on either side of the river, as they seem to meet, delude the spectator into the notion that he sees before him a still, inland loch forming a natural moat for the Castle rather than a mighty river pouring its resistless flood onwards to the ocean. From the margin of the river the banks rise in gentle slopes on either side, showing patches of greenest verdure through the over-arching leaves of beech, of birch, and of elm which fringe the water-edge and crown the grassy summits of the confronting eminences. On the left bank of the river the ruins of Blantyre Priory may be seen rising from the grey rock on which it was founded about the beginning of the fourteenth century ; while the grassy mound on the right bank is surmounted by the remains of Bothwell Castle, whose ivy-mantled walls have looked forth upon many changing epochs of Scottish history, and whose halls have been trodden by both the friends and foes of Scotland.

The ruins of Bothwell Castle have been regarded by antiquaries as affording one of the finest examples of its style of architecture in the kingdom.

The date of its erection is not accurately known, although it was certainly in existence early in the thirteenth century. The plan of the Castle, as well as the method of masonry employed, distinctly show that it was not the work of native artizans ; for in those times Scottish architecture was of the rudest description. Possibly some enterprising Southern knight had penetrated into the remote recesses of Clydesdale, and, enamoured of the locality, had annexed it to his property, and built the Norman Castle thereon. The size of the building itself would forbid the idea of its having originated with any of the Scottish nobles of that distant time ; for there were few indeed among them wealthy enough to have undertaken this task, even had they been civilized enough to conceive it. But as no authentic record exists of the original builders, all is but conjecture.

The social position of its first occupant may be imagined from the idea of its magnificence which the ruins still convey. It has been constructed as an oblong quadrangle, with inner court enclosed by vaulted buildings, probably with circular towers at the corners, of which the greater part of two remain, although but slight traces of the others now appear. An examination of the existing ruins will show that the Castle covered an area of about 240 feet in length, by 100 feet in breadth. The lateral extensions between the towers are pierced irregularly with windows, but there are not sufficient examples left to enable us to decide as to the nature and extent of the chambers these walls contained. That it was devised as a stronghold is evidenced by the strength of the outer wall, which is about 15 feet in thickness, and stands nearly 60 feet high. Despite the almost defenceless position which it occupies topographically, it is evident that no light force would be necessary to win the Castle from resolute defenders.

Yet there are few Castles on Scottish ground which have more frequently changed masters, and though we cannot tell whose brain devised or whose hands upreared its towers, the stories which are known of its chequered career link its history with that of Scotland ; and the Barons of Bothwell in chivalrous times for a long period exercised vast power both in the Council and the camp of the nation. Most of the structures of a similar kind, even if they have not their beginning recorded, have at least accurate details of their destruction ; but the date of the erection of Bothwell Castle is unknown, and the name of its destroyer can only be conjectured.

The first name associated with a Castle of some kind at Bothwell is that of Olyfard, and the connection of the family with Scotland may be traced. The family were of long Norman descent, and the name appears in " Scalacronica " amongst the Norman knights who fought on the side of William I. at the battle of Hastings in 1066, and received grants of land in Northamptonshire from the Conqueror. In 1113, when David I. of Scotland, sixth son of Malcolm Caenmòr, when

Prince, became Earl of Northampton by marriage, he came much in contact with the Olyfards, and was godfather to the heir, David Olyfard. This fortunate youth, though on the English side, was able to assist David's escape after the Battle of Winchester in 1141, and he accompanied the fugitive King to Scotland, and became a prominent member of the Scottish Court, and received many grants of lands from his godfather, the King, becoming a generous benefactor to the Church. Though Bothwell is not specially mentioned, it is evident that he had a seat there, as he gave a contribution from Bothwell towards Blantyre Priory, the ruins of which are close beside the ruined Castle. David Olyfard was made Justiciary of Laudonio, which included the lands south of the Forth and on to the Tweed. He was one of the first to establish feudalism in Scotland.

Walter Olyfard, the third Justiciary by heredity, died in 1242, and though there is no known clue as to the style and extent of Bothwell Castle in his time, it must have been a place of importance as the regular seat of the Justiciary of the South of Scotland. The statement has been made, and not disputed, that the daughter of Walter Olyfard was married to Walter de Moravia, who was ancestor of the Randolphs, Earls of Moray, and thus a new race came into possession of Bothwell Castle and the surrounding district.

In the time of Alexander II. the influence of England in the government of the northern part of the kingdom had been experienced, and the unfortunate imprisonment of William the Lion, the King's father, had suffered the English to have some claim to feudal superiority. The boldness of Alexander had prompted him to oppose their efforts, and to seek to undermine the power of the throne of England by joining with the Barons against King John. That monarch, enraged at this presumption upon the part of his vassal, gathered together an army of freebooters and desperadoes, invaded Scotland, crossing the Humber, and laying waste the provinces between that river and the Forth. The Scottish King was unable to oppose his march, and presently retired until an accession of forces should join him. Then, ordering the Castles of the knights who had joined him to be left in a defensive position, he pursued King John by way of Berwick and chased him ignominiously to his own country. At this time Bothwell Castle was in the possession of Walter Olyfard, and would doubtless be considered a post of importance, as it lay in the midst of a fruitful country, and was sufficiently apart from the highway of England to escape the destruction with which the invading armies usually overwhelmed their adversaries' dwellings.

It was not to be expected that a position of such strength as Bothwell must have been would long escape the notice of the English. The armies which overran this portion of the kingdom ere long discovered that the district of Clydesdale could remain unsubdued whilst Bothwell and Dumbarton were in the hands of the natives. Against the former of these, therefore, they directed their endeavours, and with too fatal success. The delusive hopes which the Scottish statesmen had built upon the apparent amity that existed for some years betwixt Henry III. of England and his son-in-law, Alexander III., had been rudely shattered by the attitude which the former assumed upon the question of the independence of Scotland. But Henry was too polite to risk an open rupture with Alexander, and proceeded therefore by underhand means to secure the division of the kingdom through fomenting discord while professing friendship. His schemes were interrupted by the hand of Death; but he bequeathed his policy to an able successor in the person of his son and successor, Edward I.

How faithfully that monarch fulfilled the desires of his much-lamented father need not here be told except incidentally. Every one knows that Edward endeavoured to entrap his brother-in-law, Alexander III., into rendering homage for the kingdom of Scotland; that he took advantage of every pretext for interfering in Scottish affairs during his life; that he expired in the very act of leading an overwhelming army against the defenders of her liberty; and that he directed that his tombstone should bear as its proudest motto the self-assumed title of " Malleus Scottorum "— " The Hammer of the Scots." It is not, therefore, necessary to dwell on all the details of this King's venturous career. When he visited Bothwell Castle in 1301 it was a very different place from that which the Olyfards had left about fifty years before. Sir Walter de Moravia had vast means at his command, and had determined to erect a Castle worthy of the superb position. His wife, the last of the Olyfards in Lanarkshire—the family were afterwards located at Newtyle, Kinpurnie, and Gask in Perthshire—was at the Scottish Court, and had met the second wife of Alexander II., the famous Marie de Coucy of Picardy, who was married to the King in May, 1239, at Roxburgh. Now, in 1230, the Queen's father, Enguerand III., Baron de Coucy, had just completed the splendid Chateau de Coucy, in Picardy, which evidently has been the model for the Bothwell Castle, possibly planned by Walter Olyfard, but certainly completed by Walter de Moravia, no doubt with the prompting of his wife, who may have sought to rival the Queen.

It has been shrewdly suggested that Queen Marie may have brought to Scotland some of the Mason Lodges that had been engaged on the Chateau de Coucy, and that these may have been employed on the building of Blantyre Priory and Bothwell Castle. The theory is by no means incredible, and accounts for the similarity of the plans of Chateau and Castle. In any case it seems to be fairly confirmed that Bothwell Castle was finished in a splendid fashion in 1278 or thereby.

317

The second Walter de Moravia was married to a sister of John Comyn, one of the competitors for the Scottish Crown ; and he had two sons, William, who swore fealty to Edward I. in 1291, and Andrew, the famous patriot, who supported Wallace, and fell in September 1297 at the Battle of Stirling. His son, Thomas Randolph, whose mother, Isabella, was a sister of King Robert the Bruce, was also such a conspicuous hero in the War of Independence that Robert I. conferred upon him the Earldom of Moray, and after the King's death he was Guardian of Scotland. Bothwell Castle was still the seat of the Earl, though in 1299 it had been captured by the English. The place was visited in 1301 by Edward I., who resided there for three days, and then placed Bothwell in the charge of the English warrior, Aymer de Valence, Earl of Pembroke, who was appointed Governor ; and there is a consistent tradition that the plan for the capture of Wallace was devised at Bothwell.

The career of De Valence was varied, for though Edward I. trusted him with a large command, he fell under the suspicions of Edward II., who deprived him of many of his honours. Bothwell was regarded as a safe retreat for fugitives from Scotland, especially after Bannockburn. The Earl of Hereford, who had commanded a wing of the English army at that conflict, sought to save his soldiers by falling back on the Castle for shelter. Barbour relates the incident thus :—

Bothwell Castle

Their attempt to withstand the victorious Scottish army, however, was hopeless, and they were forced to abandon the Castle. At a later date the first Earl of Moray had the strange task allotted to him to dismantle his own Bothwell Castle and also the Castles of Leuchars and St Andrews, to prevent them from being again occupied by the English. The demolition was afterwards repaired by the next noble family that came into possession of Bothwell Castle, though traces may still be found of this incident.

Similarity of patriotic feelings as well as pursuits had long held the families of Bothwell and Douglas together. They claimed a common origin from some of the Flemish families which had settled in Scotland at an early period, and their determined resistance to the encroachments of England had saved the country from conquest on several occasions. When, therefore, the race of the first Randolph, Earl of Moray, terminated by the death of John, his grandson, third Earl, who was killed at the Battle of Durham in 1346, leaving no male issue, his brother, Thomas, who does not seem to have assumed the title, died, leaving a daughter, it was not unnatural that a union of these two families should be brought about by marriage. And thus it happened that by the wedding of Archibald "the Grim," Earl of Douglas (though an illegitimate son), with the heiress of Bothwell in 1381, the Castle came into the possession of this powerful family.

Marjorie, the daughter of this marriage, was united in wedlock to the unfortunate Duke of Rothesay, son of Robert III., at the Parish Kirk of Bothwell in 1398, and though no record exists to warrant the conclusion, there is every probability that the marriage festivities took place at the Castle. For nearly a hundred years the Douglas Earls held the Castle, and the strange manner in which they came to lose it is worthy of notice.

Without accepting wholly the fanciful tales which Hume of Godscroft relates as to the origin of the Douglas family, it must be admitted that they can claim a very respectable antiquity. Their historian maintains that they were almost the only family of note that could trace back their ancestry to a purely Scottish source, but his theory will hardly bear critical investigation ; and the notion that their progenitor was a man of mark " in the days of Solvathius, about the year 767," will scarcely receive credence in these days. Hector Boetius—not the most credible of historians—relates that Malcolm Ceanmòr held a Parliament at Forfar in 1061, at which he restored the estates that had been reft from the Thanes by Macbeth, and empowered them to adopt surnames from the localities where their lands lay. Amongst them was a certain " Guliel-

BOTHWELL CASTLE

Valentine & Sons, Ltd.

mus à Douglas," who was created first Lord of Douglas, and from him are derived the many and honourable men who have borne a similar title. Their influence throughout the struggles for Scottish Independence is very visible, and their growing power upon the Border ultimately induced a rivalry with the reigning family.

Latterly the Douglases held the position of make-weight in all contests between England and Scotland ; for the series of Forts and Castles which they held throughout Lanarkshire and Dumfriesshire could oppose a formidable barrier to either party, as the Lord of Douglas willed. Perhaps the most romantic portion of their history is that which relates to the " Good Sir James," the trusty fellow-warrior of Bruce, and the chosen custodian of that monarch's heart when on its *post-mortem* journey to the Holy Land. Of him the old rhyme still declares :—

> " Good Sir James Douglas,
> Who wise, and wight, and worthy was,
> Was never over-glad for winning,
> Nor yet over-sad for timing,
> Good fortune and evil chance
> He weighed both in one balance."

But the story of the early adventures of the Douglas family belongs rather to the traditions of Douglas Castle than to Bothwell Castle, which is our present theme.

The fortunes of the Douglases culminated in the person of Archibald, fourteenth Lord and fifth Earl, and with him they began to waver and decline. Through his active service in France he had won glory and wealth, and added several titles to those which he had inherited. His full style was—Earl of Douglas, Earl of Wigton, Lord of Bothwell, Galloway and Annandale, Duke of Touraine (in France), Lord of Longueville, and Marshal of France. But when James I. returned from his long imprisonment in England to assume the Crown of Scotland, he found some of the more prominent nobles too powerful to be tolerated, and suddenly cast many of them into prison, and the Earl of Douglas among them. So far as can be judged, the chief offence of that nobleman, besides his power, was a certain freedom of speech which he used in advising the King, which that monarch could not endure. Disappointed by this treatment, the Earl retired to France, and did not return till after the assassination of the King.

He found Scotland in a most pitiable condition. The policy of James I. had taught him to elevate men of parts and understanding to places of trust in the kingdom despite their inferior birth ; and for the slight thus passed on their nobility the upper grades of the Scottish nobles did not readily forgive him. When, therefore, the Earl of Douglas found that the government of his native land had been committed to Crichton and Livingstone of Callander—men of good family, but of low degree in the peerage—whilst he had been excluded from all share in the Councils of Scotland, he was not unnaturally moved with resentment. It was shrewdly suspected by the nobles that these men had been elevated to this high position as much for the purpose of curtailing the power of the nobility as for any special faculties they possessed; and the appointment of the Earl of Douglas to the post of Lieutenant-General of the Kingdom was too evidently an extorted concession to pacify them. The Earl by this time was too far advanced in years to meddle with paltry matters of dispute. He retired in 1438 to Restalrig, and died in that year.

William, sixth Earl of Douglas, was only fourteen years old when he succeeded his father. He had inherited all the late Earl's courage and daring, and as the oppressions of the Douglas family by the Stewart Kings was a frequent topic in Bothwell Castle, the young Earl was somewhat unguarded in his speech about them. Livingstone and Crichton became alarmed, and determined to have him removed. Crichton wrote to him a hypocritical letter regretting the discord betwixt the Earl and his kinsman, the King, and inviting him to meet James II. at Edinburgh Castle, and aid him with advice. The young Earl fell readily into the trap, and set out with his retainers for Edinburgh. Crichton met him on the way, and lured him to his Castle of Crichton, which he had just erected. For two days was the feasting and revelry maintained there, and then the followers of Douglas, with David, his younger brother, and his friend, Malcolm Fleming of Biggar, joined Crichton's band, and all set forth

323

for Edinburgh. Arrived at the Castle, Douglas was introduced to the King by Livingstone, and James felt, or affected, strong attachment to the two brothers, sole heirs of an ancient line. Several days were spent in entertaining them, and every mark of attention was bestowed upon them.

At length the time arrived for the consummation of the plot. One day, while at dinner in the presence of the King, Crichton and Livingstone, with many of their followers, suddenly rose upon the Douglases, and, as their attendants had been carefully disposed of beforehand, they seized the unfortunate noblemen, carried them out to the western courtyard of the Castle, and beheaded them, without even the pretence of a trial. To give an air of legality to the foul deed, Fleming was kept for four days, then beheaded on a plea of treason. The traditional rhyme made upon the occasion is thus preserved :—

" Edinburgh Castle, Town and Tower,
God grant thou sink for sin,
And that even for the black dinner
Earl Douglas gat therein."

By this double murder the direct line of the Douglases was terminated, and the title went to the grand-uncle, mentioned by the historian of the family as " James the Gross." His tenure of the title only lasted three years, when he was succeeded by his eldest son, William, whose character more resembled that of his uncle and cousin than of his weak and imbecile father. The plot of Crichton and Livingstone had been devised astutely so as to terminate the male direct line of successors, on the notion that the possessions of the Douglases would probably be distributed amongst heiresses, and thus wipe out the family. But their scheming was overturned to some extent by Earl William, who reunited the dissevered portions of the vast estates of his family by his marriage with Beatrix of Galloway, his first cousin, and chief heiress of the alienated lands of Douglas. By this union the Earl found himself in the position of the first subject of the realm. The intention of the Stewart Kings had been to centralize all power in their hands, and hitherto they had not scrupled to reduce the independence of the greater nobles by flagrant acts of injustice. Fate had selected James II. to be the chief instrument for the overthrow of the ancient house of Douglas. The story of the King's consenting to the murder of the two young Douglases in November, 1448, has just been narrated ; but the more disgraceful murder by the King's own hand in February, 1451-2, when William, eighth Earl of Douglas, " was stabbed by King James II., and was despatched by some of his courtiers in Stirling Castle." The story is told in the account of " Stirling Castle " in this volume.

With James, ninth Earl of Douglas, brother of the murdered Earl, the proud name of Douglas of Douglas was brought nearly to extinction. Earl James, wishing to avenge the murder of his brother, called out his retainers and also his three younger brothers, and made a demonstration against the King ; but some of his allies deserted him, and when the King's forces came out under George Douglas, Earl of Angus, in May 1455, James, the ninth Earl, was defeated at Arkinholme, and two of his brothers slain, and one made prisoner. In June of this year Parliament passed sentence of forfeiture on James, ninth Earl, and other members of the family.

For a long period after 1455 Earl James remained in England, and took no action against the Scottish King. In 1483 he joined with Alexander, Duke of Albany, brother of the new King, James III., in an expedition aimed at the deposition of the King. But the times were sadly altered when Douglas found that Annandale, Nithsdale and Clydesdale alike refused to rise at his bidding. The Englishmen whom he had brought to invade the land of his birth were no match for the hardy Border warriors, and fled at their approach. The Earl, weary of the exile which he had been enduring, and ashamed of the disgrace which had fallen upon him, yielded himself prisoner to one of his old servants that a friend might have the advantage of the price put upon his head. With a refinement of cruelty James III. condemned him to be confined in the Abbey of Lindores during the remainder of his existence. He felt most acutely that his life had been wasted when he heard the dread words pronounced :—

" Go thou and join the living dead !

> The Living Dead whose sober brow
> Oft shrouds such thoughts as thou hast now,
> Whose hearts within are seldom cured
> Of passions by their vows abjured ;
> Where under sad and solemn show
> Vain hopes are nursed, wild wishes glow.
> Seek the Convent's vaulted room,
> Prayer and vigil be thy doom ;
> Doff the green and don the grey,
> To the Cloister hence away ! "

Perhaps not the least bitter of his reflections in his enforced solitude would be that his defeat had been brought about through the treachery of his kinsman, the Earl of Angus, who had joined with the King against him. The members of the Angus branch were notable for the fairness of their complexions, whilst the Clydesdale Douglases were swarthy and dark in colour. Hence the saying came into use after the fall of Earl James that " the Red Douglas had put down the Black." The family historian endeavours to turn a graceful compliment out of this fact, with which the account of the Douglases in Bothwell Castle may be terminated :—

> " Pompey by Caesar only was o'ercome ;
> None but a Roman soldier conquered Rome ;
> A Douglas could not have been brought so low
> Had not a Douglas wrought his overthrow."

The estates that had belonged to the Earl of Douglas, and were forfeited in 1455, at the time of his departure for England, fell to the Crown, and King James had taken the opportunity of partitioning these so as to secure some doubtful adherents. Crichton, the son of the Chancellor who had compassed the murders of the two Earls, received Bothwell Castle as the tardy reward of his father's treachery; and Sir James Hamilton of Cadzow, who abandoned the cause of Douglas at this time, exchanged the lands of Kingswell for those of Bothwell Forest, whilst the lands of Galloway were annexed to the Crown.

PRINTED BY J. AND J. GRAY, EDINBURGH.

INDEX

(Numbers indicate pages.)

Y

329

Index

PRINTED BY J. AND J. GRAY, EDINBURGH.